The Early Modern Englishwoman:
A Facsimile Library of Essential Works

Series III

Essential Works for the Study of
Early Modern Women: Part 3

Volume 5

Women in Service in Early Modern England

The Early Modern Englishwoman: A Facsimile Library of Essential Works

Series III

Essential Works for the Study of Early Modern Women: Part 3

Volume 5

Women in Service in Early Modern England

Selected and Introduced by
Jeannie Dalporto

General Editors
Betty S. Travitsky and Anne Lake Prescott

LONDON AND NEW YORK

First published 2008 by Ashgate Publishing

2 Park Square, Milton Park, Abingdon, Oxfordshire OX14 4RN
52 Vanderbilt Avenue, New York, NY 10017

Routledge is an imprint of the Taylor & Francis Group, an informa business

First issued in paperback 2019

A Library of Congress record exists under LC control number: 2007932065

ISBN 13: 978-0-8153-9908-7 (hbk)
ISBN 13: 978-1-138-35800-3 (pbk)

CONTENTS

PREFACE BY THE GENERAL EDITORS

Until very recently, scholars of the early modern period have assumed that there were no Judith Shakespeares in early modern England. Much of the energy of the current generation of scholars has been devoted to constructing a history of early modern England that takes into account what women actually wrote, what women actually read, and what women actually did. In so doing, contemporary scholars have revised the traditional representation of early modern women as constructed both in their own time and in ours. The study of early modern women has thus become one of the most important – indeed perhaps the most important – means for the rewriting of early modern history.

The Early Modern Englishwoman: A Facsimile Library of Essential Works is one of the developments of this energetic reappraisal of the period. As the names on our advisory board and our list of editors testify, it has been the beneficiary of scholarship in the field, and we hope it will also be an essential part of that scholarship's continuing momentum.

The Early Modern Englishwoman is designed to make available a comprehensive and focused collection of writings in English from 1500 to 1750, both by women and for and about them. The three series of *Printed Writings* (1500–1640, 1641–1700, and 1701–1750) provide a comprehensive if not entirely complete collection of the separately published writings by women. In reprinting these writings we intend to remedy one of the major obstacles to the advancement of feminist criticism of the early modern period, namely the limited availability of the very texts upon which the field is based. The volumes in the facsimile library reproduce carefully chosen copies of these texts, incorporating significant variants (usually in the appendices). Each text is preceded by a short introduction providing an overview of the life and work of a writer along with a survey of important scholarship. These works, we strongly believe, deserve a large readership – of historians, literary critics, feminist critics, and non-specialist readers.

The Early Modern Englishwoman also includes separate facsimile series of *Essential Works for the Study of Early Modern Women* and of *Manuscript Writings*. These facsimile series are complemented by *The Early Modern Englishwoman 1500–1750: Contemporary Editions*. Also under our general editorship, this series includes both old-spelling and modernized editions of works by and about women and gender in early modern England.

New York City
2008

INTRODUCTORY NOTE

If one were to judge by the sheer number of tracts and sermons addressed to or dealing with servants in early modern England, one might conclude that servant behaviour was one of the most widely-discussed subjects among clergy, economists and other writers. Although the rhetoric varies, in most of these texts the overarching theme is consistent: the need to instil in servants a sense of industry, faithfulness, and honesty, traits which were supposedly eroding with each succeeding generation. The 'servant question', as it would come to be termed in the nineteenth century, was a main source of cultural anxiety throughout the early modern period.[1] Servants as a category included agricultural labourers as well as male and female domestic servants, but by the mid-nineteenth century, female domestics overwhelmingly outnumbered male servants in Britain, and scholars believe that even before this the majority of household servants may have been female, although the lack of data makes the ratio uncertain.[2] It follows that much of the anxiety about servant morals and behaviour came to be focused on female servants.

From the wealth of textual material about female servants, I have chosen four representative texts for reproduction in this volume. I hope, first, to illustrate how books addressed to female servants evolved. Secondly, I hope to show that female servants and the ordering of the household were integral to the way labour and gender structured early modern socio-economic ideals. Of the four texts reproduced here, two are manuals explaining the duties of female servants, while two are critical, in some respects, of such books addressed to servants. These four texts reveal how the domestic roles of both servants and mistresses complicated the connections among status, economics and gender during this time. Out of dozens of books, both those about servants and those addressed to servants, the two texts that I have chosen for this edition – J[ohn] S[hirley]'s *The Accomplished Ladies Rich Closet* (1687) and Eliza Haywood's *A PRESENT* (1743) – are representative of how women's work in the household (performed by both wife and servant) appeared to symbolize their social and inward virtue. Shirley's book shows that by successfully overseeing the labour of her servants, the mistress of the house ensures the economic and social success of her husband. This approach to regulating labour in the domestic sphere is highly pragmatic and conflates moral virtue with industriousness and efficiency for both servant and mistress. Haywood's book, on the other hand, represents a common type of rhetoric aimed at instilling moral behaviour in female servants. Haywood attempts to contain the potential for social and economic disruption that female servants pose by laying out a list of dos and don'ts addressed directly to female servants. Her book balances predictions of dire consequences for disobedience with promises of social approbation and personal pride for those servants who adhere to the rules. The other two texts – the poem 'THE Woman's Labour' (1739) by Mary Collier and Jonathan Swift's parody of servant manuals, *DIRECTIONS TO SERVANTS* (1745) – can be read as criticisms of servant and mistress guidebooks. In a sobering counter-balance to the notion that the wife achieves honour by supervising her servants, Collier gives us a look at the realities of household labour from female domestics' perspective, allowing us to see the harsh consequences that household norms had on labouring women. On the other hand, Swift's parody of servant tracts draws attention to the ways in which exhortations to obedience, with their exhaustive lists of right and wrong behaviours, could easily be subverted so that servants could benefit from them economically and socially.

R.C. Richardson notes that as many as forty percent of all families from the late sixteenth century through the seventeenth employed household servants. Although the bulk of servants were found in the homes of the aristocracy and gentry, families further down the social scale also employed household servants.[3] Some scholars believe that because of a drop in opportunities for female service in husbandry, beginning in the early modern period more rural women were forced to supplement the family income by performing housework for the gentry and landowners or by migrating to larger cities to find work as household servants.[4] Also driving the increase in female domestic servants was a nascent consumer culture and higher standards of household cleanliness. The proliferation of domestic goods, in tandem with ideals of hospitality and conceptions of a well-ordered household, meant that more work was needed to prepare elaborate dinners and to clean dishes, furniture and clothing.[5]

Printed discussions of servant behaviour began to burgeon in the 1590s; most appeared in sermons giving instructions to all members of the household concerning their varied Christian duties. The family, as many writers defined it, consisted of persons living in one household who had obligations to one another under the governance of the husband. Servants and apprentices were viewed as an integral part of the family structure and were placed at the bottom of the hierarchy, along with children. Servants were to be exemplars of Christian obedience for the sake of their heavenly reward and for the sake of the commonwealth, living in God-ordained hierarchies within the family and nation. William Perkins' *Christian Oeconomie: or, a Short Survey of the Right Manner of erecting and ordering a Familie according to the scriptures* (1609) and William Gouge's *Of Domesticall Dvties Eight Treatises* (1622) are typical tracts. Devoting chapters to the reciprocity of each family member's duties, Perkins stresses that servitude itself is a natural or necessary condition for the proper functioning of a Christian society. Likewise, Richard Lucas, in *The Duty of Servants* (1685), addresses parents of low fortune who will be forced to send their children to service, reminding them that servitude is a God-ordained function for some and that parents must teach their children to be content with their future lot in life. Moreover, those who find themselves in the state of servitude are obligated to show unmitigated loyalty towards their masters. As Gouge puts it, 'both their persons and their actions are all their masters: and the will of the master must be their will and guide' (604).

Similarly, Thomas Fosset, in *The Servant's Dvtie* (1613), insists on complete self-abnegation, writing that the servant should 'obey, and to be in subiection, to haue no will of his owne … but wholly to resigne himselfe to the will of his Master' (22). Such tracts are sustained by a conviction that insubordination against masters is tantamount to disobedience to God. Gouge declares that 'masters by vertue of their office and place beare Christs image, and stand in his stead' (641). Some of the most commonly cited New Testament texts used to validate the authority of masters are Titus 2.9–10, I Peter 2.18 and Romans 13. Peter's admonition, in particular, was often cited by writers in order to authorize servant obedience: 'Servants, be subject to your masters with all fear; not only to the good and gentle, but also to the froward' (I Peter 2.18, King James Version). The Old Testament, however, is invoked as well. High turnover as servants searched for better employment was endemic. Therefore, when charging servants to stay with a master even when treated unjustly, many authors cite Jacob's long years of indenture to the deceitful Laban in exchange for Leah and Rachel. Thomas Carter, in *Carters Christian Common vvealth; Or, Domesticall Dutyes deciphered* (1627), rails against servants who 'cast off the yoake of their obedience' by searching for a better job (252) and recalls that when Hagar fled into the wilderness because of Sarah's harsh treatment, the Lord commanded her to return (Genesis 16). Many writers, however, stress that masters must treat servants humanely. Robert Cleaver, for example, in *A Godly Forme of Hovsehold Gouernement* (1598), says that they should not only provide fair wages, but should also make sure that servants have 'wholesome meat…and otherwise to helpe them, comfort them, and relieue, and cherish them, as well in sicknesse, as in health, liberally to reward their good deseruings…. [and] not to bee too seuere' (371, 374).

Most of these sermon-like tracts do not go into much detail about how, exactly, a servant might apply principles of obedience in practice; one exception is John Gother's *Instructions for Apprentices and Servants* (1699), which insists that one way for a servant to fulfill his Christian duty is to avoid 'carelessly leaving the Keys of things' lying about and to keep doors and boxes closed so others will not pilfer goods (15).Writings about the dangers of sloth, disobedience, and negligence and about the importance of looking towards one's heavenly reward continued to be popular in the early eighteenth century, as witnessed by tracts such as John Waugh's *The Duty of Apprentices and Other Servants* (1713), Zinzano's *The Servants Calling* (1725) and Thomas Wheatland's *A Manual for Servants: containing the several instances of their Duty, and the Advantages of Complying with it* (1731).

By the early eighteenth century other types of writers were expressing alarm at what they perceived as servants' mounting insolence and intractability that threatened the masters' economic prosperity and the nation's socioeconomic order. Timothy Nourse, in *Campania Foelix, or, a Discourse of the Benefits and Improvements of Husbandry* (1700), writes that 'there is not a more insolent and proud, a more untractable, perfidious, and more churlish sort of People breathing than the Generality of our Servants' (200). Although Nourse's *Campania Foelix* is devoted to improving farming and husbandry and to the art of managing estates and farms, he allocates a section of the book to insisting that servants are ruining the rural economy. Like many authors who write about servants, Nourse notes that whatever complaints England's servant population might have against its masters, servants would not grumble if they were to compare their lot with the wretched conditions of servitude or slavery in non-Christian societies, especially those of Turkey and ancient Rome. Blaming diminished productivity in the countryside on lazy servants, from thieving chambermaids to indolent day labourers on the farms, Nourse believes that high wages, arrogance and servants' practice of quitting before their contracts are up are the main reasons why the honest farmer and the middling gentry are having great difficulty earning a profit from the land. Idle servants slow productivity and hurt the nation economically by bleeding the householder so dry that he is unable to invest in the land properly.

John Bellers explains why some were born to rule and others to obey in his *Essay for Imploying the Poor to Profit* (1723):

> If there were no Labourers, there would be no Lords. And if the Labourers did not raise more Food, and Manufactures than what did subsist themselves, every Gentleman must be a Labourer, and idle Men must starve [Title Page] … But if every Man in the World had a Million of Money, there would not be one Pound of Bread, nor an Inch of Cloth, nor a Cottage the more for it, to support the Life of one Man. Therefore except a suitable Number of those Moneyed Men become Labourers, Mankind must perish through Hunger or Cold. (7–8)

Given that labourers were part of the necessary economic makeup of society, it made sense to many that ways to control them economically must be found. Economic necessity was increasingly invoked to justify regulating servant wages and terms of employment, although many writers continued to give a nod to traditional Christian reasons for demanding subservience in labourers. In many tracts both arguments work together to justify extensive legal and personal authority over servants.

Daniel Defoe is one writer who combines both arguments. He vehemently denounces what he perceives as increasing corruption in servants and the disastrous economic consequences of this corruption for the nation as a whole. In *The Great Law of Subordination consider'd; or, the Insolence and Unsufferable Behavior of Servants in England duly enquir'd into* (1724), he observes that 'The Complaint [about servants] is so general, and the Grievance so very notorious, that I need enter into no Search after Evidence of Fact' (8). One of his first compositions on the subject is *The Complete Family-Instructor in Three Parts* (1715), a series of morality tales about wives, children, husbands, and servants. In *The Great Law of Subordination consider'd* (1724), Defoe calls for the regulation of all servants and apprentices, claiming that household discipline, trade, manufacturing and farming are practically at a standstill because of servant misconduct and high wages. Among other things, he proposes that servants who curse or swear to their masters' faces be transported for twenty-one years; servants turned out for lying and saucy language, he demands, should be punished by mandatory unemployment for six months. Defoe insists that should the master fail to prosecute servant misbehaviour, he should have to pay a stiff fine.

Defoe directs much of his frustration at female servants. In *The Great Law*, for example, he calls for Parliament to regulate the wages and apparel of female servants. In *Every-Body's Business is No-Body's Business, or, Private Abuses, Publick Grievances: Exemplified in the Pride, Insolence, and Exorbitant Wages of our Women-Servants, Footmen, &c.: with A Proposal for amendment of the same* (1725), he claims that since female servants are working less and demanding higher wages, the wives of tradesmen are not able to help their husbands in the shop because they are occupied with the 'Drudgery of Houshold Affairs' (4). He goes on to note that 'our Servant Wenches are so puff'd up with Pride, now a Days … It is a hard Matter to know the Mistress from the Maid by their Dress, nay very often the Maid shall be much the finer of the two' (4). As Sandra Sherman has pointed out, in Defoe's tracts 'the servant is an agent of potential disruption, able to disorganize transmission of wealth within the proprietary class'; while Defoe assumes that ambition in the middle class is intrinsically worthy, he thinks that servants undermine the efforts of that class when they exhibit the same ambition.[6] A failure to show the proper markers of class difference in dress is not merely insubordination. It is a matter of grave national concern: the woolen trade suffers as result of such 'intollerable Pride' when 'nothing but Silks and Sattins will go down with our Kitchen Wenches' (4). To counter the argument that wearing silks and satins saves money on soap because they require fewer washings than linen and cotton, Defoe asserts, 'Servant-Maids wearing printed Linnens, Cottons, and other Things of that Nature, which require frequent washing, do not, by enhauncing the Article of Soap, add more to House-Keeping, than the Generality of People would imagine' (11).

Although Defoe and others believed that governmental control was one of the most effective ways of curtailing upward mobility and indolence in servants, some writers began to address servants' sense of self-preservation and self-interest as a way of keeping them in line. Pamphlets and tracts about servants began to appear that spun out tales of downward spirals of depravity that often began with small indiscretions on the part of the servant. The purpose of such narratives was to frighten servants into good behaviour. For example, Thomas Broughton, in *A Serious and Affectionate Warning to Servants, More especially those of our Nobility and Gentry; Occasioned by The shameful and untimely Death of Matthew Henderson: Who was Executed...for the Murder of his Lady* (1746), raises an alarm about what he perceives as an increase in servants' violence and robbery against their masters. He warns that even minor pilfering may lead to the kind of murderous greed that induced Matthew Henderson to rob and kill his mistress and, finally, to be put to death himself.

Some servants, however, began to publish tracts in which they sought to refute charges that servants were venal and dishonest. These tracts include Matthew Randall's *Reflections on the Duty of Masters, Mistresses, and Servants: in which Several irregularities are Reproved* (1725), the anonymous *Directions to Lords, and Ladies, Masters and Mistresses, for the Improvement of their Conduct to Servants* (1766) and the anonymous *The Servant's Plea. Or, a Defence of that Present just and equitable Practice of giving Servants and Labourers Wages and other Encouragements, according to their Merit* (1732). A specific response to Defoe was made by a 'Lady's woman' in *The Maid-Servants Modest Defence: in answer to a pamphlet, entitul'd Every-body's Business is No-body's Business* (1725). Robert Dodsley, a former footman, also reacted to *Every-body's Business* and exhorted masters in *Servitude: A Poem. To which is prefix'd An Introduction, humbly Submitted to the Consideration of all Noblemen, Gentlemen, and Ladies, who keep many Servants* (1729) to treat servants humanely. In most such texts, the writers suggest that unjust and abusive masters and mistresses are far more common than greedy and disobedient servants.

It is true that masters and mistresses often treated servants cruelly and with impunity. Female servants were particularly vulnerable to sexual exploitation by masters and upper servants. James Townley, who wrote under the name Oliver Grey, was a retired household servant who, in his *An Apology for the Servants. By Oliver Grey. Occassioned by the Representation of the Farce called 'High Life Below Stairs', and by what has been said to their Disadvantage in the 'Public Papers'* (1760), cites examples of physical abuse by masters over the smallest infractions, insisting that such mistreatment is far more common than servant misconduct. In one poignant example, Townley recalls the time that his master inflicted a serious gash on his head because he had taken a sip of wine behind his back. Arguing that immoral behaviour by servants does not compare to that of their masters, he is particularly outraged by the complaint that servants play 'kitchen cards' during off hours and asks how society can condemn servants for a few hands of cards when the upper classes gamble night and day. Townley is eager to defend the custom whereby visitors would give servants 'vails' (or tips); Defoe and others argued passionately against the practice, which they believed provided income that servants would merely waste on alcohol and expensive clothing. Townley, however, makes the point that vails are necessary because they can be saved to provide a pension after retirement from service. He calculates how much it costs for a servant to maintain himself modestly and compares it with the average servant wage, concluding that servants are barely able to subsist on wages alone, and, therefore, that saving vails is necessary for retirement.

Ironically, although they formed the lowest part of the household hierarchy, servants often wielded much power. Their knowledge of and access to household finances were inevitable. On larger estates and farms stewards or upper servants negotiated with tenants for rents and conducted land transactions. Thomas Seaton, in *The Conduct of Servants in Great Families* (1720), warns stewards not to accept bribes from tenants in return for an advantageous lease agreement or to lease a farm for a higher price than the landlord has agreed to and then pocket the difference. Except for a few types of servants, such as footmen and butlers in great houses, who were more or less status symbols, most servants were supposed to be invisible, staying in the background and making sure that the household ran smoothly. They were, however, in a position to manipulate household assets for their own benefit, since even kitchen and chambermaids were, in many households, responsible for buying and managing food, fuel and other household goods. One of the most common complaints against servants – which may seem to us to be fairly minor – involved their filching foodstuffs such as butter and milk, eating leftovers after household meals and taking candles and other small odds and ends for personal use. Given the relative cost of those items in a household budget, however, it was no small economic hardship for a household when candles and butter were always disappearing and thus in short supply.

As late as the end of the eighteenth century, it was commonly believed that financial ruin loomed if servants were not rigourously policed. One writer in the late 1770s, for instance, complains that

> I found that servants and housekeepers were not to be trusted … During the state of my widowhood, for want of a wife in the house when I was absent, I had already suffered to my own knowledge, to the amount of forty or fifty pounds at least, by downright thievery, so that continuing as I was, I had no prospect before me but ruin.[7]

This writer repeats what had long been a common belief: that it is mainly the wife's responsibility to supervise the servants. For example, a part of the popular *Lady's New Years Gift* (1688) by George Halifax,

Marquis of Savile, outlines the wife's Christian responsibility as a manager of the house and servants. The main purpose of conduct books such as Halifax's was to stress proper decorum and virtuous behaviour for both single and married gentlewomen. One of the earliest, Richard Brathwaite's *The English Gentlevvoman, drawne out to the full Body* (1631), is divided into such topics as proper apparel, decency, gentility and honour. The alphabetically arranged *Ladies Dictionary, being a General Entertainment of the Fair Sex* (1694), by N. H, offers entries on such subjects as famous women in history, 'Apparel or the Ladies Dressing-Room' and 'ability', under which the author discusses the physical and mental abilities of women as compared to those of men (18).

Along with listing principles of behaviour, many conduct books also stress the wife's proper role in regard to the household finances. As Craig Muldrew has noted, early modern society placed great value on 'household management, based on the virtues of diligence, honesty and thrift, to maintain the credit of a household'.[8] Richard Allestree, in *The Ladies Calling in Two Parts / by the Author of The Whole Duty of Man, &c.* (1693), cautions wives against the evil of spending money on luxury items: 'for the furniture oft consumes the house, and the house consumes the land' (196). Frittering away the profits of an estate on items such as furniture, clothing and equipage renders the very ground on which the estate rests infertile and wears out 'the soil too; those luxuries usually prey upon the vitals, eat out the very heart of an estate' (198). Even worse, a wife's lack of thrift is tantamount to 'embezl[ing] her husband's estate' (195). Therefore, she should never give her household duties over to a 'mercenary house-keeper' who, like her counterpart the land steward, will almost certainly 'raise fortunes on their Patrons ruines, and divide the spoil of the family, the house-keeper pilfering within doores, and the Bailiff plundering without' (223). The fear of deceitful servants bleeding their betters dry and then supplanting them socially was thus pervasive. The solution, as Allestree sees it, is to make sure that the mistress's servants are all 'God's servants also; this will secure her of all those intermedial qualifications in them in which her secular interest is concerned; their own consciences being the best spy she can set upon them … and the best spur also to diligence and industry' (224). He therefore advocates that the wife organize regular daily prayers for the servants so that 'the hours of praiers be fixt and constant as those of meals, and as much frequented' (224). The writer hastens to add that the wife should not set herself up as a 'catechist or preacher', explaining that her job is simply to provide the means and opportunity for prayer and devotion. A secular, economic problem of saving household money is cast in moral and spiritual terms; arranging collective prayer allows the housewife to watch her servants by gathering them in one place at regular intervals.

Writers also began to be concerned with how wives and servants could perform household tasks more efficiently and cost-effectively. Hannah Woolley was one of the first to publish such instructions. In addition to writing several collections of recipes and directions for curing various ailments, she also wrote didactic conduct books in the manner of Brathwaite. Two of her books, however, combine moral instruction with such practical aspects of household management as the best ways to keep milk fresh, to clean linen and to perform a myriad of other mundane household tasks. First published in 1673, *The Gentlewomans Companion; or A Guide to the Female Sex: containing Directions of Behaviour, in all Places, Companies, Relations, and Conditions, from their Childhood down to Old Age…Whereunto is added, A Guide for Cook-maids, Dairy-maids, Chamber-maids, and all others that go to Service* went through several editions by 1682. An earlier book, *A Guide to Ladies, Gentlewomen and Maids: Containing Directions of Behaviour, in all Places, Companies, Relations, and Conditions, from their Childhood down to Old Age* (1668), is similar.

By the mid-eighteenth century, cookbooks and instructions addressed to servants that were more or less divorced from long treatises on conduct and moral behaviour had become popular. Some writers discuss domestic service for women as a respectable, semi-professional career path, advising how to acquire a specific set of skills to help the servant find and keep profitable employment. Woolley's *The Compleat Servant-Maid; or the Young Maidens Tutor. Directing Them How they may fit and qualifie for any of these Employments. Viz. Waiting Woman, House-keeper, Chamber-Maid, Cook-Maid, Under Cook-Maid, Nursery-Maid, Dairy-Maid, Laundry-Maid, House-Maid, Scullery-Maid* was one of the first books to advance this argument. First published in 1677, from which edition I quote here, the book went through several editions by 1729. Woolley argues that if young women take care to hone their skills they will be able to find positions in the best houses. She also hints at the possibility of upward mobility, noting that by acquiring the title of a 'compleat servant-maid', a young woman will have a better chance in the marriage market: 'For there is no Sober, Honest, and Discreet Man, but will make choice of one, that hath Gained the Reputation of a Good and Complete Servant for his Wife, rather than one who can Trick up her self and like a Bartholomew Baby [a doll sold at Bartholomew Fair] is fit for nothing else but to be looked upon' (from 'The Epistle'). She implies that the would-be husband will be attracted to a 'compleat servant-maid' because marrying her would save him having to hire one. The idea that a female domestic servant might attract a husband higher up the social ladder was apparently nothing new when Samuel Richardson produced *Pamela* in 1740. Hannah Glasse, in *The Servant's Directory; or House-Keeper's Companion … to which is annexed a Diary, or House-Keeper's Pocket-Book for the entire Year* (1760), also avoids moralizing. She simply says, at the end of her preface, that she hopes that the servant will 'find every thing necessary in regard to House-hold-Affairs, and the Mistress saved a great deal of Trouble in teaching them' (viii).

By the mid-eighteenth century, several female servants were writing their own manuals. Elizabeth Raffald, in *The Experienced English House-keeper, For the Use and Ease of Ladies, House-keepers, Cooks, &c. Wrote Purely from Practice* (1769), writes from her long experience as a housekeeper for Lady Elizabeth Warburton; by well into the nineteenth century, the book had gone through over thirty editions. Raffald is highly pragmatic. In her dedication, she hopes that young women will take advantage of her experience and 'improve themselves' by learning the cooking methods that she lays out. Her main purpose is to instruct in 'plain language' not 'glossed over with hard Names, or words of high Stile'. Ann Peckham, a cook for over forty years, writes in the preface of *The Complete English Cook; or, Prudent Housewife* (1767) that she has taken special care to 'make everything easy and intelligible to the meanest understanding'; and, in *The Complete Servant-Maid* (1770?), Anne Barker, a housekeeper, proposes to provide 'plain and easy Directions' to qualify young women for service 'in General'. These books state or imply that to comply with their instructions will mean steady and profitable employment. Advice about moral behaviour continued in some books, but it was presented mainly as needful for servants to find and keep good jobs. Mary Johnson, in *The Young W[o]man's Companion; or the Servant-Maid's Assistant; Digested under the several Heads* (1753), urges honesty and faithfulness on the grounds that the servant's livelihood depends on the good will of her superiors. The result of obedience for the female servant will be a 'universal Respect' and happiness (ii).

All of these varying discourses about servants reveal a complex concern about how gender, economics and social stability were playing themselves out in the domestic space. Some writers insist that the authority of the master and mistress is sanctioned by biblical authority, arguing that servants must be obedient and honest in order to please God. Others, like Defoe, believe that government intervention is needed to control servants – especially female servants. Still other writers, such as Shirley and Allestree, approach the problem of household waste, servant idleness and thievery by making it the wife's responsibility to see that servants do their jobs. Writers such as Woolley and Haywood attempt to instil a rigourous work ethic in female servants by promising that a good reputation will ensure job security or a good marriage. As the eighteenth century wore on, many books simply concentrated on the practical aspects of running a household.

J[ohn] S[hirley]

Almost nothing is known about John Shirley (*fl.* 1685–88). *The Oxford Dictionary of National Biography* (2006) lists three John Shirleys writing at around the same time. It appears that the John Shirley who wrote *The Accomplished Ladies Rich Closet OF RARITIES* also penned an adventure story, a history and two works praising women, *The Illustrious History of Women; or a Compendium of the many Virtues that Adorn the Fair Sex* (1686) and *The Triumph of Wit* (1688).

The Accomplished Ladies Rich Closet OF RARITIES. OR THE Ingenious Gentlewoman and Servant-Maids Delightfull Companion. Containing many Excellent Things for the ACCOMPLISHMENT of the FEMALE SEX, after the exactest Manner and Method... To which is added a Second Part, Containing Directions for the Guidance of a Young Gentlewoman as to her Behaviour and seemly Deportment, &c. (1687)

In *The Accomplished Ladies Rich Closet*, Shirley follows a familiar pattern in conduct books, one which lays out the duties of a gentlewoman, including proper dress as well as proper behaviour towards parents, suitors and husband. Shirley appears to model his work closely on Woolley's *A Gentlewoman's Companion*. Like Woolley, Shirley includes collections of recipes and directions to servants on how to manage the dairy, the kitchen and the nursery, directions to midwives, several recipes for beauty treatments and cures for various ailments. The household is conceived of as fairly self-sustaining, with food, drink, birth and sickness all managed within its space. The book begins with a visual representation of the wife's all-seeing presence in her household and ends with instructions on how to police the servants. In the centre of the frontispiece, the gentlewoman peers out at the reader while the female servants perform their prescribed duties in the insets around her portrait. Although the gentlewoman looks directly at the reader, her presence at the centre implies that a panoptical gaze emanating from her ensures that the female servants under her control carry out their tasks dutifully. As the last section in the book makes clear, the servants are extensions of the wife's virtue; if any of them fail, the failure will redound to the wife, who will bear social and economic blame in the wider community. It is therefore difficult to imagine that the relationship between the mistress and her servants was as harmonious and peaceful as is depicted in the frontispiece, since any breach in a smooth-running household would have been accounted a deficiency in the wife's character. The constant battle to save, to trim excess and to stretch resources meant that the mistress of the house might see her servants as enemies whose lack of diligence threatened the household with disorder, waste and want.

Shirley's purpose in the preface is to give advice 'such as must contribute to the Advancement of each Individual Female ... in whatsoever state or condition, even from the Lady, to the inferior Servant-Maid'. When addressing various servants, Shirley usually includes a short section that exhorts them to be clean, orderly and honest. He directs the bulk of his advice, however, to the gentlewoman. After a discussion of her duties towards parents, suitors and husband, his last chapter concerns servants and the ordering of the household. Shirley warns the housewife not to delegate too much responsibility to 'second Management', presumably head housekeepers, but to make sure that servants 'do what is fitting, and that they lavish not out, nor waste that wherewith you intrust them ; for this being neglected, the fault will be charged upon your self' (232). Wives must make sure that 'nothing ... be wasted or squandered away by the resort of idle people, that too frequently flatter and wheedle your Servants to your disadvantage' (232–3). In matters of dress, the wife must prohibit servants from wearing fashions above their station and, instead, make sure that they appear neat and clean, 'which will redound to both their credits' (232). The servants' wastefulness will be 'charged' as a moral flaw to the wife, but if the servants behave well, that will be to the mistress's 'credit'. These charges and credits have both moral and economic implications. The moral fault charged to the wife brings nothing less than public humiliation: 'In the Kitchen it is requisite that you see no Necessaries are wanting, nor the seasoning of Meats, and other things in due time neglected, least by that defect you happen to be disgraced at your own Table' (233). Judgement occurs at the wife's 'Table', the epicentre of communal hospitality where her virtue is evaluated according to her decorum: how well her table is laid out, how well the food is cooked and how generous the portions are. Shirley includes a long chapter (VII) on the wife's conduct and deportment during dinner both at home and abroad. Her ability to entertain guests successfully within the house is extremely important to the husband's reputation and standing in the community, as it is even today in many cases, especially in politics and business.[9]

The Accomplished Ladies Rich Closet was first published in 1687 with a second edition in the same year; four more editions appeared by 1699 and one more in 1715, making seven in all. In editions after

1687 not many changes were made, although each one claims to have new information important for the female sex not seen in the previous volumes. The 1691 edition has added chapters containing information about how herbs, fruits and other plants may aid in preserving life. The 1696 edition adds a few recipes for making artificial pearls, sapphires and other jewels. Some information was taken out in later editions, and those after 1687 shorten the last chapter on how the wife should instruct the servants. My choice of copy for this facsimile edition was limited by my belief that it is important to include the expanded information on the wife's duties pertaining to servants that is present only in the 1687 editions. I have chosen the copy held by The British Library because it is the most legible throughout. The copy of the second edition of 1687, held by the Folger Shakespeare Library, has been microfilmed for UMI, but its pages are tightly bound, making it difficult to read many words in the inside margins.

Mary Collier

Mary Collier (*c.*1689–after 1762) is one of the first labouring-class female poets to publish in England. In the preface of the 1739 edition of 'THE Woman's Labour', a person identified only as M.B. emphasizes that Collier is not seeking literary distinction with her poetry. M.B. does acknowledge that the author hopes to gain a 'small Sum' of money from the volume, but gives the impression that she does so only to alleviate serious financial distress or penury. M.B. thus de-emphasizes the subversive implications of a labourer's turn to verse by denying that the author entertains any hopes of upward mobility by writing poetry.

Most of what we know about Collier comes from the preface to her second volume of poetry, *Poems on Several Occasions by Mary Collier, Author of the Washerwoman's Labour, With some remarks on Her Life* (1762). This volume includes 'THE Woman's Labour' from the 1739 edition along with several new poems. In the preface to the 1762 volume, which she penned herself, Collier tells the reader that she was born to 'poor, but honest Parents' who taught her to read. As she grew up, she 'bought and borrow'd' histories, including 'Fox's Acts and

Monuments of the Church' and books by Josephus. After her father died, she began her life as a washerwoman in Petersfield. 'THE Woman's Labour' caught the attention of a gentlewoman for whom Collier worked and who encouraged Collier to publish it. Collier tells us that she did so at her own expense and, although she does not explain exactly what happened, she reports that she earned almost nothing from 'THE Woman's Labour' because 'others [had] run away with the profit'. She relates that she now lives in a garret, being forced to retire from domestic service because of infirmities brought on by old age.

'THE Woman's Labour' in *THE Woman's Labour: AN EPISTLE TO Mr. STEPHEN DUCK; In ANSWER to his late Poem, called THE THRESHER'S LABOUR. To which are added, The Three WISE SENTENCES, TAKEN FROM The First Book of ESDRAS, Ch. III. and IV.* (1739)

'THE Woman's Labour' is a specific response to Stephen Duck's 'The THRESHER's LABOUR' in *Poems on Several Occasions* (1736). Duck had created a sensation in the literary world as a 'natural genius' because he was an agricultural worker without formal education who could write poetry.[10] In 'The THRESHER's LABOUR', the poet chronicles the field labourers' seemingly never-ending and harsh toil at harvest time. In one part, the speaker observes that while the men work, the female field workers are mostly gossiping. Collier's poem is an indignant rebuttal that not only details how hard the women actually do work in the fields, often having no choice but to bring their babies with them, but also describes the additional back-breaking labour done in their own homes and the washing and cleaning that they must do in the homes of the farmers or landowners.

Collier devotes a large portion of 'THE Woman's Labour' to the char-work performed for the farmer's or gentleman's wife. Once the female field workers are through with the harvest, 'Respite none' they 'find', for they must now go 'abroad, a Charing often' (12). The poet's description of the washing and cleaning allows us to examine more fully the complex interplay between female servants and the mistress of the house. Collier's poem is significant because it allows us to see how household labour, for women of all stations, was central to wider economic and social relations. When the poet describes her gender and class oppression, she is condemning an economic system that expected middle and upper-class women to extract excessive labour from domestic servants. We can look at Shirley's directions to the wife through the lens of Collier's poem: the mistress's disregard for the servants' exhaustion and welfare in the poem stems from her awareness that her own housekeeping is tightly bound up with perceptions of her social virtue.

In the poem, the charwomen rise before daylight and stand patiently in the cold until the live-in maid, who is herself 'quite tir'd' and overworked, lets them into the house (12). Once inside, the servants begin their tasks with the vigour and industry that is praised in servant manuals:

> Briskly with Courage we our Work begin;
> Heaps of fine Linen we before us view,
> Whereon to lay our Strength and Patience too;
> Cambricks and Muslins, which our Ladies wear,
> Laces and Edgings, costly, fine, and rare,
> Which must be wash'd with utmost Skill and Care;
> With Holland Shirts, Ruffles and Fringes too,
> Fashions which our Fore-fathers never knew. (13)

The mistress commands the women that 'we mind / Her Linen well, nor *leave the Dirt behind:* / Not this alone, but also to take care / We don't her Cambricks nor her Ruffles tear' (13–14). The mistress asks the impossible:

> And *these* most strictly does of us require,
> *To Save her Soap, and sparing be of Fire*;
> Tells us her Charge is great, nay furthermore,
> Her Cloaths are fewer than the Time before. (14)

The poet's mild disapproval of the mistress's extravagant dress – 'Fashions which our Fore-fathers never knew' – echoes the many conduct books that warn against vanity of dress and the economic burden on the husband's estate and the entire nation when wives purchase costly clothing. Here, the poet adds a human dimension to the cost: a large portion of 'poor Woman-kind' is oppressed because of the intense 'Drudgery' involved in caring for this type of clothing (6).

The work involved in washing was prodigious, as Hill has pointed out.[11] Washing was an ordeal that usually stretched over two or three days. Usually done in the kitchen, it disrupted cooking, since kettles used for cooking had to be commandeered for the clothes. Large amounts of water had to be fetched, many times from long distances, as did the wood with which to heat it. In *A PRESENT FOR A Servant-Maid*, Haywood instructs servants to collect water three or four days in advance in order for impurities to settle (71). The realities of eighteenth-century laundering meant that delicate fabrics often did not survive many washings. Caroline Davidson notes that most households spent a large proportion of their income on laundry, partly because soap made from animal or vegetable fats was very expensive. She observes that even the upper classes often used the much more caustic lye, saving soap for small or favourite items of clothing.[12] In *A Gentlewoman's Companion*, hoping to save the employer's money, Woolley warns servants doing laundry to be 'Sparing of your Soap, Fire and Candle' (216). In the poem, from the mistress's perspective the maids waste the precious soap, ruin the clothes by using water that is too hot, scrub too hard and leave the fabric threadbare; however, when the women attempt to save soap, she complains that the clothes remain filthy. Many servant manuals attempt to solve this problem; Shirley recommends washing starch-point laces by bringing them through 'four Lathers' (106) and Haywood advises the maids to use 'moderate Heat; for if it be too hot, it scalds the Dirt into the Linnen' (72). Instead of rubbing the linen 'very hard', she insists, the maids should let the 'Strength of the Lather and the Motion you give it' take the place of scrubbing (72). Later on in the century, Glasse, in *The Servant's Directory*, approaches this problem by detailing a complicated process for cleaning muslin and lace that involves several rounds of soaking in hot water, brushing the fabric gently, then rinsing, thus requiring several kettles of water to be on hand. No matter what method was used, the work was extremely time-consuming and harsh.

In 'THE Woman's Labour', while the charwomen are washing, the mistress provides '*perhaps* a Mug of Ale' to the women 'To cheer our Hearts, and also to inform / Herself, what Work is done that very

Morn' (13). This mistress does not give her duties over to a housekeeper, a practice Shirley and Haywood warn against, but checks on the women herself. John Goodridge notes that the mistress arrives several hours into the work and that her 'meagre bribe' of ale is an obvious ploy to spy on the servants' progress.[13] The weak ale is less than adequate to provide strength for the kind of work that the women must perform. As the poet laments, the constant motion and the heat go on all day until 'Not only Sweat, but Blood runs trickling down / Our Wrists and Fingers' (14). Nonetheless, the women cannot stop – the work 'demands / The constant Action of our lab'ring Hands' (14). When middle-class women adopt higher standards of cleanliness and fashionable dress in order to confirm their social status, the work for labouring women takes on a nightmarish quality. After the maids have washed, they are not done: 'The *Washing* is not all we have to do: / We oft change Work for Work as well as you [the male field laborer]' (15). The maids must also work in the kitchen, where 'Our Mistress of her Pewter doth complain, / And 'tis our Part to make it clean again' (15). Although polishing the pewter goes on for hours, it is 'not the worst we hapless Females do: / When Night comes on, and we quite weary are, / … / Pots, Kettles, Sauce-pans, Skillets, we may see, / Skimmers and Ladles, and such Trumpery, / Brought in to make complete our Slavery' (15). The physical action of cleaning takes its toll: 'On Brass and Iron we our Strength must spend; / Our tender Hands and Fingers scratch and tear' (15–16). In her directions to the scullery maid, Woolley draws up a list of kitchen items not to be overlooked: 'wash and scowre all the Plates and Dishes which are used in the Kitchen, also Kettles, Pots, Pans, Chamber-Pots, with all other Iron, Brass, and Pewter materials' (217). One can imagine the mistress in Collier's poem reading from this book aloud as she instructs the charwomen. Some books recommend sand or bran for cleaning dishes, but Shirley advocates cleaning 'Plate' by rubbing it with 'Chalk and Vinegar' (108). These cleaning materials probably account for the scratching and tearing of the speaker's hands in the poem. For the middle-class wife, elaborate dinners, such as the ones that Shirley lays out in *The Accomplished Ladies* (126–7; 141–5), are a sign of her social virtue and indicate her worth in the domestic sphere. To the female servants, the dishes that help the wife to fulfil her role are simply ‘Trumpery’ or worthless trinkets that wear out their bodies.

The poet laments that for her and her fellow female labourers, ‘All the Perfections Woman once could boast, / Are quite obscur’d, and altogether lost’ (16). The notion that women are creatures whose grace, daintiness and beauty place them naturally in the home, away from the concerns of the harsh public world of work, applies only to the privileged. Women of the higher classes are able to exhibit ideals of femininity by damaging the bodies and minds of lower-class women through constant and severe labour. In ‘THE Woman’s Labour’, the mistress’s harshness toward her servants arises from the pressure that she herself feels to maintain an ideal domestic atmosphere by dressing fashionably and being a gracious and generous hostess. By ending the poem at the landowner’s house, Collier shows how her oppression benefits an economic system that is patriarchal – from the exhausting underpaid work in the landowner’s fields to the unpaid domestic labour in her own home (by which the male field worker and landowner benefit) to that in the landlord’s home, where his wife, in order to enhance her husband’s (and therefore her own) status, nearly drives her female servants to physical and mental collapse. The poet compares her life of labour to ‘Danaus’ Daughters’, who must fill ‘Bottomless Tubs of Water’[14] and who, in the end, are poorly recompensed for their ‘Toils and Pains’ (17).

Initially printed in 1739, ‘THE Woman’s Labour’ also appeared in Collier’s *Poems on Several Occasions* (1762) along with additional verses. ‘THE Woman’s Labour’ seems to have been forgotten until recently.[15] Only four copies of the 1739 edition exist, together with three of the 1762 version with its set of additional verses. I have elected to reprint the 1739 edition housed at The British Library because of its legibility and availability for copying.

Eliza Fowler Haywood

Eliza Fowler Haywood (1693–1756) supported herself by her pen for over twenty years, writing plays, novels, journals, translations, conduct books and pamphlets. She is best known for her early novels, including

Love in Excess; or the Fatal enquiry (1719), *The British recluse* (1722), *The injur'd husband* (1723), *Fantomina; or, Love in a Maze* in *Secret Histories, Novels, and* Poems (1725) and *The city jilt; or, the alderman turn'd beau* (1726). For a time, she collaborated with Defoe on a series of sensational pamphlets (1720–25) about a deaf-mute man, Duncan Campbell, who professed to have prophetic powers. She also translated many continental romances, including *Letters from a lady of quality to a chevalier* (1721). Many of her early romances portray heroines brought to ruin or death by deceitful men who seduce them. After Haywood was ridiculed for these works by Pope in *The Dunciad* (1728), she wrote mainly novels of domestic fiction such as *The history of Miss Betsy Thoughtless* (1751) and *The history of Jemmy and Jenny Jessamy* (1753). Haywood also published the monthly journal *The female Spectator* (1744–46) and wrote conduct books such as *Epistles for the ladies* (1749), *The wife* (1756) and *The Husband. In answer to The Wife* (1756). Haywood published at least 60 works.

A PRESENT FOR A Servant-Maid. OR, THE Sure Means of gaining LOVE and ESTEEM. Under the following Heads ... To which are added, DIRECTIONS for going to MARKET: ALSO, For Dressing any Common Dish, whether FLESH, FISH, or FOWL. With some Rules for WASHING, &c. The whole calculated for making both the Mistress and the Maid happy (1743)

No doubt inspired by the success of books written for female domestic servants, Haywood published *A Present for a Servant-Maid*, apparently basing it on an extremely popular tract, Richard Mayo's *A Present For Servants, From their Ministers, Masters, or Other Friends* (1693; nineteen editions by 1821). Mayo takes a variety of approaches in order to control subversive female servants. He delivers familiar didactic rhetoric under headings such as 'The Servant's Reverence to their Masters', 'Of cheating and defrauding' and 'How Wicked Servants waste their Time'. Mayo also uses the time-tested argument that servants are relatively well off compared to those in past ages. He assures servants that they are in fact blessed, since they are not subject to the temptations of their betters: 'Did you but consider their [masters' and mistresses'] Temptations to Idleness, and thereby to almost all other sins, you would see that God has delivered you from many snares … By appointing you a moderate Labour … your Souls are not in danger of flattering the Great' (62). As an added bonus, servants' minds are free from daily worries about money and property, whereas masters are driven to distraction because they 'have great Rents to pay, and the Money hardly got to pay them with; they have Meat and Drink to provide for you … one trespasses on their Fields, and another defrauds them of their Debts … They have Losses to be made up abroad, and Houses to be repair'd at home' (63). Employing this same line of reasoning, Haywood asks female servants to take pity on their masters by considering the 'exorbitant taxes, and other Severities of the Times, [which] have, for some Years past, reduced our middling Gentry, as well as Tradesmen, to very great Straits' (32). The financial losses of the wealthy do not touch the servants, who are 'entirely free from all Incumberances, all Distractions of Mind, have only to do your Duty quietly … without Danger of having your Repose disturbed' (32). This type of discourse predominates in the book, while the collection of recipes and directions on going to the market and doing the laundry take up a little over one-fourth of the volume.

Haywood appeals to servants' self-interest by insisting that a good reputation will keep them with good families or help them find husbands. Under the heading 'Apeing the Fashion', Haywood warns against spending wages on 'rich Cloaths' because this will make it more difficult to find a husband, who will be looking for a wife with the reputation for 'Honesty, Industry and Frugality' (24–5). Wearing fashionable clothing carries the risk of having the servant's reputation called into question by those who would compare the 'Profits with your Purchases' and conclude that the clothing was obtained by fraud (25). When Haywood describes how servants sometimes find bargains on food or household items and pocket the difference, she asserts that guilt over such acts will eventually create a mental breakdown of sorts that might betray the servant to her mistress and cause 'your Character [to be] utterly destroyed' (27). By losing her reputation, the servant will lose any chance of employment, be forced into petty fraud, and then into even greater thievery; eventually, she will suffer a 'shameful Death', presumably by hanging (27). Haywood treats female domestics as individuals with agency and assumes that they desire to better themselves, abandoning earlier rhetoric that called for servants to give up control of their own will and personality utterly. Haywood continues to insist that servants please the master and mistress at all times, but she also recognizes that they have hopes and desires of their own. Her purpose is to present appropriate ways to control or channel ambition, holding out the hope of an advantageous marriage, of finding employment in wealthy and noble families or of resigned complacency. As we will see in Swift's text, however, efforts to bring about internalized subservience have the potential to produce the opposite effect.

A PRESENT FOR A Servant-Maid was first published in 1743 and went through seven editions by 1749. A work published in 1771 as *A New Present For A Servant-Maid* by 'Mrs. Haywood' is a reissue of the 1743 edition with several changes. The compiler, who is not identified, expanded the book from 74 pages to 292 by adding many more recipes. In this edition, the advice on moral behaviour is much shorter than in Haywood's 1743 edition. The 1771 text was published only twice in the eighteenth century. Both Mayo's *A Present For Servants* and Haywood's 1743 edition have been reproduced together in a facsimile edited by Randolph Trumbach (New York & London: Garland 1985). After examining copies from several libraries, including the now-missing copy that was held at The New York Public Library, I have chosen to reproduce the first edition formerly held at The New York Public Library (fortunately available there on microfilm) because it is one of the most complete and legible.

Jonathan Swift

Born in Ireland to English parents, Jonathan Swift (1667–1745) is best known for his brilliant satirical works such as *A tale of a tub* (1704), attacking what he saw as the abuses of religion and learning, as well as *A modest proposal* (1729) and *Gulliver's Travels* (1726). As first a Whig and then a Tory, as an Irish patriot and as a priest in the Anglican Church of Ireland, Swift composed many polemical pamphlets, essays and Pindaric odes about politics and religion. Seeking preferment in the Anglican Church in England, he left Ireland in 1688. He was never to obtain an ecclesiastical position in England; instead, he was ordained a priest in the Church of Ireland in 1695, and was appointed Dean of St Patrick's Cathedral in Dublin in 1713. He died in 1745, some years after suffering from a paralytic stroke.

DIRECTIONS TO SERVANTS IN GENERAL; And in particular to The BUTLER, COOK, FOOTMAN, COACHMAN, GROOM, HOUSE-STEWARD, and LAND-STEWARD, PORTER, DAIRY-MAID, CHAMBER-MAID, NURSE, LAUNDRESS, HOUSE-KEEPER, TUTORESS, or GOVERNESS (1745)

Although Swift penned serious works about the need for servants to be industrious and faithful, such as 'Laws for the Dean's Servants' (1733), his popular *DIRECTIONS TO SERVANTS* is almost a direct parody of Haywood. On the one hand, the book satirizes servants, portraying them as self-serving and indifferent to the chaos and ruin that their tactics produce. On the other, it is a criticism of the ruling class itself, a class whose financial mismanagement and immoral behaviour have allowed the reversal of the household's balance of power. Swift is quick to recognize that many of Haywood's rules can be read subversively, and his book highlights the impossibility of instilling values in servants who would then always and automatically serve their betters' interests and create a socioeconomic utopia. For example, Haywood cautions servants against taking the dinner leftovers for themselves. She explains that servants try to get away with such behaviour by blaming the loss of the food on the household pets. Such dishonest servants ensure that the 'poor Cat or Dog has the Blame, who, before you were aware, stole all out of the Dish' (31). By giving elaborate and detailed examples of how 'bad' servants cover up their acts of thievery and other misconduct, Haywood is disseminating insider information about how servants might use the system to their own advantage. The dilemma recalls the complaint that prisons actually serve as schools for criminals – crooks learn all sorts of tricks of the trade while incarcerated. Of course, Haywood writes such examples with the belief that the reader will inevitably want to see herself as different from the thieving servants and take these examples as moral lessons.

Swift, however, envisions the servant reading these instructions and identifying with the bad servants. So, when he discusses the same issue – servants taking food for themselves – he takes Haywood's example one step further: 'Never send up a Leg of a Fowl at Supper, while there is a Cat or a Dog in the House that can be accused of running away with it' (38). He advises holding back the main course itself so that the servants can eat it. Why stop at holding back the leftovers when you can use the same excuse to get even more and better food? Swift's 'instruction' in this example reveals the slippage of meaning in servant tract warnings. Swift's tone is close to Haywood's and reveals that the difference between prescription and proscription of certain behaviours can be muddied.

Shirshendu Chakrabarti has pointed out that the two worlds in Swift's text – upstairs and downstairs – although supposed to form a hierarchical power structure, become a 'powerful metaphor for movement up and down, for the equivocal nature of social mobility' (115). Swift's advice to the maid, for example, to use her mistress's riding hood and cloak to go to market on a wet day in order to save the servant's own clothing is doubly subversive. On the one hand, by wearing her mistress's expensive cloak to market, the servant will likely ruin it, requiring her employer to purchase another one. On the other, when dressed in her mistress's clothing, the servant is indistinguishable from her, erasing class differences (at least temporarily) and revealing the artificiality of class lines. As Swift describes the master's and mistress's relationships with their chambermaids and footmen, the servants become impossible to tell from their betters as they pick up the social habits that, in turn, elicit emulation from the gentry themselves. As the narrator says to the footman, 'You are sometimes a Pattern of Dress to your Master, and sometimes he is so to you. You wait at Table in all Companies, and consequently have the Opportunity to see and know the World, and to understand Men and Manners' (46). In other words, the footman, because of his proximity to many people of distinction, is able to pick up nuances in fashion and manners to such a degree that his own master will sometimes rely on him for the latest in upper-class behaviour. The narrator of *DIRECTIONS* underscores the implications of this statement by casually explaining that all this may lead the servant to 'pick up a Fortune, Perhaps your

Master's Daughter' (46). The author realizes that the similarity of servants, especially upper servants, to those above them threatens to blur class distinctions. In addition, the servant may become a member of the upper class in reality if he is able to gather a fortune because of inside knowledge or if his behaviour mirrors that of a gentleman to the extent that he is able to marry a woman higher in status.

Throughout his book, Swift taps into his society's deepest anxieties about servants. Because idleness was deemed one of the worst offences, much of *DIRECTIONS* assumes that the servants run the household according to their own convenience, putting their own leisure ahead of everything else. As he tells the cook, 'As soon as you have sent up the second Course, you have nothing to do in a great Family until Supper: Therefore ... take your Pleasure among your Cronies until Nine or Ten at night' (43–4). If dinner is running late, the cook-maid should 'put the clock back, then it will be ready to a Minute' (42). But Swift does not simply invert hierarchies. His subversive directions appear to conform outwardly to the ideological intent of conventional warnings to servants. In doing so, he exposes their logical contradictions. For example, Swift appears to reverse the usual exhortations that servants be honest when purchasing food at the market: 'If you are employed in Marketing, buy your Meat as cheap as you can', he says, and then he advises that, when giving an account to the master, servants 'be tender of your Master's Honour, and set down the highest Rate' (38). He explains that keeping the money saved on buying the meat at a lower cost is actually a good practice, since it enhances the master's sense of his own status for him to think that he has bought a high-priced piece of meat to set before company. The servant's decision to hold back the price difference is presented not as greed, but as a commendable desire to put the master's honour first. Swift suggests that, when one rule must be favoured over another, the rule that will benefit the servant may be kept in good conscience.

DIRECTIONS, therefore, exposes the logical contradictions within the ideals of household thrift and hospitality. When Swift says that the cook should 'Always keep a large Fire in the Kitchen when there is a small Dinner', he justifies his instruction by pointing out that when the 'Neighbors [see] the smoak [they] may commend your Master's Housekeeping' (41), meaning that the community will believe that the master entertains often and generously. On the other hand, when a large company does happen to dine at the master's house, 'then be as sparing as possible of your Coals, because a great deal of the Meat being half raw will be saved, and serve next Day' (41). The irony is that because much money has been wasted by burning fuel so as to appear hospitable, stingy portions of meat must then be served when guests do attend dinners. Swift reveals how many instructions to servants were impossibly contradictory. We had been reminded of this truth in 'THE Woman's Labour', when the poet related how the mistress urges the servants to get the clothes clean and keep them from tatters while simultaneously saving soap and avoiding rubbing. Domestic thrift and hospitality often clash, and in most cases, as Collier has shown, it is the servants who suffer. Collier's mistress must maintain her reputation for keeping a good table, which means saving on cleaning materials and wages for the charwomen. Swift's text, however, portrays a household in which servants exploit the contradictions to their own benefit.

DIRECTIONS TO SERVANTS was first published in 1745 and went through ten editions by 1778. In the nineteenth century, the book was reprinted in Swift's collected works. In 1843, John Jackson published a humorous revision of Swift's work entitled *Hints to servants: being a poetical and modernised version of Dean Swift's celebrated "Directions to servants"; in which something is added to the original text, but those passages are omitted which cannot with propriety to be read aloud in a kitchen, by an upper servant*. An edition of Swift's *DIRECTIONS* came out in 1925, and in 1964 the book was published with humorous illustrations by Joseph Low. A more recent edition, with a foreword by Colm Tóibín, appeared in 2003. After examining copies from several libraries, I chose the copy of the first edition held by The British Library because it is one of the most complete and legible.

Acknowledgements

I am indebted to the following librarians and institutions for their generous assistance in helping me locate the best texts to use for the facsimile editions. I thank each of them for taking the time to examine carefully copies of the texts: Maggie Powell and Susan Walker, The Lewis Walpole Library, Yale University; Rebecca Cape, the Lilly Library, Indiana University; Bettina Smith, The Folger Shakespeare Library; Ellen Cordes, Beinecke Rare Book and Manuscript Library, Yale University.

I would also like to thank The British Library, London, and The New York Public Library, New York, for granting me permission to reproduce texts from their collections. Finally, I would like to thank the series' general editors, Anne Lake Prescott and Betty S. Travitsky for their many helpful suggestions.

Notes

1 See Hill (1996) and Sambrook (1999 and 2005).
2 Richardson (2004).
3 Hill (1994), 125–6; (1996), 35–9.
4 See Snell (1985) and Hill (1994).
5 Hill (1994), 37–40, Hecht (1956), and Davidson (1982). On the cultural desire to maintain social credibility through hospitality and a well-ordered house, see Muldrew (2000).
6 Sherman (1995); also Robbins (1986).
7 Quoted by Vickery (1998), 128, from Thomas Wright (ed.), *Autobiography of Thomas Birkenshaw in the County of York, 1736–1797* (London, 1864), p. 146.
8 Muldrew (2000), 158.
9 See Vickery (1998) and Muldrew (2000) for discussions of how people during the period thought of public and private space.
10 For a thorough discussion of plebeian poets in the eighteenth century, see Christmas (2000).
11 Hill (1994), 110–13.
12 Davidson (1982), 144.
13 Goodridge (1995).
14 For killing their husbands, Danaus' daughters were punished in the underworld by having continually to pour water into jars with holes.
15 One of the earliest studies of the poem was made by Landry (1989).

References

Wing S3498 [Shirley]; ESTCT52659 [Collier]; ESCTI98873 [Haywood]; ESTCT69637 [Swift]

Armstrong, Nancy (1989), *Desire and Domestic Fiction: A Political History of the Novel*, London: Oxford University Press

Arnold, Bruce (1999), *Swift: An Illustrated Life*, Dublin: Lilliput Press

Barker, Hannah and Elaine Chalus (1997), *Gender in Eighteenth-Century England: Roles, Representations, and Responsibilities*, New York: Longman Publishing

Baudino, Isabelle, Jacque Carré and Cécile Révauger (2005), *The Invisible Woman: Aspects of Women's Work in Eighteenth-Century Britain*, Aldershot: Ashgate

Bennett, Judith (1988), 'History that Stands Still: Women's Work in the European Past', *Feminist Studies* 14: 269–83

Chakrabarti, Shirshendu (1996), 'Master and Servant: Social Mobility and the Ironic Exchange of Roles in Swift's *Directions to Servants*', in Alvaro Ribeiro S.J. and James G. Basker (eds), *Tradition in Translation: Women Writers, Marginal Texts, and the Eighteenth-Century Canon*, Oxford: Clarendon Press

Christmas, William (2001), *The Lab'ring Muses: Work, Writing, and the Social Order in English Plebeian Poetry in England, 1730–1830*, Newark, DE: University of Delaware Press; London: Associated University Presses

Darby, Barbara (2000), 'The More Things Change … The Rules and Late Eighteenth-Century Conduct Books for Women', *Women's Studies: An Interdisciplinary Journal* 29.3: 333–55

Davidson, Caroline (1982), *A Woman's Work is Never Done: A History of Housework in the British Isles, 1650–1950*, London: Chatto & Windus

Davidson, Jenny (2001), 'Swift's Servant Problem: Livery and Hypocrisy in the Project for the Advancement of Religion and the *Directions to Servants*', *Studies in Eighteenth-Century Culture* 30: 105–25

Ehrenpreis, Irvin (1962–83), *Swift: the Man, and His Works, and the Age*, 3 vols, London: Methuen

Evett, David (2005), *Discourses of Service in Shakespeare's England*, New York: Palgrave Macmillan

Ezell, Margaret (1987), *The Patriarch's Wife*, Chapel Hill, NC: University of North Carolina Press

Ferguson, Moira (1995), *Eighteenth-Century Women Poets: Nation, Class, and Gender*, Albany, NY: State University of New York Press

Fite, Patricia Paulette Lonchar (1996), '*The Illustrious History of Women* (1686) by John Shirley: A Critical Edition with an Introduction and Notes', Ph.D. dissertation, Texas A&M University

Flint, Christopher (1998), *Family Fictions: Narrative and Domestic Relations in Britain, 1688–1798*, Stanford, CA: Stanford University Press

Goodridge, John (1995), *Rural Life in Eighteenth-Century English Poetry*, Cambridge: Cambridge University Press

Hartman, Mary (2004), *The Household and the Making of History*, Cambridge: Cambridge University Press

Hecht, Jean (1956), *The Domestic Servant Class in Eighteenth-Century England*, London: Routledge

Hill, Bridget (1987; 1994), *Women, Work and Sexual Politics in Eighteenth-Century England*, Montreal and Kingston: McGill-Queen's University Press

——— (1996), *Servants: English Domestics in the Eighteenth Century*, Oxford: Clarendon Press

Kittridge, Katherine (ed.) (2003), *Lewd and Notorious: Female Transgression in the Eighteenth Century*, Ann Arbor, MI: University of Michigan Press

Korda, Natasha (2002), *Shakespeare's Domestic Economies*, Philadelphia, PA: University of Pennsylvania Press

Kussmaul, Ann (1981), *Servants in Husbandry in Early Modern England*, Cambridge: Cambridge University Press

Landry, Donna (1989), *The Muses of Resistance: Laboring-Class Women's Poetry in Britain, 1739–1796*, Cambridge: Cambridge University Press

Lehmann, Gilly (1999), 'Politics in the Kitchen', *Eighteenth-Century Life* 23: 71–83

McBride, Kari Boyd (ed.) (2002), *Domestic Arrangements in Early Modern England*, Pittsburgh, PA: Duquesne Press

Maclean, Virginia (1981), *A Short-Title Catalogue of Household and Cookery Books Published in the English Tongue, 1701–1800*, London: Prospect Books; Charlottesville, VA: distributed by the University Press of Virginia

McMinn, Joseph (1991), *Jonathan Swift: A Literary Life*, Basingstoke: Macmillan

Mendelson, Sara and Patricia Crawford (1998), *Women in Early Modern England, 1550–1720*, Oxford: Clarendon Press

Milne, Anne (2001), 'Gender, Class, and the Beehive: Mary Collier's "The Woman's Labour" (1739) as Nature Poem', *ISLE: Interdisciplinary Studies in Literature and Environment* 8.2:109–29

Muldrew, Craig (2000), *The Economy of Obligation: the Culture and Credit of Social Relations in Early Modern England*, London: Macmillan Press

Murray, John Middleton (1955), *Jonathan Swift: A Critical Biography*, New York: The Noonday Press

Nokes, David (1985), *Jonathan Swift: A Hypocrite Reversed*, Oxford: Oxford University Press

Northrop, Douglas A. (2002), 'The Lively Heroine: Eliza Haywood's Later Novels as Conduct Books', in *Proceedings of the Tenth Annual Northern*

Plains Conference on Earlier British Literature, Barbara Olive and David Sprunger (eds and introd.), Moorhead, MN: Concordia College, 32–41

Overton, Mark (2004), *Production and Consumption in English Households, 1600–1750*, London; New York: Routledge

Owens, Judith Hildreth (1977), 'Philosophy in the Kitchen', *Eighteenth-Century Life* 3: 77–9

Richardson, R.C. (2004), 'Social Engineering in Early Modern England: Masters, Servants, and the Godly Discipline', *CLIO:* 33.2: 163–87

Richetti, John (1987), 'Representing an Under Class: Servants and Proletarians in Fielding and Smollett', in Felicity Nussbaum and Laura Brown (eds), *The New Eighteenth Century: Theory, Politics, English Literature*, New York: Routledge, 84–98

Robbins, Bruce (1986), *The Servant's Hand: English Fiction From Below*, New York: Columbia University Press

Sambrook, Pamela (1999), *The Country House Servant*, Stroud: Sutton Publishing in association with the National Trust

——— (2005), *Keeping Their Place: Domestic Service in the Country House, 1700–1920*, Stroud: Sutton Publishing

Saxon, Kirsten T. and Rebecca P. Bocchicchio (eds) (2000), *Passionate Fictions of Eliza Haywood: Essays on Her Life and Work*, Lexington, KY: University Press of Kentucky

Schofield, Mary Anne (1985), *Eliza Haywood*, Boston, MA: Twayne

Sharpe, Pamela (ed.), (1998), *Women's Work: the English Experience, 1650–1914*, London: Arnold Publishers

Sherman, Sandra (1995), 'Servants and Semiotics: Reversible Signs, Capital Instability, and Defoe's Logic of the Market', *ELH* 25: 551–73

Snell, K.D.M. (1985), *Annals of the Labouring Poor: Social Change and Agrarian England, 1660–1900*, Cambridge: Cambridge University Press

Spedding, Patrick (2004), *A Bibliography of Eliza Haywood*, London: Pickering and Chatto

Stead, Jennifer (1980), "'Quizzing Glasse: Or Hannah Scrutinized", in *'First Catch Your Hare…': The Art of Cookery Made Plain And Easy'*, facsimile reprint of the first edition of *The Art of Cookery Made Plain and Easy*, by Hannah Glasse, London, 1747, London: Prospect Books

Swift, Jonathan (1925), *Directions to Servants*, with decorations by John Nash, Waltham Saint Lawrence, Berkshire: Golden Cockerel Press

——— (1964), *Jonathan Swift's Directions to Servants*, with drawings by Joseph Low, New York: Pantheon Books

——— (2003), *Directions to Servants*, with a foreword by Tóibín Colm, London: Hesperus

Vickery, Amanda (1998), *The Gentleman's Daughter: Women's Lives in Georgian England*, New Haven, CT: Yale University Press

Wall, Wendy (2002), *Staging Domesticity: Household Work and English Identity in Early Modern Drama*, Cambridge: Cambridge University Press

JEANNIE DALPORTO

J[ohn] S[hirley], *The Accomplished Ladies Rich Closet* (Wing S3498) is reproduced, by permission, from the British Library copy (shelfmark 1037.e.25). The text block of the original measures 136 × 69 mm.

Pages and lines where the British Library copy is blotted:

Title page.1:	Closet	167.31:	Woman
Title page.16:	Diseases	183.22:	*Holy Men*
Title page.17:	-Maids	183.23:	be in private
Title page.18:	Washing,	183.24:	self is
Title page.19:	Gold	183.25:	on those
Title page.20:	Cook-	183.26:	*inclinable*
Title page.24:	Directi-	183.27:	*a Day holy set a-*
Title page.25:	delivery	183.28:	peculiarly
Title page.26:	relates		designed for
Title page.28:	Containing	183.29:	ought on no day
Title page.29:	Young Gentle-		to
Title page.30:	Deportment, &	183.30:	keep it with the
Title page.31:	Boddington	183.31:	not only your
Title page.32:	1687	183.32:	Actions
82.20:	it	184.20:	him pray
100.25:	appear	184.21:	v.13. And
100.26:	water	184.22:	blessings
106.12:	Starch	184.24:	With
125.3:	for	184.25:	; for
141.2:	White	184.26:	of Heaven
141.17:	quarter	184.27:	things shall be
141.25:	Amber	184.28:	And this much
141.26:	salt	184.29:	in-struct you
142.14	Bones	184.30:	your
150.25:	and	185.19:	as
166.26:	material	219.7:	constant
166.27:	observed	228.7:	to be
167.30:	sprawling		

John Long

June the

1st 1792

Angel Sarah

Long

1793

The
Accomplished
Ladies
Rich Closet
of
RARITIES
or the
Ingenious
Gentlewoman
&
Servant Maids
Delightfull
Companion
London Printed for
N Bodington & J Blare

The Accomplished Ladies Rich Closet

OF

RARITIES:

OR THE

Ingenious Gentlewoman and Servant-Maids Delightfull Companions.

Containing many Excellent Things for the ACCOMPLISHMENT of the FEMALE SEX, after the exactest Manner and Method, *Viz.*

1. The Art of Distilling. 2. Making Artificial Wines. 3. Making Syrups. 4 Conserving, Preserving, *&c.* 5. Candying and Drying Fruits, *&c.* 6. Confectioning. 7. Carving. 8. To make Beautifying-waters, Oyls, Pomatums, Musk-balls, Perfumes, *&c.* 9. Physical and Chyrurgical Receipts. 10. The Duty of a Wet Nurse; and to know and cure Diseases in Children, *&c.* 11. The Compleat Chamber-Maids Instructions in Pickling, making Spoonmeats; Washing, Starching, taking out Spots and Stains, Scowring Gold or Silver Lace, Point, *&c.* 12. The Experienced Cook-Maid, or Instructions for Dressing, Garnishing, making Sawces, serving up together, with the Art of Pastry. 13. Bills of Fare 14. The Accomplished Dairy-Maids Directions, *&c.* 15. The Judicious Midwives Directions, how Women in Travail before and after delivery ought to be used; as also the Child; and what relates to the Preservation of them both.

To which is added a Second Part, Containing

Directions for the Guidance of a Young Gentlewoman as to her Behaviour and seemly Deportment, *&c.*

LONDON, Printed by *W. W.* for *Nicholas Boddington* in *Duck-Lane*; and *Josiah Blare* on *London-Bridge*. 1687.

Licenſed,

Aug. 26.
1686.

Rob. Midgley.

Pilulæ *Londinenſes*, or, the *London Pills*.

MAde by the Author Dr. *Richard Brown* (of long ſtanding in the College of Phyſicians) and ſold at his Houſe in *Winchester* Street, *London*, for the ſake of the Publick, who have had their Bodies miſerably tormented by the unwholſome Phyſick of illiterate Quacks and Mountebanks, which has been obtruded upon the World, for divers years laſt paſt, under the Name of Pills, Elixirs, Spirits, *&c.*

THE PREFACE TO THE READER.

Reader,

IN consideration that variety is most taking, especially of such things as are highly necessary, I have thought it convenient not only for Delight, but for the Accomplishment of the Female Sex, to set forth what must undoubtedly turn to their advantage, and consequently more than a Preface can express, or a sudden conception bring forth, if seriously and deliberately considered, to a degree of Practice; for indeed without industry, the smallest matter cannot be brought to perfection. Things Natural and Artificial owe their Original to Labour and Industry; the first to the visible and insensible workings of Nature; the second to that of the Creature; nor without these could the World subsist. But to come nearer the subject-matter.

In the following Treatise you will find not only approved Rules, Instructions and Directions for particular persons, whose ability and leasure may contribute in an extraordinary manner to the highest Acquirement, but such as are suitable to all degrees and capacities; such as must contribute to the Advancement of each Individual-Female, to a Station that may render her acceptable in the eyes of great ones, or at least create her a good repute, and pronounce her happy, though moving in a lower sphere. All that we can term Accomplish'd *in Female conduct, is briefly to be found in the following Pages; digested into so easie and plain a method, that it will, no doubt, insensibly attract the desire of the Reader to make an Essay; and that*

Essay being found both profitable and delightful, will carry her further in the progress of Pleasure and Advantage, till she confesses the time and cost was well bestowed; and becomes an Admonisher of others to make the like improvement; nothing of this nature being more exact in directing the Female Sex in what is seemly and profitable from Infancy to extremity of Age, and is a fit Companion upon all commendable occasions, in whatsoever state or condition, even from the Lady to the inferiour Servant-Maid, being a Directory, *in which nothing necessary for the Accomplishment and Qualification of the Sex is omitted, in relation to Education, Breeding, good Manners, Courtly deportment, prudent Conduct and Management of Affairs, being the very Quintessence of what ever has been practised or published, and more perhaps than can probably be expected in so small a Book. But thinking no labour too much to advantage the fair Sex, I have travelled through the World of Curiosities, to furnish out this Cabinet of Rarities, in hopes it will find a kind acceptance, and turn to the advantage of those who rightly consider it. In expectation of which, I remain,*

LADIES, *&c.*

Yours to serve you

in what I may,

John Shirley.

The

The Accomplished Ladies Rich Closet of Rarities, &c.

CHAP. I.

Rules and Directions for a Gentlewoman in the Art and Way of Alimbecking, Distilling and making sundry sorts and kinds of Waters, Physical, Chyrurgical, and pleasantly useful on divers occasions; With the Order, Manner of Composition, and quantity of Ingredients, &c.

ALimbecking and Distilling are held by many to be Learned, or taken by the Ancients from the Operation of the Sun in it's effectually Exhaling the Sublunar moisture, and Rarifying the gross and indigested Vapours in a more subtil Region; and indeed Distillations participate of a Solar vertue, as being by their penetrating qualities, and insensible Operations, more quick, subtil and enlivening. Wherefore I have thought it highly convenient to give Directions in this

Chapter how to Distill and draw off su Waters from Herbs, and other Cordial matters, as may contribute to the preservation of Health, and wherewith a Gentlewoman, being furnished, may be instrumental in saving the lives, or at least in doing good to her poor Neighbours: And in this case the Simples that are to be put into the *Still* together to draw off your compound Waters, which indeed are the most effectual in their Operations, ought to be considered: the several Directions for which, take as followeth.

A distilled Water, good to prevent the Danger of Infectious Air, Plague, Pestilence, &c.

Take the buds, or green husks of Walnuts, or the leaves of that tree a handful, of Rue the like quantity, and as much Baum: bruise them, and add of Mugwort, Celendine, Angelica, Agrimony, Pimpernel and wild Dragons, or Snap-dragons, each half a handful, bruise them as the former, and being put into an Earthen-pot or Glass, pour on them a Gallon and a half of white or Rhenish-wine, and let them stand four days, afterward putting the Wine and Herbs in an Alembeck; draw off the Quintessence: or it may be done, for want of conveniency, in a cold Still.

The

The Famous Water, called Dr. Stevens's *Water, is made to the best advantage; thus.*

Take a gallon of French Wine, of Cloves, Mace, Carraways, Coriander and Fenel-seeds, Gallinga, Ginger, Cinamon, Grains, Nutmeg, Anniseed, of each a dram; to these add Camomile, Sage, Mint, Rue, red Roses, Peletory of the Wall, wild Marjorum, wild Thyme, Lavender, Penyroyal, the Roots of Fennel, Parsley and Setwall, of each four ounces; and having bruised them, put them into two quarts of Canary, and the like quantity of Ale; and then having stood sixteen hours, with often stirring, draw off the Quintessence by Alembeck over a soft fire.

This Water is a wonderful fortifier of Nature in all cold Diseases, preserving Youth, comforting the Stomach, and is given with success to such as are afflicted with the Stone or Gravel.

Cinamon-Water is properly made thus.

Take half a pound of Cinamon, bruise it and steep it in a quart of white Wine, a quart of Rose-water, and a pint of Muscadel, twelve hours, with often stirring; and from this Alembeck three pints, which will not be only pleasant, but fortifie nature, and restore lost vigour.

To make Rosemary Water.

Take the Flowers and Leaves of Rosemary in their prime, half a pound and four ounces of Elicampane Roots, a handful of Red Sage, three ounces of Cloves, the same quantity of Mace, and twelve ounces of Anniseeds: beat the Herbs together, and the Spices separately, putting to them four gallons of White-wine; and after a weeks standing, distill them over a gentle fire.

Spirit of Wine; how to make it.

To Distill, or rather Alembeck Spirit of Wine, is to draw off any Wine you think fit over a gentle fire to what height you please, by often rectifying it, and is very good moderately taken, in cold distempers, or to mix with Cordial Waters of a cooler nature.

To make Treacle-water excellent good, in case of Surfeits, or the like disorders of the Body.

Take the Husks of green Walnuts, four handfuls of the juyce of Rue, Cardus, Marigolds and Baum, of each a pint; green Petasitis Roots one pound, Angelica and Masterwort of each half a pound; the Leaves of Scordium four handfuls, old Venice-Treacle and

and Mithridate, of each eight ounces; six quarts of Canary, of Vinegar three quarts, and of Lime-Juyce one quart: which being two days digested in a Bath in a close Vessel, distill them in Sand, *&c.*

A Cordial Mint-Water is thus made.

Take two handfuls of Mint green, two handfuls of Cardus, and one of Wormwood, and soak them in new Milk; being bruised, and after three or four hours infusion, draw off the water by way of distillation, and keep it close stopped for your use, it being excellent good in case of pains in the Belly or Stomach.

An Excellent Water for Sore Eyes, or to Restore the sight.

Take Smallage, Rue, Fennel, Vervein, Egremony, Scabeous, Avens, Hounds-tongue, Eufrace, Pimpernel and Sage, of each a handful; Roach-Allum half an ounce, Honey a spoonful, dissolved in Rosewater: distill them in a cold Still; and when you use it, put in a little Allum and Honey, and suffer it to dissolve, washing your Mouth with it Evening and Morning.

An Excellent Water for a Canker.

Take of the Bark of an Elder-Tree, Sorrel and Sage, of each two handfuls: stamp them well, and strain out the liquid part, mingling it with double the quantity of White-wine, and often with a feather dipped in it, wash the Sore, *&c.*

A Water very good for a Fistula.

Take a pint of White-wine, an ounce of the Juyce of Sage, Borace in Powder three peny weight, Camphire-powder the weight of a groat: boil them two hours over a gentle fire; strain them through a Woollen-cloth; and being cold, wash therewith the place grieved.

An Excellent Water to cleanse any filthy Ulcer.

Take of the Water of Plantane, and that of Red Roses, each a pint; the Juyces of Housleek, Nightshade and Plantane, of each a quarter of a pint: Red Roses half a handful, Myrtle, Cyprus-nuts, of each half an ounce; of the Rind of Pomgranet three drams, St. *John*'s Wort half a handful, Flowers of Molleyn half as much, Myrrh, Frankincense, each a scruple; Honey of Roses a pound

pound and four ounces: Diftill them toge-ther, and of the Water take a pint, and dif-folve in it fix ounces of Conferve of Rofes, and one ounce of Syrup of dry Rofes, with twelve drops of the Oyl of Brimitone, and wafh the place grieved.

An Excellent Water for the Heats and Inflam-mation of the Eyes.

Take of Aloes, Epatick, fine Sugar, Tut-ty-ftone powdered, each an ounce; of red and white Rofewater, each a pint: put them in a double glafs, and fet them in *Balneo Ma-ria* five or fix days, often fhaking them, and with a feather dipped in it, wafh your Eyes as often as you fee occafion, as likewife your Forehead and Temples.

An Excellent Water for a fore Leg, or for a Can-ker in any part or place.

Take of Woodbine-leaves, Ribwort, Plan-tane, Abinte, of each a handful Clarified; Englifh Honey three fpoonfuls, Roach-Allum an ounce: put them into three quarts of Run-ning-water, and let them feeth till a third part be confumed; then ftrain out the liquid part, and keep it in a new glazed Earthen-pot for your ufe, wafhing the afflicted place with it twice a day.

A Water

A Water to turn back the Rhume that afflicts the Eyes.

Take of red Rose-water six ounces, White-wine and Eyebright-water, of each the like quanantity; *Lapis-Tuttiæ* three scruples, Alloes Epatick the like quantity, fine Sugar two ounces: put them into a glass with a narrow neck, and set them in the Sun for the space of thirty days, shaking them twice a day, and then with the liquid part wash the Eye-lids, Temples, Forehead, and the Nape of the Neck.

An Excellent Water to cool the Liver and Heart; as also in case of a Feaver, Surfeit or Ill digestion.

Take two handfuls of Wood-sorrel, the like of Barbary-leaves, half a dozen Plantane-roots washed and sliced, two ounces of Mellion-seed; of Comfry and Borrage-flowers, each an ounce: steep them in a gallon of fair water, well sweetned with Sugar-candy, and distill them, giving the party grieved two ounces of the Water with an ounce of the Syrup of Citron or Lemon.

An Excellent Water for an Internal Bruise.

Take two handfuls of Scabeous-flowers of Peny-royal, Camomile, Smallage and Bay-leaves, each a handful; Myrrh pulverized, half an ounce; Harts-horn two ounces, and two quarts of Malaga-wine: bruise the Herbs, *&c.* in the Wine, and then distill them altogether, and let the party drink two ounces of the Water Morning and Evening.

An Excellent Water for the Stone, to provoke Urine, and prevent Stoppage, &c.

Take two quarts of new Milk, Saxifrage, Parsley, Peletory of the Wall, Mother Time, green Sage, Radish-roots sliced, of each a handful: steep the Herbs and Roots over night in the Milk, and distill them the next morning; which done, mingle six spoonfuls of the Water, with as much White-wine, into which grating a third part of a Roasted Nutmeg, drink it off, and so continue to do divers times, and you will find extraordinary benefit thereby.

Poppy-Water; how to make it.

Take two pound of red Poppy-leaves, half an ounce of bruised Cloves, and the like quantity

quantity of ſliced Nutmeg: ſteep theſe in a quart of Canary, and after two hours ſtanding, put them into your *Still*, and draw off the Water over a gentle fire.

Cordial Angelica-Water is made thus.

Take of *Cardus Benedictus* a handful well dried, of Angelica-roots three ounces, of Nutmeg, Cinamon and Ginger, each an ounce, of Myrrh half an ounce, and one dram and a half of Saffron, of Cardamums, Cubebs, Galingal and Pepper, of each a quarter of an ounce; bruiſe them and ſteep them in two quarts of Canary, and draw them off with a common *Still*.

Aquamirabilis *is thus made.*

Take three pints of White-wine, of the Juyce of Celandine and *Aquavitæ*, each a pint; Cardamer and the Flowers of Melilot, a dram of each; of Cubebs, Gallingal, Cloves, Mace and Ginger, of each a dram: bruiſe them and put them to the Liquor, where ſoaking all night, the next morning ſet them on a *Still* in a glaſs *Alimbeck*, and draw off the Quinteſſence.

[The Water prevents the Putrefaction of the Blood; is good in caſe of the ſwelling of the Lungs; removes the Heart-burn, and pur-

purgeth Flegm and Melancholy, *&c.*] Divers other Waters of Physical Vertue I might mention, but having many things yet to propose, and intending brevity, I shall proceed from Distilled Physical Waters to give Directions for making Artificial Wines, *&c.* And as for such Waters as are for Beautifying, I shall treat of them in another place.

CHAP. II.

Instructions for a Gentlewoman how to make Artificial Wines and other pleasant Liquors, necessary and profitable both for Sale, and to be kept in private Houses for the Accommodation of Friends, &c.

AS there are many pleasant Liquors made rather Artificial than Natural, so it will not be amiss to say something of them, which for variety may not prove pleasant only, but profitable, and are very commendable to be kept in the House for the Entertainment of friends and strangers, who being perhaps rarely used to such, will set a value on them above any other: But to the purpose.

To

To make Cherry-Wine.

Stone your Cherries before they are too ripe, press them in a Preſs, or through a clean cloth, and let the Juyce ſettle, then draw it off, and bottle it up with half an ounce of Loaf-ſugar, and a piece of Cinamon in each bottle, and tying the Cork down, let it ſtand ſix weeks; and then being opened, it will drink pleaſant and brisk.

Hypocras is made thus.

Take a gallon of White or Rheniſh-wine, and put to it two pound of Loaf-ſugar, Cinamon, Mace, Pepper, Grains, Gallingal and Cloves, of each a quarter of an ounce; bruiſing the Spices, and putting them into the Wine; in which they having been cloſe covered for the ſpace of ten days, draw off the Wine, and renew it with other Wine, and an addition of Sugar, and ſo you may do three or four times, but the firſt is the beſt; nor is there a pleaſanter liquor imaginable.

To make Wormwood-Wine.

Take a gallon, or what quantity you think fit, of the ſmalleſt White-wine, put into it the peel of two Lemons, half an ounce of Mace,

Mace, and a quarter of an ounce of Cinamon, adding a pound of white Sugar to each gallon, and ſtop them up cloſe in a Veſſel; and after they have ſtood ſix days, you may draw off the Wine, and put it up in bottles.

Rasberry, Strawberry, or Curran-wine, may be made as that of Cherries, but the liquor being boiled up with the Sugar before the Spices are put in, will keep the longeſt. An excellent Liquor may be likewiſe drawn from Plumbs, of pleaſant taſte, diſſolving in ſome of the Liquor hot two or three ſpoonfuls of new Ale Yeſt to make it work, and afterward keep it in a cool place, that it may Rarifie the better.

Goosberry-wine is made the ſame way, only adding ſome blades of Mace, and ſlices of Ginger: As for the Wine of Engliſh Grapes, only Rarifie it with fine white Sugar-candy beaten into Powder. And ſince there are other pleaſant Liquors beſides theſe, I think it not improper to ſay ſomething of thoſe that are moſt in requeſt.

To make the beſt ſort of Mead.

Take a quart of Spring-water, and three quarts of ſmall Beer, as clear as may be; add to them a pound and a half of clarified Honey, two ounces of the diſtilled Water of ſweet Marjorum, three or four ſprigs of Roſe-

Rosemary and Bays: boil them together on a gentle fire, ever scuming off what rises to the top, and then put it into a vessel to purge, six days after which bottle it up for your use.

To make Stepney, a Liquor formerly much in use.

Take a gallon of spring-water, and stone a pound and a half of the best Raisins of the Sun, and putting to them half a pound of fine Sugar, press upon them the Juyce of three Lemons; slicing likewise the peel, and adding to the Water a quart of White-wine; boil it, and when it is boiling-hot, pour it into a pot upon the Raisins, Sugar, *&c.* and stopping it close, let it stand six hours; after that stir it about, and let it stand two days more, at the end of which strain it, and press the Raisins; and when you find the Liquor clear, put it up into bottles for your use.

Cock-Ale is thus made.

Take a young Cock, and having stoned four pound of Raisins of the Sun, boil them and him in fair water, and then slice four Nutmegs, adding to them an ounce of Mace, and half a pound of Dates; beat them well, and put them into two quarts of Canary; and having added to them the boiled liquor, in in which the Cock muſt be boiled in a manner to pieces: ſtrain the liquor, and preſs what is ſolid; and after your Ale has done working, pour it in, and ſtop it down cloſe; two quarts is ſufficient for a Barrel, then bottle it up, and in a month it will be fit to drink.

To make Rack, an Indian *Liquor.*

Take a quart of Water, a pint of Brandy, and a pint of Canary; add half an ounce of beaten Ginger, and the like quantity of Cinamon, the Juyce of four Lemons, and two ounces of Roſewater, with half a pound of fine Loaf-ſugar; put into it a hot Toaſt, it being well ſtirred, it is the Prince of Liquors.

Choccolate is made with *Choccolate*, Milk, Eggs, White-wine, Roſewater, and Mace or Cinamon, which the party fancies; they being all boiled together over a gentle fire, two ounces of *Choccolate*, eight Eggs, half a pound of Sugar, a pint of White-wine, an ounce of Mace or Cinamon, and half a pound of Sugar, anſwering in this caſe a gallon of Milk.

Many other Liquors there are, as *Metheglin*, *Perry*, *Syder*, *Bracket*, *Tea*, *Coffee*, &c. But the way of making them being vulgarly known, I ſhall ſpare my Inſtruction, and proceed to Directions for making Syrups.

CHAP. III.

Instructions for a Gentlewoman in preparing and making Physical and Cordial Syrups, pleasant and profitable on sundry occasions, &c. *Highly necessary to be kept in Families for the preservation of Health,* &c.

SYrups are of two kinds, one Physical, and the other pleasant and useful on sundry other occasions: But of these I shall treat without distinction, the use of them being so publickly known, and indeed it is improper here to incert it: but to proceed.

To make Syrup of Clove-Gilliflowers.

Take the red part of the Flowers, separated from the white, to the quantity of half a peck; let them soak a night in spring-water, then boil them, and add to them a gallon of Water wherein they were boiled, and into which, after boiling, they have been strongly pressed, twelve pound of white Sugar, and half a pint of Rosewater, then boil up the Liquor with the Sugar into the thickness of a syrup, and keep it for your use. Some there are that make it without fire, but in my opinion this way must be the best for keeping.

To

To make Syrup of Violets.

Take the Flowers of the blew Violets, clipping off the Whites, and to a pound of them add a quart of boiling-water, and four pound of white ſugar; ſtirring them together, and ſtopping them cloſe in an Earthen-veſſel four days, then ſtrain them, preſſing out the liquid part; which being moderately heated on a gentle fire, will thicken into a ſyrup.

To make Syrup of Wormwood.

Take Roman Wormwood (the Leaves only) half a pound, Leaves of red Roſes the flowers two ounces, Indian-ſpike three drams, of the beſt White-wine a quart, and the like quantity of the Juyce of Quinces, or for want of it Syder: bruiſe and infuſe them for the ſpace of twenty ſix hours, then boiling them till the liquid part is half conſumed; ſtrain out the remainder, and adding two pounds of ſugar; boil it up into a ſyrup.

To make Syrup of Lemons.

Take a gallon of the Juyce of ſound Lemons, ſtrain it and let it clarifie, and boil it up with ſix or ſeven pounds of fine ſugar till it it be of the thickness of a syrup, and sweet enough for your purpose.

An Excellent Syrup to preserve the Lungs, and for the Astma.

Take of Nettle-water and Coltsfoot-water each a pint, Anniseed and Liquorish-powder of each two spoonfuls, Raisins of the Sun one handful, sliced Figs, number four: boil them together till a fourth part be consumed, strain the liquid part, and make it up into a syrup, with a pound of white Sugar-candy bruised into powder, and take two spoonfuls of it each morning fasting.

An Excellent Syrup to open Obstructions, and help the shortness of Breath.

Take Hysop of the first years groth, and Peny-royal, of each a handful; stamp them, and strain out the Juyce, and add of English Honey the like proportion: heat them in a Pewter dish over a chafing-dish of Coles till the Juyce and Honey be well incorporated, and making it continually fresh; let the party afflicted take early each morning, and late each night, two spoonfuls.

To

To make Syrup of Roses by Infusion.

Take of the Water of Infusion of white Roses five pounds, clarified Sugar four pounds, and boil them with a gentle fire to the thickness of a syrup, then soak two pounds of fresh white Roses in six pound of warm water, suffering them to stand for the space of twelve hours close covered, then ring them out, and put in other fresh Roses, and so continue to do till the Water has the perfect scent of the Roses, and then the Water is fitting for the Sugar to be dissolved in, and used as aforesaid. This Syrup draweth from the Entrails thin choler, and waterish humours, and is therefore fitting to be taken moderately by children, aged persons, and such as are afflicted with the super-abundance of either Choler or Phlegm.

How to make Catholicum Majus.

Take of the four great cold seeds cleansed, and of white Poppy-seeds each a dram, Gum-Dragant three drams, red Roses, yellow Saunders, Citron and Cinamon each two drams, Ginger one dram of the best and choicest, Ruburb and Diacridium each half an ounce, Agarick, Turbith, of each two drams, white Sugar dissolved in Rosewater, wherein two ounces of Senna have been concocted, one pound, make them into Tables of three ſcruples, and let one Table be the doſe. [It gathereth humours from all parts of the Body, and expells them without moleſting health, or impairing of the ſtrength, but rather fortifying nature, *&c.*]

Syrup of Radiſh; how to make it.

Take of the Roots of Garden and wild Radiſhes, of each an ounce; of Saxifrage, Kneeholm, Lorage, Sea-Holly, Pettywhin, O Cammack or Ground-Furz, Parſley, Fennel, each half an ounce: the Leaves of Betony, Pimpernel, wild Time, Tendercrops of Nettles, Creſſes, Samphire, Venus-hair, of each a handfull: the fruit of Sleepy Night-ſhade and Jubebs, of each twenty: the ſeed of Baſil, Burr, Parſley, of Macedonia, Carroways, Seſeli, yellow Carrots, Grommel, Bark of Bay-tree Root, of each a ſcruple; Raiſins ſtoned, Licoras, of each a dram: boil them in ten pounds of water till four of them be conſumed, then ſtrain it, and with four pounds of Sugar, and half the quantity of clarified Honey, make the liquid part into a Syrup over a gentle fire, adding an ounce of beaten Cinamon, and half the quantity of grated Nutmeg. [This being taken at convenient times, expelleth Gravel and Stone,

and

and ſcowreth the Kidneys,if it be mixed with other lenitive and ſcowring matters; and alſo provokes Urine.]

Syrup of Vinegar compound; how to make it.

Take of the beſt Wine-Vinegar a gallon, boil it, and take off the ſcum that ariſes; then ſtamp Indive, Maiden-hair and Wood-ſorrel, with Barberys or green Grapes; preſs out the Liquor, and put it into the Vinegar, to the quantity of a quart; boil them up till a fourth part be conſumed, then add ſix pounds of Sugar, or ſo much as will make it into a Syrup, and give two ſpoonfulls at a time with ſucceſs, in caſe of any hot diſtemper or feavoriſh diſorder of the Body, or to expell groſs phlegmatick humours.

Oxymel ſimple; how to make it.

Take of the cleareſt Water and clarified Honey, of each four pounds; boil them till half the Water be conſumed, then add of Wine-Vinegar two pounds, and ſuffer them to boil to a ſyrup. This ſyrup extenuateth the groſs humours, takes away ſlimy matter, and opens all Obſtructions and *Aſtma*, that is, Obſtruction of the Lungs, with Phlegm, from whence ariſeth ſhortneſs of breath.

Syrup of Barberys is made thus.

Take your Barberys picked from the ſtalks, boil them to a pulp, then ſtrain and rarifie the Juyce; then boil it up, being ſix pounds, with ſix pounds of fine Sugar into a ſyrup: or if you find that will not thicken it ſufficiently, you may add more.

To make Syrup of Cowſlips.

Take a gallon of the Diſtilled ſimple Water of Cowſlips, and put into it half a peck of the flowers clean picked, the yellow part only; boil them up with the Water, and add to the liquid part, after it is ſtrained from them, ſix pound of ſugar, heating it over the fire till it became a ſyrup.

To make Syrup of Maiden-hair.

Take the Herb ſo called to the quantity of ſix ounces, ſhred it a little, and add of Liconiſh-powder two ounces and a half, ſteep them twenty four hours in three quarts and a pint of hot water: add five pounds of fine Sugar to the Liquor, after it is boiled and conſumed a third part, and ſet it again on the fire til it become a ſyrup.

To

To make Syrup of Licoris.

Take of the Root of Licoris newly drawn from the ground two ounces, ſcrape it into Powder of Coltsfoot, four ounces; of Maidenheir and Hyſop, each half an ounce: infuſe them twenty four hours in three quarts of Water, then boil them till a half part be conſumed: which done, ſtrain out the remainder, and with a pound of clarified Honey, and the like quantity of Loaf-ſugar, boil it up into a ſyrup.

To make Syrup of Cittron Peels.

Take of the Peels of yellow Cittrons a pound, of the Berrys, or Juyce of the Berrys of Cherms, a dram; ſteep them a night in Spring-water to the quantity of two quarts, then boil them till a half part be conſumed; and taking off the ſcum, ſtrain it, then boil it up to a ſyrup, with two pound and a half of Sugar.

To make Syrup of Harts-horn, or rather Harts-tongue.

Take of the Herb called *Harts-tongue*, the Roots of both ſorts, of Bugloſs, Polipodium, of the Oak, Bark of Caper-roots, Tamaris,

Hops, Maiden-hair, Baum, of each two ounces: boil them in five quarts of Spring-water till a fifth part be consumed; to which add four pounds of fine sugar, and boil it up to a syrup.

To make Syrup of Cinamon, (which is excellent good in case of Faintings or cold Distempers.)

Take of the best Cinamon four ounces; bruise it and steep it in three pints of White-wine, and a pint of small Cinamon-water, three days by a gentle fire, add three pound of Sugar when it is strained, and boil it up to a syrup.

To make Syrup of Quinces.

Take three quarts of the Juyce of Quinces, let it be well setled and clarified; boil it over a gentle fire till half be consumed, then add three pints of Red-wine, with four pounds of white Sugar, and a dram and a half of Cinamon, and of Cloves and Ginger two scruples, and boil them up into a syrup.

To make Syrup of Hysop.

Take a handfull of the Herb so called, Figs, Dates and Raisins, of each an ounce: boil them in three pints of Water till a third part be consumed, strain and clarifie the remainder with the Whites of two Eggs, adding two pound of fine Sugar, and so make it up into a syrup, and it will continue good a twelvemonth.

To make an Excellent Syrup for a Cough or Cold, or to restore decaying Lungs.

Take two quarts of Spring-water, put into it an ounce of Sydrack, half an ounce of Maiden-hair, two ounces of Elicampane-roots sliced: boil them in an Earthen-vessel till half be consumed, add more to the liquid part, strained off two pound of Sugar, and boil it up into a syrup; two spoonfulls of which take morning and evening, it being a wonderfull restorative.

To make Syrup of Elder, now greatly in use.

Take the Elder-berries fresh, when they are full ripe, strain out the Juyce, boil it till a third part be consumed; scum it clean, and add to a gallon an ounce of Mace and six pounds of Sugar, boiling it up to a ſyrup.

To make Syrup of Roſes.

Take a gallon of fair water, and a quart of White-wine, put into them when they boil, a peck of red Roſes pickt, and let them boil till they appear white: then preſs them, and put them into the liquid part, and boil it often, adding the Whites of two Eggs well beaten, and a pound of Sugar to each pint of Liquor; and when you find it ſufficiently thick, preſerve it in Glaſſes or Earthen-veſſel cloſe ſtopped, for your uſe.

To make Syrup of Vinegar.

Take of the Roots of Smallage, Fennel, Endive, of either three ounces; of the Leaves of Anniſeed, Smallage, Fennel, Endive, half an ounce of each: boil them gently in three quarts of Spring-water till half be conſumed, then ſtrain and clarifie it with three pound of Sugar, and add a quart of White-wine Vinegar, and boil it up to a ſyrup.

To make Syrup of Saffron.

Take a pint of Endive-water, two ounces of Saffron finely beaten, ſteeping it in the Water for the ſpace of two days; at the end

end of which ſtrain out the Saffron, and with a pound of Sugar, boil it up to a ſyrup.

To make Syrup of Mint.

Take the Juyce of ripe Quinces, and of Pomgranets, of each a pint and a half: dried Mint half a pound, and of the Leaves of red Roſes two ounces; let them ſteep a day and a night in the Liquor: boil it then till half is conſumed, and add four pound of Sugar to make it into a ſyrup.

Theſe, as the moſt material, I thought fit expreſly to mention; what remains, a Gentlewomans diſcretion by theſe Rules may direct her to perform. And ſo I proceed to give Directions for Preſerving and Conſerving, &c.

CHAP. IV.

Instructions for a Gentlewoman in Preserving and Conserving Fruits, Flowers, Roots, and what else is usefull on sundry occasions for setting out Banquets, &c.

PReserving of Fruits, Roots and Flowers, *&c.* to be at hand for ornament or taste, is, no doubt, a curious Art. Wherefore that a Gentlewoman should not be ignorant of such curiosities, I shall incert many Directions worthy to be observed, and at the same time speak something of Conserving, *&c.*

To Preserve Mulberries.

Strain two quarts of the Juyce of Mulberries, and add to it a pound and a half of sugar; boil them together over a gentle fire, till they become in a manner a syrup, then put into it three quarts of Mulberries, not over ripe; and after they have had one boil, take them off, and put them together, with the Liquor, into an Earthen-vessel, stop them close, and keep them for your use.

To

To Preserve Goosberries.

Take them before they be over-ripe, cut off their ſtalks and tops; and if you have leaſure, ſtone them; then laying in an Earthen-veſſel a Layer of ſugar, lay upon it a Layer of Goosberries; and ſo do between every Laying, till your Veſſel be almoſt full: then add about a pint of Water to ſix pound of Goosberries; and the Goosberries having before been ſcalded, ſet them in this manner over a gentle fire, and let the ſugar melt: when being boiled up, you may ſtop them up, and reſerve them for your uſe.

To Preserve Cherries.

Take your Cherries when they are in their prime, and ſcattering ſome Sugar and Roſe-water at the bottom of your Preſerving-pan; put them in by degrees, ſtill caſting in your ſugar, remembring there be put an equal weight of either; and being ſet on a quick fire, you may add a pint of White-wine, if you would have them plump; and when you find the ſyrup boil'd up ſufficiently, take them off, and put them into your Gally-pots for uſe.

To Preserve Apricocks.

Obſerve when they are moderately ripe to pare and ſtone them, laying them a night in your Preſerving-pan amongſt Sugar, it being layed in Lays, and in the morning put a ſmall quantity of fair Water or White-wine, and ſet them on Embers, and by increaſing a gentle fire, melt the Sugar; when being a little ſcalded, take them off, and letting them cool; ſet them on again, and boil them up ſoftly till they are tender and well coloured, at what time take them off, and when they are cool put them up in Glaſſes or Pots for your uſe.

To Preserve green Walnuts.

Obſerve to gather them on a dry day, before they have any hard ſhell, and boil them in fair water till they loſe their bitterneſs; then put them into cold water, and peel off their Rine, and lay them in your Preſerving-pan with layings of Sugar to the weight of the Nuts, and as much water as will wet it, ſo boil 'em up over a gentle fire; and again being cool, do it a ſecond time, and put them up for your uſe. This way Nutmegs, with their green Husks, are Preſerved.

To

To Preserve green Pippins.

Obſerve to take them e're they are too ripe, chuſing the greeneſt, pare them and boil them in water till they are exceeding ſoft, then take out the cores, and mingle the pulp with the water, ten Pippins and two pound of Sugar being ſufficient to boil up a Pottle of water; and when it is boiled to a thickneſs, put in the Pippins you intend to Preſerve, and let them boil till they contract a greener colour then natural. And in this manner you may preſerve Plumbs, Peaches, Quinces, or any thing of that kind that you are deſirous to have green and pleaſant.

To Preserve Barberries.

Obſerve that you chuſe the faireſt bunches, gathered in a dry day, and boil ſeveral bunches in a Pottle of Claret till they are ſoft: ſtrain them then, and add ſix pound of Sugar and a quart of Water; boil them up to a ſyrup, and put your Barberries ſcalded into the liquor, and they will keep the year round.

To Preserve Pears.

Obſerve that you gather thoſe that are ſound, not over-ripe, and laying at the bottom

tom of an Earthen-Pot or Pan a laying of Vine-leaves, lay another laying of Pears upon them, and ſo do till the Pot is full: then to a pound of Pears add half a pound of Sugar, and as much fair Water as will diſſolve it over a gentle fire; where ſuffer them to boil till they are ſomewhat ſoft, and then ſet them by for your uſe.

To Preſerve Black Cherries.

Pluck off the ſtalks of about a pound, and boil them in Sugar and fair Water till they become a pulp, then put in your other Cherries, with ſtalks, remembring to put half a pound of Sugar to every pound of Cherries; when finding the Sugar to be boiled up to that thickneſs that it will rope, take them off and ſet them by, uſing them as you ſee convenient.

To Preſerve Eringo-Roots.

Take of the Roots that are fair and knotty two pound, waſh and cleanſe them, then boil them over a gentle fire very tender, after that peel off their out-moſt Rind, but beware of breaking them after they have lain a while in cold water; put them into your Sugar boiled up to a ſyrup, allowing to each pound of Sugar three quarters of a pound of Roots; which boiling a ſhort time over a gentle

gentle fire, you may set them to cool, and then put them up for your use.

As for Elicampane-Roots, scrape and cut them thin to the pith, in lengths about your finger, and put them into water, which you must often shift to take away the bitterness; at which rate being used twenty days, put three quarters of a pound of Sugar to every pound of Roots, the Roots being first boiled tender over a gentle fire till you find the Sugar has sufficiently taken; and then being cool, put them up in a Gally-pot or Glass: And much at the same rate you may manage any thing of this or the like nature, as Grapes, Peaches, Plumbs, *&c.*

Conserving Flowers or Fruits is somewhat different from this: Wherefore for your better instruction, I shall say something concerning it.

To Conserve or keep any sort of Flower, as Roses, Violets, Cowslips, Gilleflowers, &c.

Take your Flowers well blown and clean picked, bruise them very small in a Mortar, with three times the weight of Sugar; after which take them out, and put them into a Pipkin; and having thorowly heated them over the fire, put the Conserve up in Gally-pots for your use.

To

To Conserve Strawberries.

Strain them, being first boiled in fair water, and boil the pulp in White-wine and Sugar as much as is convenient to make them stiff, *&c.* And thus you may Conserve any sort of Fruit, the difference not being great between this and making Fruit Paste; of which I shall speak hereafter.

CHAP. V.

Instructions for a Gentlewoman in Candying Fruits, Flowers, Roots, &c. *As also in drying Fruits, and other things necessary to be observed, after the exactest and newest Mode and Method,* &c.

CAndying Fruits, Roots and Flowers, being an excellent way of rendering them pleasant and lasting, is the next thing intended to be discoursed on: Directions for which take as followeth.

To Candy Ginger.

Take the fairest pieces, pare off the rind, and lay them in water twenty four hours; and

and having boiled double-refined Sugar to the hight of Sugar again; when it begins to be cold, put in your Ginger and ſtir it till it is hard to the Pan; when taking it out piece by piece, lay it by the fire, and afterward put it into a warm Pot, and tye it up cloſe, and the Candy will be firm.

To Candy Orange-peel.

Take Peels of the beſt Civil Oranges, the meat being taken out, and put them into Water and Sugar boiling hot; where being well ſoftned, boil Roſe-water and Sugar up to a hight, till it becomes Sugar again; then draw your Peels through it, and dry them in an Oven or Stove, or before the fire.

To Candy Cherries.

Take them before they are full ripe, ſtone them, and having boiled your fine Sugar to a hight, pour it on them gently, moving them, and ſo let them ſtand till almoſt cold, and then taken out and dried by a fire, *&c.*

To Candy Elicampane-Roots.

Take them from the ſyrup in which they have been Preſerved, and dry them with a cloth; and for every pound of Roots, take a pound

pound and three quarters of Sugar: boil it to a hight, and dip your Roots into it when hot, and they will take it well.

To Candy Barberries.

You muſt take them out of the Preſerve, and waſh off the ſyrup in warm water, then ſift fine Sugar on them, and put them into an Oven or Stove to dry, ſtirring or moving them the mean while, and caſting more Sugar upon them till they are dry.

To Candy Grapes.

You muſt take them after they are Preſerved, and uſe them as the former.

To Candy Eringo-Roots.

Take the Roots pared and boiled to a convenient ſoftneſs, and to each pound add two pound of fine Sugar, clarifie it with the Whites of Eggs that it may be tranſparent; and being boiled to a hight, dip in your Roots two or three at once, and afterward dry them in an Oven or Stove for your uſe. And in this faſhion you may Candy any thing as to Fruits or Roots, to which Candying is proper. And as for Flowers, which that way are pleaſant and ornamental, you may Candy dy them after the following manner with their ftalks and leaves, *viz.*

Take your various forts of Flowers, cut the ftalks, if they are extraordinary long, fomewhat fhorter; and having added about eight fpoonfulls of Rofe-water to a pound of white Sugar, boil it to a clearnefs; and as it begins to grow ftiff and cool, dip your Flowers into it; and taking them out prefently, lay them one by one in a Sieve, and hold it over a chafing-difh of Coles, and they will dry and harden.

To dry Plumbs, Pears, Apples, Grapes, or the like.

You muft firft Preferve them, then wafh or wipe them; after which fet them upon Tin Plates in a Stove, or for want of it an Oven, not too hot, and turn them as you fee occafion, obferving ever to let them have their Stalks on.

Thefe things more efpecially being fit to be underftood by a young Gentlewoman, I have fpoken of them in order: And fince there are many other things neceffary, of which I have faid nothing, I fhall proceed to give Inftructions, as they occur, which I hope will prove altogether as profitable.

CHAP.

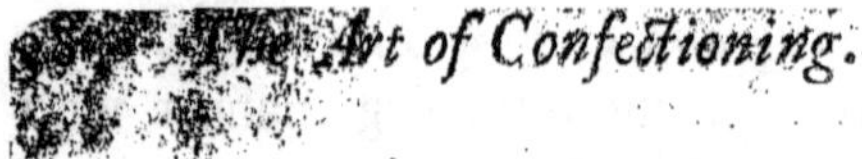

CHAP. VI.

Instructions for a Gentlewoman in making of Marmalade, Paste of Fruit, Artificial Fruit, Jellies of Fruit, Quiddanies, Fruit-cakes, Honey, Conserve for Tarts, Maccaroons, Comfits and Confections, after sundry forms and manners.

To make Marmalade of Oranges.

PAre your Oranges as thin as may be, and let 'em boil till they are soft in two or three waters, then take double the number of good Pippins; divide them, and take away the core; boil them to pap without losing their colour: strain the pulp, aud put a pound of Sugar to every pint; then take out the pulp of the Oranges, and cut the peel, and boil it till it is very soft: bruise it in the Juyce of two or three Lemons, and boil it up to a thickness with your Apple-pap, and half a pint of Rose-water.

To make Paste of Cherries.

Boil the Cherries till they come to be very soft, and strain the pulp through a fine Sieve,

Sieve, and add a pound of Sugar to a pint; ſtiffen it with Apple-pap, and boil it up to a hight, then ſpread it upon Plates and dry it.

To make Marmalade of Grapes.

Take the ripeſt Grapes, gathered in a dry day, ſpread them upon a Table where the Air and the Sun may come at them; after which take from them the ſtalks and ſeeds, boiling the Husk and Pulp, or Juyce in a Pan, with often ſcuming, whilſt it is reduced to a third part, and then let the heat be gentle; and when you find it thickned, ſtrain it through a Sieve; and boiling it once more, add a ſmall quantity of fine ſugar, or the Powder of white Sugar-candy, and ſo put it up in Pots covered with Paper for your uſe.

To make Honey of Mulberries.

Take the Juyce of the black Mulberries, and add to a pound and a half of their Juyce two pound of clarified Honey, and boil them up with often ſcuming till a third part be conſumed.

To make Jelly of Quinces, Currans or Gooſeberries.

Take the Fruit, and preſs out the Juyce, clarifie

clarifie it, and add to each quart a pound of ſugar, clarified and boiled up to a Candy hight; then boil them together till a third part be conſumed; then add a pint of White-wine, wherein an ounce of Cherry-tree or Plumb-tree Gum has been diſſolved, and it will make it a perfect Jelly.

To make Lemon-Cakes, or Cakes of Lemons.

Take fine Sugar half a pound, to two ounces of the Juyce of Lemons, and the like quantity of Roſe-water; boil them up till they become Sugar again, then grate into it the rind of hard Lemons; and having well incorporated them, put them up for your uſe into coffins, *&c.* being cold, and cover 'em with Paper.

Artificial Walnuts are thus to be made.

Take a Sugar-plate and print it like a Walnut kernel, yellowing the in-ſide with Saffron; then take ceraced Sugar and Cinamon, and work them with Roſe-water, in which Gum-dragon has been ſteeped, into a Paſte, and print it in a Mould made like a Walnut-ſhell; and when the kernel and ſhell are dry cloſe them together with Gum-dragon or Gum-Arabick, and they will deceive the gueſt, who will take 'em for real Whlnuts.

To

To make Artificial Oranges and Lemons.

Take Moulds of Alablafter made in three pieces, bind two of them together, and let them lye in the water an hour or two; boiling to a hight, in the mean time as much fugar as will fill them : the which being poured into the Mould, and the lid put quickly on, it by fuddainly turning will be hollow : And fo in this cafe to the colour of the Fruit you caft, you muft colour your fugar in boiling.

To make red Quince-Cakes.

Take the fyrup of Quinces and Barbarys, of each a quart; cut into it about a dozen Quinces free from rind and core: boil them till they are very foft, then ftrain the pulp or liquid part, and boil it up with fix pound of fugar till it be Candy-proof; then take it out and lay it upon Plates, as thin as you think convenient, to cool.

Clear or tranfparent Quince-Cakes are made thus.

Take a pint of the fyrup of Quinces, and a quart of that of Barberries: boil and clarifie them over a gentle fire, keeping them free from fcum; then add a pound and a quarter

quarter of Sugar to the Juyce, Candying as much more, and putting it in hot, and so keeping it stirring till it be near cold, at what time spread it and cut it into Cakes as the former.

To make Marmalade after the Italian *fashion.*

Take about thirty Quinces, pare them, take out their cores, and put to them a quart of water and two pound of sugar; boil them till they are soft, then strain the juyce and the pulp, and boil them up with four pound of sugar till they become sufficiently thick.

To make white Quince-Cakes.

Clarifie your sugar with the Whites of Eggs, putting to two pound a quarter of a pint of water; which being boiled up, add dry sugar, and highten it to a Candy: then the Quinces being pared, cored and scalded, beat them to pulp, and put them into the boiling sugar, not suffering them to boil long before you take them off, and lay them on Plates.

To make Maccaroons.

Blanch a convenient quantity of Almonds, by putting them into hot water: beat them fine

fine in a Mortar, ſtrewing on them as you beat fine ſeraced Sugar; and when they are well mixed, add the Whites of Eggs and Roſe-water; and when they are of a convenient thickneſs, drop the Butter on Wafers layed on Tin-plates, and bake 'em in a gentle Oven.

To make a Leach of Almonds.

Take half a pound of Almonds blanched, beat them in a Mortar, and add a pint of new Milk, and ſtrain them: add more, two ſpoonfulls of Roſe-water, and a grain of Musk, with half an ounce of the whiteſt Iſing-glaſs, and ſtrain them a ſecond time for your uſe.

To make Sugar ſmell like Spice.

Lay lumps of Sugar under your Spice, or ſprinkle them with ſome of the Diſtilled-water.

To make a Quiddany of Plumbs, Apples, Quinces, or any other Fruit that is proper.

Take a quart of the Liquor of the Preſerved Fruit, and add a pound of the Fruit raw, ſeparated from the ſtone, rind or core: boil it up with a pound of Sugar till it ſtands upon a knife-point like a Jelly.

To make a Conserve for Tarts of any Fruit that will keep all the Year.

Take the Fruit you intend, peel off the rind, and remove the core or ſtone, then put them into a Pot, and bake them with a ſmall quantity of Water and Sugar: being bak'd, ſtrain 'em through a ſtrong cloth; adding Cinamon, Sugar and Mace, very finely ſeraced, boil them on a gentle fire till they become as thick as a Jelly, and then put them up into Pots or Glaſſes ſtopped cloſe, and they will have their proper taſte at any time.

To Preſerve Medlers.

Take the Fruit and ſcald them in fair water till the Skin may be eaſily taken off, then ſtone them at the head, and add to each pound a pound of Sugar, and let them boil till the Liquor become ropey; at what time take them off, and ſet them by for your uſe.

To make Sweet-meats of any Apples.

Make your Jelly with thoſe that are moſt ſoft and pleaſant, then cutting other Apples round-ways, put them into a Glaſs or Pot and let them ſtand ſix days, then boil 'em with

with the addition of a quarter of a pound of Sugar to a pound of Liquor, not breaking them, but ſeaſoning them further with the Juyce of Lemons, Oranges, Cloves, Mace, and Perfuming them with a grain of Ambergreaſe.

To make each ſort of Comfits, vulgarly called Covering-ſeeds, *&c. with Sugar; obſerve as followeth.*

You muſt provide a Pan of Braſs or Tin, to a good depth, made with Ears to hang over a Chafing-diſh of Coles, with a Ladle and Slice of the ſame Mettal; then cleanſe your Seeds from droſs, and take the fineſt Sugar well beaten: put to each a quarte. of a pound of Seeds, two pounds of Sugar; the Seeds being firſt well dried, and your Sugar melted in this order, put into the Pan three pounds of Sugar, adding a pint of Spring-water, ſtirring it till it be moiſtened, and ſuffer it to melt well over a clear fire till it ropes, after that ſet it upon hot embers, not ſuffering it to boil, and ſo from your Ladle let it drop upon the Seeds, and keep the Baſon wherein they are continually moving, and between every Coat rub and dry them as well as may be; and when they have taken up the Sugar, and by the motion are rolled into order: dry them in an Oven, or before a fire, and they will be hard and white.

Thus, Gentlewomen, have I let you underſtand the depth of Curioſities of this kind, and ſuch as are ſutable to be done by your ſelf, or at leaſt to be obſerved whether they are done as they ought by thoſe you imploy to perſorm 'em, whether your Houſe-keeper or Woman; for if your ſelf appear ignorant herein, thoſe that perform it will either have your want of underſtanding in contempt, or not perform as they ought. Wherefore leaving them to be conſidered and practiced by you at leaſure, I ſhall proceed to the remaining Curioſities in their order. And firſt, as to what belongs properly, eſpecially in many caſes, to your ſelf, leſt by too long abſtenance your Appetite ſhould be paul'd. I invite you to a Table furniſhed with dainties; and really let you underſtand what your Behaviour muſt or ought to be abroad or at home; and how, if it comes to your turn, you muſt handle your Knife and Fork, *&c.* in Carving the ſeveral ſorts of Fowl, Fiſh and Fleſh, of Beaſts, *&c.*

CHAP.

CHAP. VII.

Instructions for a Gentlewoman in her Behaviour at the Table, abroad and at home, with the Terms and Manner of Carving Fowl, Flesh, of Beasts and Fish, with Directions to know the choicest pieces in either, and such as are most acceptable.

THough you may think it ſtrange, and altogether a matter that might have been ſpared to inſtruct you as to Behaviour in a Marriage ſtate; yet let me tell you, though I ſhall hereafter ſay ſomething as to this Point, yet the Behaviour of Youth differs from that of riper years; and ſince it is an Introduction to other matters, let your wonder ceaſe, and obſerve what follows.

Being at the Table in your due place, obſerve to keep your Body ſtrait, and lean not by any means with your Elbows, nor by ravenous Geſture diſcover a voracious Appetite: Knaw no bones, but cut your Meat decently with the help of your Fork; make no noiſe in calling for any thing you want, but ſpeak ſoftly to thoſe that are next, or wait to give it; nor be ſo diſ-ingenious as to ſhew your diſlike of any thing that is before you if ſtrangers be at the Table; eſpecially at anothers Table, Eat not your Spoon meat ſo hot that it makes your Eyes water, nor be ſeen to blow it. Complain not of a queazy ſtomack; wipe your Spoon every time you dip it in the diſh; if you eat Spoon-meat with others, eat not too faſt, nor unſeemly; neither be nice or curious at the Table by mincing or mimping, as if you liked not the Meat or the Company; where you ſee variety, yet reach not after them, but ſtay till you have an opportunity, and then ſhew an indifferency as to your choice; and if it chance to happen you have a Plate with ſome piece you fancy not preſented, wait your opportunity till it be taken away and changed; nor be inquiſitive (for that is uncomely) to know what ſuch a Fowl or ſuch a Joynt coſt, nor diſcourſe of Bills of Fare; take not in your Wine or other liquor too greedily, nor drink till you are out of breath, but do things with decency and order. If you are abroad at Dinner, let not your hand be firſt in any diſh, nor take your place unſeemly; neither be induced to Carve, though the Miſtriſs of the houſe out of a complement intreat it, unleſs you ſee a neceſſity for it; and whenever you Carve, keep your fingers from your mouth; throw not any thing over your ſhoulder, neither take or give any thing on that ſide where a Perſon of Quality, or one

much

much above you is ſeated; nor reach your arms over other diſhes to reach at what you like better. And ſo leaving what elſe is requiſite in this kind to be obſerved, I proceed to give you, Firſt, the Terms of *Carvers*. Secondly, the manner of *Carving*; and, Thirdly, Directions to know the beſt pieces, *&c.* And of theſe in their order.

Firſt, That you may the better be enabled to direct thoſe you appoint to Carve, if you Carve not your ſelf, the moſt expert in that dextery give the following Terms, by way of diſtinguiſhment, and properly in the cutting up all manner of ſmall Birds: the direction for it is Thighing them, as Larks, Woodcocks, Pigeons, *&c.* Directions for cutting up a Plover, is to mince it; a Quail and Partridge, to wing them; a Pheaſant, to alay it; a Curlew, to untie it; a Bittern, to unjoynt it; a Peacock, to disfigure it; a Crane, to diſplay it; a Hern, to diſmember it; a Mallard, to unbrace it; a Chicken, to unfruſt it; a Swan, to lift it; a Gooſe, to rear it: And ſo in Fleſh of Beaſts, as Creek that Deer, Unlace that Coney, Leach that Brawn. So in caſe of Fiſh; As Chine the Salmon; String the Lampry; Splat the Pike; Sawce the Place and Tench; Splay the Bream; Side the Haddock; Culpon the Trout; Tusk the Barble; Tranſon the Eel;

Tame the Crab ; Barb the Lobſter ; Tranch the Sturgeon, and the like, or much to the ſame effect, in caſe of others not mentioned. But paſſing them over for brevities ſake, I come to the ſecond thing to be conſidered, which is the manner of cutting up.

If you take it upon you to Carve a Swan, called in the proper term Lifting, ſlit him down-right in the middle of the breaſt, and through the back, from the neck to the rump, laying the ſlit ſides downward in the diſh, without tearing the fleſh, and ſerve the ſawce up in Sawcers.

The term of Carving a Gooſe is to rear or break her in this manner. Take off the legs very fair, then cut off the belly-piece round, cloſe to the lower end of the breaſt, and with your knife lace her down on each ſide a thumbs breadth from the breaſt-bone, taking off the wings with the fleſh you firſt laced, raiſing it cleaver from the bone, then cut up the merry-thought, and another piece of fleſh which you formerly laced ; turn the carkaſs, and divide it at the back-bone above the loin ; then lay the rump end of the back-bone at the fore end of the merry-thought, with the fleſhy ſide upward, and the wings on each ſide contrary, that ſo the boney ends of the legs may ſtand up in the middle of the diſh, and the wings on their out-ſide, putting under the wing Pinions, the two long

pieces

pieces of flesh, *&c.* and let the ends meet under the leg-bones.

In carving or dismembring a Hern. Lace her down the breast, and take off both the legs; then raising up the flesh, take it clean off with the Pinions; then sticking the head in the breast, set the Pinion on the contrary side of the carkass, and the legs on the other side, so that the ends of the bones may meet cross over it.

In cutting up a Bustard or Turkey. The leg being raised up very fair, open the joynt with the sharp point of your knife, and lace down the breast on both sides without taking off the leg or the pinion; then raise up the merry-thought, and between the top of the breast-bone and the merry-thought, lace down the flesh on both sides, and raise up the flesh called the Brawn; turn it outward on both sides, but neither cut it off nor break it; then cut off the wing-pinions at the body joynt, and stick on each side the pinion, in the place where you turned out the Brawn, cutting off the sharp end, and taking the middle-piece, that will fit the place. And in this manner a Capon or a Pheasant may be cut up; but cut not off the Pinions of the former, the divided Gizard serving to supply the place where the Turkies wings were put.

In unbracing a Mallard. Obſerve that you raiſe up the pinion and leg, not taking them off: raiſe likewiſe the merry-thought from the breaſt, and lace it down ſloapingly on each ſide the breaſt, and looſening the joynts, leave it undivided.

In diſplaying a Crane. Unfold the legs, and cut off the wings by the body-joynts, then ſawce both the wings and legs with powder of Ginger, Muſtard, Salt and Vinegar: and ſo a Bittern may be unjoynted, or any other Fowl of that nature.

Your Partridge or Plover minced, *&c.* white Wine, Powder of Ginger and Salt is a proper ſawce.

In unlacing a Coney. Turn the belly upwards, cutting the belly-pieces from the Kidneys, then with the point of your knife looſen the kidneys, and fleſh between, to either ſide of the bone; when turning up the back-ſide of the Rabit, cut it croſs between the wings, and lace it down cloſe by the bone on either ſide; then open the fleſh from the bone againſt the kidney, and opening the legs, ſlit them from the Kidney to the rump, and lay them cloſe in order.

A Pig being chined, is generally divided into four quarters, the Head divided, and the Ears taken off, and the reſt left to the diſcretion of the Carver.

A Salmon is chined down the back, or laced on each ſide the back-bone, and divided into Mediums and Extremities, greater or leſſer, at diſcretion. And thus far having given you an inſight into the terms and methods of *Carving*, I ſhall let you in the next place know what is to be done in the diſtribution of what is carved, that it may find the better acceptance: As,

Thirdly, If you have a friend at the Table you would oblige more than another, and Chicken-broth be the firſt diſh, the breaſt is to be preferred, and next the leg; for in all boiled fowl, the leg is accounted better than the wing; though in roaſted ones, if they be wild-fowl, the wing is chief: and the reaſon that is given is, becauſe it is exceeding tender by means of its continual motion; and add, as a curioſity on the other hand, that the legs of tame-fowl not uſing the wing, but too often ſcratching, are to be preferred as the beſt nouriſhment; though it is generally held in wild and tame fowl, as Pullets, Turkies, Capons, Geeſe, Duck, Mallard, Pheaſant, Dotril, and the like, that the merry-thought and the wing is beſt, however they are moſt acceptable, and the next part that which is laced on the breaſt-bone.

As for Butchers meat. In roaſt Beef, that which is within ſide the Surloin is moſt prized; and in other piece, that which is curi-

ouſly

ously ſtriped with fat and lean; and ſo in boil'd Beef.

In a Loin of Veal the Nut-piece or Kidney-piece is the beſt to be preſented.

In a Leg of Mutton there is a little round bone on the inſide, above the handle, that is fit with the meat upon it to be preſented, and is in great eſteem among the curious: As it appeared by a Gentleman, who after long courſing being extreme hungry, and finding that bone untouched in a cut Leg of Mutton, refuſed to eat by reaſon he fancied Booriſh people had had the firſt handling of it, or otherwiſe their diſcretion would have directed them to have taken that piece.

A Shoulder of Mutton being cut between the handle and the flap, the fat Nut there found is the choiceſt piece, and worthieſt to be preſented. And in a roaſted Pig the Women eſpecially prefer the under Jaw and the Ear, though on the other hand the Neck and middle-piece is preferable.

In a Hare, Coney or Leverit, the back-piece, juſt in the middle, is held of great eſteem, though ſome nicely covet the piece by the ſide of the tail, commonly called the Huntsman's piece.

In all Fiſh without ſhells, the Jole, or that part next to the head, is to be eſteemed; and in a Lobſter or Crab, the claw.

If

If Fiſh or ſliced Fleſh be in Paſte, 'tis proper to touch it with your Knife, Fork or Spoon; and raiſing it conveniently, lay it upon a Trencher or Plate in the beſt order, not by any means delivering it to the hand of the party with your Knife, Fork or Spoon, but on a Plate.

All ſorts of Tarts, Cuſtards, wet Sweet-meats and Cakes, being cut in the diſh wherein they were ſerved up, muſt be layed likewiſe with the point of a Knife handſomely on a Plate and preſented.

Thus having ſhewed you how to behave your ſelf, and, in ſome part, to manage good cheer; it will be highly neceſſary to conſider, that a young Gentlewomans Beauty is an ornament next to that of her Virtue; and though Nature is prodigally laviſh in furniſhing your Faces with charms, yet ſeeing ſhe is deficient, and caſualties impair the perfection of your lovely Sex, I think fit to impart ſuch Secrets, as by harmleſs ways what is wanting or diſordered, may be ſupplied or repaired: In which the following Treatiſe will direct you.

CHAP.

CHAP. VIII.

The Closet of Beauty, or Modest Instructions for a Gentlewoman in making Beautifying Waters, Beautifying Oyl, Pomatums, Reparations, Musk-balls, Perfumes, and other Curiosities: Highly necessary and advantageous in the Practice, &c.

GEntlewoman, Imagine not that I undertake this Treatise to create in you the least self-conceit or extravagant opinion of your Merits, by putting into your hands an opportunity to render your selves more beautifull, if possibly it may be, but to preserve what you have, at least from the ruins of time, or any unfortunate accident for neatness on this side the Region of Pride is to be observed in that as well as in Apparel; nay in a cleanly observance, even Health it self is concerned. But to proceed.

If Hair, that comely Ornament of your Sex, be wanting, occasioned by Sickness or defect of moisture, &c. To recover it.

Take the Ashes of Hysop-roots, the Juyce of Marshmallows, and the Powder of Elicampane-roots, of each an ounce: boil them in in half a pint of White-wine, with a dram of the Oyl of Tartar, till half be consumed, and with the remainder Anoint the ball'd place, and the Hair will be restored.

To preserve the Hair from falling off.

Burn Pigeons dung to Ashes, of which take the quantity of an ounce, put them into a pint of water where Wood-ashes have soaked: then add two ounces of the Juyce of Senagreen or Housleek, and one of fine Sugar-candy, and half an ounce of Rosemary flowers: boil them together, strain them well, and wash the place six or seven times, and the Hair will not only remain firm, but what is fallen off will renew.

If Hair grow too thick or unseemly in any part of the Body.

Take Gum Arabick, and boil it to the thickness of a Salve in the Juyce of Hemlock, and lay it on the place Plaster-wise; and when it is taken off, which must not be under two days, it will bring off the Hair by the roots, not permitting any more to grow in that place.

To make the Hair fair and beautifull.

Cleanse it from dust by washing it in Rose-Vinegar, then boil an ounce of Turmerick, the like quantity of Rubarb, with the leaves of Bay-tree cut small, to the quantity of a handfull, boiled in a quart of water, wherein half a pound of Allom has been dissolved; and by often washing your Head with the decoction, it will make your Hair fair and lovely, unless it be a deep red, or exceeding black.

To cleanse the Skin of the Face and make it beautifull.

Take and distill the Blossoms of Pease and Beans with the like quantity of the flowers of Fumitory and Scabeous, and wash the Face with it morning and evening, anointing it afterward with a small quantity of Oyl of Myrrh; and by often using it, you will have cause to admire the effects. Rosemary flowers boiled in White-wine have likewise their wonderfull quality in this kind.

To take away Freckles.

Take the Galls of two Cocks, a handfull of Rye-flower or Meal, a pint of Verjuice, two

two ounces of Plantane-water, and one of the Oyl of Bitter Almonds: boil them, and ſtrain out the liquid part, when a third part is conſumed, then boil it again till it becomes a kind of an Ointment; and often anointing the Face therewith, will remove 'em.

To make a clear, white and ſmooth Skin.

Take an ounce of Barrows greaſe, the Whites of two Eggs, half an ounce of the Aſhes of Bay-tree roots or leaves, a quarter of an ounce of Honey of Roſes, and a quarter of a pint of Plantane-water: boil them till they become an Ointment, and uſe it to the end above mentioned.

To take away Sun-burn.

A handfull of Spaniſh Salt diſſolved in the Juyce of two Lemons, is a ſpeedy remedy, the Face and Hands being often rubbed with it, and it as often ſuffered to dry upon them.

To take away Wrincles, and make the Face look youthfull.

Take of Brandy, or Spirit of Wine, a quarter of a pint; of Bean-flower and red Roſe-water, each four ounces; Water of Lillies, four ounces; the Juyce of Briony-roots, two ounces;

ounces; and of the Decoction of Figgs, two ounces: Incorporate them over a gentle fire, and use it as a Wash.

To take away the red Spots, occasioned by the Small Pox.

Wash your Face with Juyce of Lemon; in which beaten Alom and Bay-salt has been dissolved; and to wear out the Pits, or prevent them gnawing deeper, as you grow in years, Take half a pint of the Spirit of Vinegar, an ounce of Mustard-seed, a quarter of a pint of the Juyce of Marshmallows, and a handfull of Bran: boil them together, and put the liquid part in a Viol; with which wash your Face morning and evening, and you will find the effect will answer the trouble.

To take away Pimples and Redness in the Face.

Dissolve half an ounce of Alom in the White of an Egg, and a spooefull of Vinegar: beat it together till it is well mixed, and when you go to bed, lay it Plaster-wise upon the place, and your desire will be effected.

To

To take away the hot swelling of the Face.

Boil Rosemary-blossoms, or leaves of Gronndsil and Chamomile in White-wine, and not only wash your Face in the Juyce, but lay the Herbs stamped with a small quantity of Oyl of Roses, Pultis-wise, to the place afflicted.

To restore a Ruby Face to it's former complexion.

Take the yolks of two Eggs, an ounce of fresh Butter, four drams of Camphire, half a pint of Rose-water, an ounce of the Oyl of Bays: mingle them well by heating them over a fire; and anoint the Face with the Oyntment, for they will produce, if well beaten and kept stirring, and strained through a Woollen cloth an Oyl, *&c.*

To make the Hands soft and white.

Take of Bean and Lupin-flower, of each a handfull; of Starch, Corn, Rise and Orice, and sweet Almonds, two ounces: beat or grind them together, and with the Powder wash your Hands often.

To make an Excellent Wash-ball for the Hands and Face.

Tke two ounces of *Calamus-aramaticus*, of Rose-flowers, and the flowers of Lavender, each a handfull; three ounces of Orice, and an ounce of Cyprus: beat them well, scrape into the Powder of them, being sifted, as much Castle-sope as will make it into Balls, when mollified with Rose-water.

To prevent marks of the Small Pox in the Face.

Boil Cream and Honey of Roses to an Oyntment, and therewith anoint the places, during the Patients sickness, where you fear the deformity.

To make Teeth white and continue sound.

Take of the Powder of Roach-Allum a quarter of an ounce, the like quantity of the Powder of fine Pumice-stone, half as much Bay-salt, and half a quarter of a pint of the Juyce of red Sage: boil them over a gentle fire till they appear thick, and with the residue rub your Teeth every morning, washing your Mouth with Water and Honey.

For want of this, boil a like quantity of Rosemary, Sage and Alum, in Spring-water; rub

rub your Teeth therewith, and waſh your Mouth with the Juyce or Water of Ladys-Thiſtle root, or the root of Hore-hound, and it will reſtore the Gums, and preſerve the Teeth white and firm.

A fine Pumice-ſtone only will make Teeth, if ſound, as white as Ivory, by gentle rubbing.

To cauſe ſweet Breath.

Take four ounces of Cummin-ſeed, as much of Anniſeed, with half as much of the tops of Lavender: bruiſe them and boil them in Wine, ſweetned with white Sugar-candia drink, when you riſe and go to bed, an ounce of the liquid part, and in ten or twelve days your Breath will be as ſweet as ever, unleſs the Lungs are putrefied.

If your Eyes are Blood-ſhot, to remove that unſeemly grievance.

Take two ounces of the Roots of red Fennel, ſtamp them aud preſs out the Juyce, and mingle it with half an ounce of clarified Honey: heat them gently over the fire till they become an Oyntment, anoint therewith the Eye-lids, and drop a drop with a feather into each Eye: and in ſo doing, and waſhing them with White-wine or Eye-bright-water, the redneſs will vaniſh. A

A rotten Apple, Bole-armorick and Bread, made into a Poultis, by braying them in a Mortar, and laying them over the Eyes, wetted a little with Eye-bright-water, between two fine cloths, will do the same; as also remove an Inflammation.

If by the Wind, or sharpness of the Air, clefts happen in your Lips.

Take Deers Suet an ounce, the like quantity of *Spermaceti*; add thereto an ounce of the Juyce of Housleek or Senegreen, and make them into an Oynment, and anoint your Lips, or any part of your face so afflicted; it will likewise serve for your Hands, *&c.* doing it when you go to bed, and drawing on a pair of soft Gloves.

To restore a singular Complexion in the Face where it is wanting.

Take green Hysop, when the flowers are on it, stamp it, and strain out the Juyce: sweeten it with white Sugar-candia, and boil it up with a third part of the Juyce of Pomgranets; and when it is clarified, use your self to drink six spoonfulls of it in warm Ale morning and evening, and you will find the advantage.

To remove any ill scent from out of the Nostril.

Snuff up or inject with a Sirringe White-wine, wherein Ginger, Cloves and Calamint have been boiled, and provoke your self to sneeze with the Powder of *Piritrum*, steeped in the Juyce of Senegreen, and afterward dried to it's original dryness in the Sun.

To make a sweet Water to be used by Gentlewomen on sundry occasions.

Take a pint of the Water of Mugwort, half a pint of the distilled Water of Peach-blossoms, drop into them when warm eight or nine drops of the Oyl or Spirit of Cloves, and as much of Nutmegs: stop it close, and shake it when you use it.

To take away Warts, very troublesome, on sundry occasions.

Take the Juyce of Senegreen and Purslain, adding to it an ounce of both together, ten or twelve drops of Oyl of Tartar, and wash the Warts with it when hot, and they will fall away.

To

To kill black-headed Worms in the hands or face.

Take half a pint of Wormwood-water, an ounce of the Ashes of Suthern-wood, and half an ounce of black Sope: boil them till the moisture be so far consumed, that they come to a thickness: then add an ounce of Oyl, make them into an Oynment, and anoint the place where they be, which you may perceive by their black heads, and they will, by often doing it, dye and waste away.

To take away Freckles, Morphew or Scars in the face.

Take half a pint of the Spirit of Wine, Rosemary-flowers two ounces, the Juyce of Elder-leaves two ounces, and the Marrow of Sheeps-feet or Hogs-feet two ounces; boil them till a third part be consumed, and anoint your face therewith. Or for want of it, Take of the Oyl or Oyntment of Cittern four ounces, and two of Pomatum; anoint your face with them when well incorporated, and six hours after wipe it off, and wash your face with Bean-flower or Rosemary-flower water.

In case of a Ring-worm in the Face.

Take half a quarter of a pint of the Vinegar

gar of Squills, a quarter of an ounce of the Juyce of Sellendine, three drams of the Oyl of Tartar, and as much of the Powder of Alloes: heat them over the fire till they become thick, and lay some of it Plaster-wise to the place grieved.

To cleanse the Body and make it comely.

Take red Roses two handfulls, of red Sage and Lavender-flowers the like quantity; a handfull of Featherfew, and as many Bay-leaves: boil them in Spring-water, adding a handfull or two of Salt, and wash your self as warm as with conveniency you may.

To Curl the Hair.

Take three ounces of Pine-nut kernels, dry them and beat them into Powder, then add to them half a pint of the water of Wall-flowers, and two ounces of the Oyl of Myrtle: boil them into a thickness, and straining out the liquid part, anoint the Hair, and roll it up; and so you will find it will in twice or thrice doing keep the curl.

To make Hair black.

Take two ounces of the Juyce of green Walnuts, as much of that of red Poppeys;

an ounce of the Oyl of Myrtle, and of that of Costomary, the like quantity: boil 'em to an Oyntment, and anoint the Hair therewith often, and it will effect your desire.

If, Gentlewomen, your Breasts be over-large, (and by that means troublesome) to reduce them,

Make an Oyntment of Roach-Allom and Oyl of Roses, with a small quantity of Scabeous-water, and they will contract themselves by being often anointed.

To make a sweet Bath.

Take the flowers or peels of Cittrons, the flowers of Oranges and Gessamine, Lavender, Hysop, Bay-leaves; the flowers of Rosemary, Comfry, and the seeds of Coriander, Endive and sweet Marjorum; the Berries of Myrtle and Juniper: boil them in Spring-water, after they are bruised, till a third part of the liquid matter is consumed, and enter it in a Bathing-tub, or wash your self with it warm, as you see occasion, and it will indifferently serve for Beauty and Health.

To make Musk-bags to lay amongst your Cloaths.

Take the flowers of Lavender-cotton six ounces, Storax half an ounce, red Rose-

leaves

leaves two ounces, Rhodium an ounce: dry them and beat them to Powder, and lay them in a bag wherein Musk has been, and they'l cast an excellent scent, and preserve your Cloaths from Moths or Worms.

To make Musk-balls.

Take of the flower of Almonds six ounces, Castle-sope six ounces: wet them in Rose-water, and infusing two grains of Musk, make the Paste up into balls without heating.

To make Burning Perfume.

Take an ounce of Storax, the like quantity of Mace, Cinamon and Nutmeg: bruise them together, and add the Powder of Cassa, and two ounces of the Oyl of Myrrh, or more if that suffice not to make it into rolls; or instead of it, you may use Virgins Wax; and being set on fire, it will cast a pretious scent.

To make a scent of Rosemary.

Take your Perfumer, and heat it over a chafing-dish of coles; put into it, being pretty hot, two spoonfulls of Rose-water, half a handfull of Rosemary-tops, and six drams of of Sugar, and all the house will be scented.

Another Excellent Perfume; how to make it.

Take a quarter of a pint of Rose-water, two grains of Amber-grease, two peny weight of Sugar, and a grain of Civit: beat them together, and put them into your Perfuming-pot over the fire, and it will send forth a delicate odour.

An Excellent Perfume good against Infectious Air, and exceeding pleasant; how to make it.

Observe to take half a quartern of Spike-water, as much of Rose-water; a quarter of an ounce of Cloves, with seven or eight Bay-leaves shred; add six grains of Sugar, and boil them in your Persumer.

To make Musk-Cakes.

Take half a pound of red Roses; bruise them well, and add to them the water of Basil, the Powder of Frankincense, making it up with these a pound; add four grains of Musk; mix them well to a thickness, make them into Cakes, and dry them in the Sun.

Thus,

Thus, Gentlewoman, have I made you sensible of such Curiosities, as are not only pleasant, but as highly advantageous. And now least you should be wanting in what is further necessary in the preservation and restauration of Health, I shall give you some admirable Receipts in Physick and Chyrurgery, that you may be helpfull to your self and others: Such they are, as have been often administred, and used with success; and such as, if rightly and seasonably applied, can do no harm; nor are they unfit for the Closet of a Gentlewoman, therefore accept them in good part.

CHAP. IX.

Instructions for a Gentlewoman in many Excellent Receipts, Physical and Chyrurgical, tending to the restauration and preservation of Health, in old and young, according to the best approved Rules and Methods, safe and easie in the Application, and successfull in the Operation.

IF any person be afflicted with the Griping of the Guts, Take Juniper-berries, Fennel, Anniseeds, Bay-berries, Tormentilo, Bistwort, Balaustius and Pomgranet-seeds, of each an ounce: bruiſe them, adding of Roſe-leaves a handfull: boil them in Milk, preſs out the liquid part, and add more the yolk of an Egg, and ſix grains of *Laudanum*: prepare it warm, and give it Cliſter-wiſe.

For Pains in the Head.

Take a Roſe-cake, ſteep it in Bettony-water, and apply it to the Forehead and Temples cold, often wetting it, and the Pain will abate.

In caſe of an Ague.

Take Rye-meal, temper it well with the yolk of an Egg, then ſpread it Plaſter-wiſe, and ſtrow upon it the Powder of Juniper-berries, and lay it to the parties Wriſts, giving him to drink a draught of hot Ale, wherein blew Lilly-roots have been ſteeped a night, and a white Flint-ſtone red hot quenched, and let him or her thereupon go into a hot bed; and by ſeveral times uſing it, the advantage will appear.

Or, Take two quarts of ſmall Ale, ſhread into it a handfull of Parſley, and the like quantity of red Fennel, of Centory and Pimpernel, each half a handfull: boil them in the Ale till a third part be conſumed; ſweeten it then with Sugar-candy, and let the party ty drink it hot upon the approach of the cold fit.

For the yellow Jaundice.

Take a large Onion, make it as hollow as you can; put into the cavity a quarter of an ounce of Venice-Treacle, and as much Honey, with a dram of Saffron: set the Onion on a gentle fire, and when by often turning it is sufficiently roasted, press it together with what was in it, and let the party grieved take a spoonfull of it for three days together in White-wine.

For the black Jaundice.

Take Sage, Parsley, Groundsil and Smallage, and boil them in Pottage with Swines-flesh; and in often eating it, the grievance will be removed.

For a dry Cough.

Take Anniseeds an ounce, the like quantity of Ash-keys, as many Violet-flowers, and the Powder of Licoris: beat them together, when dried, till they be a Powder; then put them into a pint of White-wine, sweetning it with two ounces of white Sugar-candia: boil them into an Electuary, and let the party take the quantity of a Walnut every morning fasting, drinking after it a glass of warm Ale or Milk.

To make green Ointment.

Take a pound of Barrows grease, add to it an ounce of Verdigrease, of Salgem half a scruple: make them up into an Ointment over a soft fire, and it is used with success in case of old sores or bruises.

To break an Imposthume or Swelling.

Take an ounce of the Roots of white Lillies, half a large Onion, and half an ounce of Barrows grease: stamp them together, and being fryed, lay it hot to the place.

To remove the humour that occasions the Green-sickness in Virgins and young Widows.

Take a quart of Claret, a pound of blew Currans, a handfull of young Rosemary-tops, with half an ounce of Mace: bruise them, and boil the liquid part to a pint, and let the party afflicted drink half a pint hot morning and evening for a week together.

Sir

Sir Philip Parry'*s Emplaister; how to make it, and its Virtue.*

Take of Olive-oyl two pounds, red Lead one pound, white Lead one pound; beat and ſerace them; of Caſtle-ſope twelve ounces: incorporate them in an Earthen pot well glazed, then ſet them on a gentle fire for an hour and half, ſtirring them continually till the matter become the colour of Oyl, and ſomewhat dark. Try it on a Plate, if it cleave not thereto, it is enough, then ſpread it on your Linnen, or dip the Linnen into it, and ſmooth it with a ſlek-ſtone, and it will not loſe it's Virtue in many years.

This Plaiſter, applied to the Stomack, provoketh Appetite, taketh away the grief or pain. Applied to the Reins, it ſtoppeth the Bloody-flux, the Running of the Reins, the Heat in the Kidneys, and the weakneſs of the Back, and is good for Swellings, Bruiſes, Aches, &c

A moſt Approved Plaiſter for the Rupture.

Take of Alloes and Cittron one ounce, Dragons blood an ounce, Myrrh an ounce, Maſtick, Bole-Armonick, Gum-dragant, of each three ounces; make them into a Powder, and with the Juyce of red Houſleek, work them into a Plaiſter.

A Salve Excellent to draw and heal, &c.

Take a penyworth of Turpentine, as much Virgins Wax as a Walnut, the like quantity of fresh Butter, a spoonfull of Honey: melt them into a pan, and strain the substance into fair water, and make it into a Roll for your use.

An Excellent Emplaister for a new or old Sore.

Take of Rosine four ounces, melt it, then of Turpentine take an ounce, and two ounces of Wax, the like of Sheeps-suet cleared from the skin, and a spoonfull of Olive-oyl: boil them over a gentle fire, and then strain them into water, and apply them as a Salve.

Dr. Morsus *Emplaister, commonly called* Oxecrotium.

Take Ship-Pitch, Saffron, Colophony, Bees-wax, of each three ounces; Turpentine, Galbanum, Amoniacum, Myrrh, fine Frankincense, Mastick, of each an ounce and three scruples: lay your Galbanum a night in Vinegar, then boil and strain it; melt your Gums, and mingle them by stirring: put in last your Turpentine, and being well incorporated, make it into Rolls, and use it in

case

case of Pains, Aches, Bruises, Strains, Dislocations, and to strengthen the Nerves, *&c.*

Oyl of Rosemary-flowers; how to make it, with it's Virtual Operation.

Take a good quantity of Rosemary-flowers, stamp them and put them into a Glass with strong Wine: stop the Glass close, and set it in the Sun six days, then distill the Flowers and Wine with a soft fire, and the effect will produce both Water and Oyl; separate them, and keep the Oyl close in a Glass.

This Oyl is good against the inveterate Head-ach, it comforteth the Memory, and preserveth the sight, by being drank in a Glass of Wine, or dropped into the Eyes: being dropped into the Ears, it helpeth Deafness, and is good in case of the Dropsie, yellow Jaundice, Rising of the Mother, &c.

An Excellent Powder to provoke Urin, and send forth the Gravel and Stone.

Take a Flint-stone and beat it in a Mortar to a fine and subtil Powder, serace it and keep it in a Bladder till you have occasion to use it, then take half a dram fasting in a Glass of White-wine or Ale, and keep your self warm.

A Powder to ease the Pains of the Gout.

Take of fine Ginger two drams, four drams of dried Elecampane-root, Licoras half an ounce, Sugar-candy three ounces: beat them to a fine Powder, and ſerace them, drinking off the Powder, a dram at a time faſting in a Glaſs of Ale.

A Water for eaſing the Pains in the Teeth.

Take of red Roſe-leaves half a handfull, Pomgranet-flowers the like quantity, two Galls thin ſliced; boil them in three quarters of a pint of red Wine, and half a pint of fair Water, untill a third part be conſumed; ſtrain them, and hold a ſpoonfull at a time in your mouth, and lay a hot cloth to your cheek dipped in the liquid part, *&c.*

An Excellent Water for the Ulceration of the Yard.

Take Water wherein Iron has been often quenched, a quart of Roſe-water, four ounces of Pomgranet-piles and flowers of each, three drams; of Plantane and Houſleek, each an ounce and a half; of Honey of Roſes, Turpentine, each half a pound; Allum ſix ounces, white Copperas three drams: boil them

them till half be consumed, then add Verdigrease three ounces: strain them, and gently boil them again; then letting them settle, take the thin and rarify'd part, and inject it with a Syringe, anointing the place grieved with the other part.

An Ointment to cleanse Sores either old or new.

Take two ounces of Turpentine, wash it well in a Barly-water, put to it the yolks of six new-laid Eggs, Honey of Roses, or common Honey four ounces: mingle them well over a gentle fire till they become an Ointment, and then dip the Tents or Pledgets in it, and apply them.

Flos Unguentorum; *how to make it; together with it's Excellent Virtue.*

Take Rosin, Perrosin, of each half a pound; Virgins Wax, Frankincense, of each four ounces; Mastick half an ounce; Stags-suet four ounces; Camphire two drams: Pound, and melt them over a gentle fire, then strain them into a Pottle of White-wine; and when it is lukewarm, put thereto three ounces of Turpentine, stirring it till it be cold, and then put it up for your use.

It is exceeding good for old Wounds, in order to the

the ingendring good flesh, and cleansing them; wasting likewise the bad flesh, and is good for all manner of Imposthumes in the Head, and in the Body; also for Strains in the Sinews: It draweth out Thorns or Splinters of Bones; it healeth Botches and Scabs, and is good for the Noli me tangere; *and is an excellent Sear-cloth for the Gout, Sciatica or Aches in any part of the Body.*

For a Scald, or any Burn, an Excellent Ointment.

Take of Cream a quart, Fern-roots a handfull: slice and wash the Roots, and then boil them in the Cream in an Earthen-pot till they Jelly, and at what time there is an occasion to use it: Ferment it with a *Spatula*, and apply it on a Linnen-cloth, often renewing it.

An Excellent Ointment to asswage Pain, and cool any extraordinary Heat by what means soever it happen.

Take of white Carrate four ounces, Oyl of Roses ten ounces, red and white Saunders, red Roses, Myrrh, Olibanum and Mastick, of each two drams; Camphire half a dram, Turpentine two ounces and a half, and make them into an Unguent.

A

A Tobacco-Salve for any fresh Wound.

Take of the Juyce of green English Tobacco a quart, of Olive-oyl a pint, of Wax and Turpentine, each an ounce and half; an ounce of Verdegrease: boil them over a gentle fire for an hours space, and make them up in Rolls for your use.

Note, That the best Cloth for Plaister is new Lockram, and the worst Calico, or such cloth as has been starched.

For the shrinking of the Nerves or Sinews, a Plaister.

Take of Water-cresses and Cammomile, each a handfull; stamp them and fry them with a handfull of Wheaten-meal, and two ounces of Honey; then spread them on a cloth, and apply them to the place as hot as may be well endured.

A Dredge Powder, that purgeth Choler, Phlegm and Melancholy.

Take of Turbith one ounce, Ginger, Cinamon, Mastick, Gallengale, grains of Paradise, Cloves, Anniseeds, the Herb called *Mercury's Finger* and *Diagredium*, of each half an ounce: the leaves of Senna two ounces,

Loaf-

Loaf-sugar four ounces; dry them that they may be pulverized, and mingling them well, take a dram in a morning fasting either in a glass of White-wine or warm Ale.

An Excellent Powder to purge the Head by Sneezing.

Take of the Roots of Sneezing-wort or Bartram an ounce, *Castorum* half an ounce, of white Elebore and black Elebore, each an ounce; Marjorum a handfull: dry them and make them into a Powder, using the Powder moderately as you see occasion.

An Excellent Powder for the Falling-sickness.

Take a Mans Scull that has not been above a year buried: bury it in hot Embers till it become white, and easie to be broken: Then take off the uppermost part of the head to the top of the crown, and beat it into Powder; then grate a Nutmeg, and put it to it, with two ounces of the blood of a Dog dried and powdered: mingle them together, and give the grieved party a dram morning and evening in White-wine or new Milk.

An Excellent Powder for hollow Ulcers.

Take Frankincense, Mastick, Myrrh, Sarcocol, Bole-armorick, Dragons blood and Barly-meal, of each an ounce: make them into a Powder, and sprinkle a little of it in the Ulcer, *&c*: and bind it up: which often doing, will fill it with flesh.

A Powder to Incarnate any Wound.

Take of Hog-Fennel half an ounce, Flowerdelize five drams, Myrrh three grains, the greater and lesser Centaury, of each two drams: Round *Aristolocia*, *Tuttiæ*, *Oppoponax*, Meal of *Orobus*, each two drams and a half: beat them into fine Powder, and strew them upon the wound as you see occasion.

An Excellent Powder to stay the Bleeding of Wounds, &c.

Take Quick-Lime, Dragons Blood, Alloes, Frankincense, Copperas, of each four drams: incorporate them, and being finely powdered with Cobwebs, and the White of an Egg: apply the Powder by sprinkling it in the wound.

An Excellent Poultis for any Ach, Sprain or Dislocation.

Take of Smallage, Marshmallows, Cammomile and Groundsil, each a handfull well picked: stamp them and fry them in six ounces of Barrows grease with the yolks of two Eggs, and apply them as hot as may be well endured to the place grieved.

An Excellent Powder in case of the Small Pox, or any Infectious distemper.

Take half an ounce of English Saffron, dry it till it may be pulverized, add to it six grains of Bezora-stone, a dram of Myrrh, and an ounce of white Sugar-candy: Incorporate them, and let the party take a dram at a time in White-wine, not exceeding a spoonfull.

An Excellent Confection to preserve against the Plague, or any Pestilential disease; as also from the effects of bad Airs.

Take green Walnuts, number six; Baum and Rue, of each a handfull; Plantane and Bettony the like quantity: bruise them with fine Sugar and Spirit of Wine, then dry the whole matter in an Oven or Stove till it becomes

comes as solid as Conserve of Roses, and let the party take fasting as much as a Hazle-nut.

For the Consumption, an Excellent Receipt.

Take the Hearts of three Sheep new killed, cleansed from the blood and strings: soak them a night and a day in White-wine, dry them again, and put them into a new-glazed Pipkin, covering them above and below with Rosemary-branches: then add Cloves, Sugar, Harts-horn, of each three ounces, and four ounces of white Sugar-candy, and as much Asses Milk as will cover them; then stop them close with Paste, and let them stand in an Oven the Baking of Houshold-bread; after that press out the liquid part, and take a spoonfull morning and evening.

An Excellent Drink for the Windiness of the Stomack or Spleen.

Take a handfull of Broom-buds, the like quantity of Anniseeds; of the Roots of Scabeous an ounce: boil them in a quart of new Ale, sweeten the liquid part with brown Sugar, and drink half a quartern hot at a time morning and evening, or when you find your self oppressed; and in so continuing it for a week, you will find great relief.

The

The Lord Denise's *Excellent Medicine for the Gout; how to make and apply it.*

Take four handfulls of Burdock-leaves with the stalks on, shread them and bruise them: strain out the Juyce and clarifie it, adding half the quantity of Olive-oyl, and keep it close stopped in a glass; and as you use it, apply it with a hot cloth to the place grieved.

To make Gascoign-Powder.

Take of white Amber, Seed, Pearls, Harts-horn, Eyes of Crabs and white Corral, of each half an ounce; of the black Thighs of Crabs, calcined before they are boiled, two ounces; adding to every ounce before mentioned an ounce of Oriential Bezoar: bruise and serace them to a fine Powder, and it is excellent, two scruples of it drunk in a spoonfull of Wine, to expell evil vapours from the brain to comfort and corroborate the heart, and restore a decaying constitution; and for the better keeping, you may make it into Lozenges with the Jelly of Harts-horn and Saffron.

For

For the Dropsie.

Take Setwell, *Calamus-aromaticus* and Galingale, of each an ounce; of Spicknard, half an ounce: bruise them, and hanging in a bag, let them be covered with two gallons of Ale, the which at four days end let the party drink morning and evening.

To make an Excellent Water for any Disease in the Eyes.

Take half a pint of White-wine, and as much of white Rose-water; of the Water of Celendine, Rue, Eyebright and Fennel, each two ounce; of Prepared *Tuttiæ* six ounces; of Cloves as many; of Sugar-rosate a dram: mix them over a soft fire, and being clarified, wash your Eyes therewith as you see occasion.

To break the Wind.

Take the Juyce of red Fennel and Anniseed in warm Ale.

To prevent spitting Blood.

Take Rue, Smallage, Mint and Bettony; boil them in new Milk, and drink the liquid part as hot as you can.

To

To stay Bleeding at the Nose.

Take the Juyce of Bettony, with a small quantity of Salt in it, and snuff it up your Nose, and stop it in with the Herb, the Juyce of young Nettles; and Sugar is good upon the like occasion.

To kill a Fellon.

Take the hard roasted yolk of an Egg, and beating it with a roasted Onion, lay it to the place grieved.

To make an Excellent Salve for a Scald, Burn, Cut, or any old Sore.

Take a pint of Olive-oyl, half a pound of Bees-wax, red Lead three ounces, red Wine two ounces, and Deers-suet three ounces: boil them together in a glazed Earthen-vessel till they are of a darkish colour, and then make it up into a Salve for your use.

To remove the Pain of the Tooth-ach.

Take Henbane-seed, Hysop-seed, and the Powder of the root of black Helebore: bruise them together, and make them up into small pellets with a little Tarr or Turpentine: If the

the Tooth be hollow, ſtop it in with Lint; if not, let it lye between your Cheek and Gumm.

For the Feaver.

Take two handfulls of Wood-ſorrel, the like of the Leaves of Barberries: boil them in Spring-water, ſweeten it with Sugar, and give the party two ſcruples of Bezora-powder in a quarter of a pint of it, and it wonderfully prevails againſt the diſtemper.

Many more things there are that remain fitting for a Gentlewoman to know; but not to be tedious, I ſhall refer them to your Servants in their ſeveral places and ſtations: And ſuppoſing you by this time to have reaped the fruits of a chaſte and happy Marriage, and bleſſed with a tender, yet ſmiling, Offſpring, that it may flouriſh. Taking my leave, Madam, of you, I ſhall proceed to give your Nurſe and Nurſery-Maid inſtructions and directions; and ſo to the reſt in order.

CHAP.

CHAP. X.

The wet Nurse her Duty and Office; and how she ought to be qualified that undertakes so great a charge: With directions how she ought to use her self as to her Diet; and by what means to keep her Milk in good temper, &c.

AS for Directions to a dry Nurſe, whoſe buſineſs it is to look after a Gentlewoman when ſhe lyes in; it will not be amiſs to wave them, ſince few that undertake ſuch a charge are ignorant what is neceſſary as to Uſage and Diet: Nor is the Midwife in that caſe wanting to give Directions, if the Gentlewoman her ſelf (as few are after the firſt Lying in) were ignorant in that affair. Wherefore intending to ſay ſomething of it in treating of the Duty and Office of a Midwife, I willingly here omit it, and proceed to the Charge and Office of a wet Nurſe, whoſe care it is to bring up Children till a conveniency offer to wean them: And firſt, I ſhall deſcribe what manner of Perſon a good Nurſe ought to be.

In this caſe a good Nurſe ought to be of a middle ſtature, plump of body, though not over corpulent; of a ſanguine complection, pleaſant and cheerfull, clear skinn'd and well-proportioned. For

For her Conditions, they muſt be ſutable: Anger muſt be a ſtranger to her, and her delight naturally in Children; not drowſie nor ſelf-conceited; her Age muſt be a Medium, between five and twenty and forty, being one that has been well Educated; and ſee ſhe want for nothing; for if ſhe be neceſſitated, the Child muſt pine; or if Sickneſs happen through accident or diſorder, her Milk is injured thereby: Yet Temperance muſt be her greateſt care, for fear by exceſs of meat or drink the Milk be corrupted or inflamed; and in all things her care of her charge muſt let her Prudence appear. Take a Woman whoſe Child was a Boy, to Nurſe one of that kind, and on the other ſide the contrary, conſidering ſhe ought not to be with child during the diſcharge of this great Office, leaſt ſhe ſpoil both her Nurſery and that ſhe goes with.

A Nurſe in this caſe ought in her Diet to avoid ſalt Meats, Onions, Garlick, Leeks, Muſtard, too much Salt, Vinegar, or Pepper, and ſuch like things as create bad nutriment, or inflame and heat the blood. Strong drink immoderately muſt be ſhunn'd, for that will occaſion a ſuper-abounding of Choler in the Child, as Cheeſe and Fiſh, will Melancholy and Phlegm: nor ought ſhe to ſleep ſuddainly after Meals, but be active and in motion, to create a natural digeſtion; a good Air ought to be chosen for the more kindly respiration; for a gross Air is frequently the occasion of a dull wit and much corpulency, and a pure thin Air of the contrary, the Air on many occasions being advantageous or disadvantageous to the faculties of Life, or passions of the Mind in their several operations, it being a kind of a food to the Intellectuals.

As for the Milk, divers things are to be considered, but the chief is wholsome and moderate Diet; and to correct defects, Let her observe if her Milk be too hot, which often appears by the Childs frowardness; if so, let the Nurse take in her Posset-drink Salad or Pottage, Endive, Succory, Lettice, Sorrel, Plantane, or such like cooling Herbs: If she find it too cold, which will appear by the Childs over-drowsiness, let her do the like with Cinamon, Vervine, Bugloss, Mother, Time or Burrage.

To cause Milk where it is wanting, Take part of the Hoof of the fore-foot of a Cow calcined to Powder; a dram of which let the Nurse drink morning and evening in warm Cows Milk or Ale.

For want of the former, Take Lady-Thistle, stamp it, and squeeze out the Juyce; which boiled in Milk, an ounce to a pint you may conveniently take, drinking it off warm. And thus being carefull in seasonably ordering the Child in dressing, undressing, and what

in

in the like nature is convenient, no doubt it will thrive and come to perfection.

The best Colour of a Child, when new-born, is red, which soon turns to a Rosey; for those that are white, if they live, will be subject to diseases. A little crying, if not too often, eases the brain of watery-matter, and inlarges the Lungs; but too much crying occasions Catarrhs and Ruptures. The first month it must only suck often, changing the breast, but not over-charging it's stomack; after which a pap of white Bread and Milk seasonably given, between whiles, will strengthen it; and let there be an hour between sucking and feeding, using it in that manner till the Teeth come.

The Teeth coming forth by degrees, give it more solid food, not denying it Meat that is small cut, and may be easily chewed: Keep it well swathed, and beware it stand not too soon for fear of distorting the Legs. In such places as bathing of Children is convenient, omit it not; from the seventh month, twice a week, till it is weaned.

At a twelvemonth old, if it be healthy, wean it, not giving it suddainly strong food, but by degrees; and the first seven years Diet ought to be such as, by it's nourishment, causeth growth.

And from this I shall proceed to say somewhat of Diseases incident to Children, and prescribe Remedies which Nurses ought to use on sundry occasions.

CHAP. XI.

Of Distempers in Infants; and how to Remedy them: Together with Directions to the Nursery-Maid in the discharging her Duty and Office, &c.

CHildren in their tender age are subject to many distempers; wherefore a Nurse ought to be skilfull in Medicines, such as are prevalent on sundry occasions, by reason a Child may be lost before a Physitian can be had. Wherefore I shall give her Instructions what to do in the most dangerous cases.

For the Epilepsis or Convulsion.

Take Majesterie of Cole a scruple, of Male Piony-roots a scruple, and as much of Leaf Gold: work them into a Powder, and give it the Child in a spoonfull of Breast-Milk.

For the Chafing of the Hips.

Change the Clouts often, ſprinkling on them Litherage of Silver, Seed and Leaves of Roſes, Frankincenſe and burnt Allum made into a Powder, or anoint them with white Ointment and Diapompholigos.

To remove the Stoppage of Urin.

Take Saxifrax-roots ſix drams, Calcine them with an ounce of the Blood of a Hare: bruiſe them into a Powder, and give the Child from a ſcruple to half a dram in a ſpoonfull of White-wine.

For the Strutting of the Navel.

Uſe a Plaiſter or Poultis of Cumming, Lupins and Bay-berries beaten into Powder, and wet with White-wine.

For the Inflamation of the Navel.

Take a quarter of a handfull of Mallows, ſtamp them with half an ounce of Barly-meal, and with Fenigreek and Lupins, two ounces of each: make them into a Cataplaſm with Oyl of Roſes, and apply them to the place grieved.

To destroy Worms.

Take of Worm-seed two drams, and of Coralline and Harts-horn prepared, each a dram; Roots of Piany, Dittany, Majestery of Coral, each a scruple: make them into a Powder, and give a scruple at a time in a spoonfull of Peach-flower water.

For Vomiting.

Take a quarter of an ounce of Honey of Roses, and the like quantity of Syrup of Mint, and give it the Child at four times.

For the Hickets.

Take Mastick an ounce, Dill and Frankincense, of each two drams; Cummin-seed a dram: make them small, and apply them with the Juyce of Mint upon a plaster or sodd of Flax.

For hard breeding of Teeth.

Rub the Gums with your finger dipped in Honey, or give the Child Candle made of Virgins Wax to nable on, and Foment the cheeks with the Decoction of *Althæa*, Cammomile-flowers, and the seed of Dill.

For

For the Bladder in the Gums.

Take Lintills husked, beat them into powder, and lay them upon the Gums, or take half an ounçe of the flower of Mellium, make it into a Lineament and apply it.

To prevent squint Eyes.

Hang a Picture, and set a Candle on the contrary side; or use to cocker the Infant on that side till Eye-strings contract.

For a scald Head.

Take the Scab off gently with a cleanser, moistning the skin with Hogs-grease upon Colewort-leaves; or rather take the Juyce of Fumitory, Dock, Coleworts and Elecampane, of each half an ounce, with Litherage, Oyl of Rue, Hogs-grease and Wax, make a mollifying Ointment: then take Starch two ounces, Rosin half an ounce; boil them in water, and lay them upon the scall'd places Poultis-wise, suffering them to lye there several days: then suddainly pull them off, and use mollifying things to correct the distemper, *&c.*

In case of a Feaver.

Give the Infant a quarter of an ounce of

Syrup of Violets, and as much of that of Wood-sorrel, for the Measles or Small Pox: Give them Saffron, and a small quantity of Manna in Milk, or a spoonfull of White-wine, And thus much for the principal distempers in Children.

As for the Nursery-Maids business, to whose care Children are frequently committed, when capable of running about, it is to love and cherish them, to see they have what is fitting in due season, to keep them within compass and government, to see they carry their legs and bodys strait and even, and that they disorder themselves by no untoward tricks and actions, but that they be cleanly and neat; and if she discovers any alteration in complection, constitution or habit of body tending to sickness or other discommodity, either to apply fit remedies her self, or inform those of it who delivered them to her charge without delay, least a Remedy come too late. She is to keep them within bounds, but not be churlish nor dogged to them, but rather to be merry and pleasant; contriving such Pastimes as may best sute with their age and constitutions; keeping their Apparrel in good order, and not shewing too much love to one, nor disregard to the other: And by this means a Maid will gain Love and Applause from all parties.

CHAP.

CHAP. XII.

The Compleat Chamber-Maids profitable Instruction as to her behaviour in Managing of Affairs, making choice Spoon-meats, Pickling Sawces, Washing and Starching Tiffany, Lawn, Sarcenets, Silks, Point, &c. *Scowring Gold and Silver Lace, taking Spots out of Silk, Wollen, Linnen, Stuffs, Perfuming,* &c.

A Chamber-Maid that would be preferred, gain, or continue a good opinion, must in the first place be grave and respectfull to those whom she serves, neat in her habit, loving to her fellow-servants, and affable to all declining wanton gestures that may render her suspected of Levity. That she keep all things in her Chamber in good order, and have them in readiness on all occasions to take off the care of the Mistriss: Skilled likewise she must, or ought to be, in buying fine knacks, and be just in returning her accounts. If there be no Butler, she must see all things decently managed for the Accommodation of the guest in the Parlour and Dining-room; and above all, have a regard to the Linnen, Plate, and other furniture under her Command: And besides her skill in Dressing and Attiring her Mistriss, be skilfull in making Spoon-meats, Pickling things usefull for Sawces, or Garnishing, Washing and Starching Tiffanies, Lawns, black and white Sarsnet, Points, and other curious Lace: As likewise she ought to be skilfull at making such scowring Materials as will cleanse Silver or Gold Lace, Silver or Gold Plate, take Spots out of Linnen, Silks, Stuffs or Cloth. And because these are in a manner secrets, I shall lay down Instructions for as many as are materially usefull: And first of Spoon-meats.

To make a French *Barly-Posset after the newest fashion.*

Boil half a pound of *French* Barly in two quarts of new Milk; and when the Milk is near boiled away, add three pints of sweet Cream, then boil it a quarter of an hour, and sweeten it with fine Sugar: put in three or four blades of Mace and a piece of Cinamon: this done, take a pint of White-wine, and pour the liquid Cream into it, frothing it up.

To make an Excellent Broth.

Cut off the wings and legs of two Cocks, wash and parboil them till the scum appear: take them out and wash them in cold water, then with a pint of Rhenish-wine, and two quarts

quarts of ſtrong Broth, put them into a Pipkin; add two ounces of China-root, an ounce and a half of Harts-horn, with a ſmall quantity of Cloves, Nutmegs, Mace, Ginger, whole Pepper and Salt: ſtop the Pipkin cloſe, and ſetting it in a pot of boiling water, ſo that that water get not into it for the ſpace of ſix hours; then pour out the Broth, and ſqueeze the Juyce of Lemons into it and ſerve it up.

To make Pottage of French *Barly.*

Take a pound of Barly very clean, put it into three quarts of Milk whilſt boiling; then add a quart of Cream, an ounce of Salt, ſix blades of Mace, and a piece of Cinamon: let them boil a little, and become thick: ſerve it up with white Sugar ſcraped thereon.

To make Pannado, *after the beſt faſhion.*

Take a quart of Spring-water, which being hot on the fire, put into it ſlices of fine bread, as thin as may be: then add half a pound of Currans, a quarter of an ounce of Mace: boil them well, and then ſeaſon them with Roſe-water and fine Sugar, and ſerve them up.

To make an Excellent White-pot.

Take two quarts of Cream, boil in it a ſhort time half an ounce of Mace, a piece of Cinamon, and half a Nutmeg; then cut a white peny loaf exceeding thin, then lay the ſlices at the bottom of a diſh, and cover them with Marrow: add likewiſe a dozen yolks of Eggs to the Cream, well beaten in Roſe-water, and ſweeten it with a ſufficient quantity of Sugar: then take out the Spices, beat up the Cream well, and fill a broad Baſon in which the Bread, Raiſins and Marrow was layed, and bake it; when it is enough, ſcrape white Sugar on it and ſerve it up.

All ſtrengthning Jellies are made by boiling ſuch Fleſh as are of a tender and gluttenous ſubſtance till it is in a manner diſſolved in the Broth, and adding Wine, Sugar, Spice, Salt, or as you will have it ſeaſoned, and ſerving it up with Sipits or alone. More I might mention of this kind, but intending largely to treat of *Cookery*, I ſhall wave them, and proceed to the next, which is Pickling Fruits and Flowers, *&c.*

To Pickle Cucumbers, ſo that they may wear a laſting green.

Take your Cucumbers of a moderate ſize, waſh

wash them in water and salt, there letting them steep six hours; then boiling Wine-vinegar, Dill and Fennel-tops, Coriander-seeds, Cloves and Mace, with a little Bay-salt, and a pint of the Juyce of Mint: put them into it when warm, and stop them up for a month.

To make French *Beans a lasting green.*

Boil them in water, and a small quantity of salt, till they are a little soft; then having sharp Vinegar, Pepper and Bay-leaves ready boiled, with some blades of Cinamon: put them into it, and stop them up as the former. Thus Broom-buds, Ash-keys, green Grapes, green Plumbs, Gooseberrys, Currans, and the like, may be Pickled, though the latter must be only scalded.

To Pickle Barberries.

Take the fairest bunches, dip them into warm water, and then make a Pickle with a pint of sharp Vinegar to a gallon of Water that has been well boiled and scumed, and to each gallon add a quart of Bay or Spanish salt; and putting in the Barberries, keep them down with a stone. So Quinces, Apples, green Walnuts and Olives are Pickled.

To Pickle Mushrooms.

Take a quart of Water and a pint of Vinegar, put your Mushrooms, the smallest, boiling hot into it; and when they have contracted a kind of a softness, take them out and put them to the sharpest Vinegar, with whole Pepper, long Ginger, Mace and Bay-leaves. And thus you may Pickle Clove-gilleflowers, Primroses, Roses, Cowslips, green Peaches, or the like.

As for Sampher, it is boiled in salt and water to a little tenderness, and then put up with a Pickle made of half Vinegar and half Water and Salt, boiled up to a hight. And thus much for Pickles.

To wash Tiffanies.

Take the finest Crown-soap, Soap them on their Hems or Laces, and with a gentle hand pass them through three Lathers, forbearing to wring or wrince them; but keeping them from the Air, dry them over the flame of Brimstone: then to a pound of Starch, add a quarter of an ounce of Smalt, if you think convenient, but on necessity as much Allum as a Hazle-nut: boil it to a fineness, and charge it lightly on your Tiffanies, and dry them, being wet therewith, by a fire,

still

ſtill clapping them in your hands; and when they are very clear, ſhape them by the pattern you took before they were waſhed, and iron them with a ſmooth, though quick Iron, till they ſhine, and you will find little difference as to the gloſs between them and new. Some there are, that inſtead of Starch, uſe Gum-water.

Lawns are uſed in the like manner, only they are Ironed on the wrong ſide, and on a damp cloth.

To waſh Sarſnet.

If white, ſpread it upon a ſmooth clean board long-ways; Soap it well, but let the Soap lye thin; then with a ſmall hard bruſh raiſe a gentle Lather by bruſhing it the right way of the Silk; and turning it in order, do the other ſide in the ſame manner, then cleanſe it with fair water, and make a new Lather hot, and renew it three times with turning; then caſt the piece into hot water where Gum has been diſſolved, and a ſmall quantity of Smalt infuſed; let it lye there covered a convenient time; then folding it ſmooth, dry it as well as you can by clapping it between your hands, then dry it over Brimſtone, and ſpreading it on the Table, Iron it with a hot Iron on the right ſide.

Black

Black Sarſnets in waſhing are managed the ſame way, only they are wrinced generally in ſmall Beer, without any Gum, and ironed upon a Wollen-cloth.

The Modiſh way to Waſh and Starch Point-laces.

Put your Points into a Tent, and make a ſtrong Lather with Caſtle or Cake-ſoap, then with a ſmall ſoft bruſh dipped therein, rub your Point well,continuing to waſh it on both ſides till it have paſſed four Lathers; wrince it then in fair water, and afterward paſs it gently through blew water; then Starch it over on the wrong ſide lightly with very thin Starch, and follow it with your bruſh; after that ſuffer it to dry, and with a round bodkin open the holes or parts that in waſhing were cloſed; as alſo the Gimp or over-laying, and not ſuffering it to be too blew: gently iron it on the wrong ſide, and ſet it out to advantage.

Coloured Silks may be waſhed as white Sarſnet, avoiding the blew water, or drying over Brimſtone.

To take a Spot or Stain out of Silks, Worſted or Woollen.

Take two ounces of Caſtle-ſoap, half an ounce of Bone calcined, half an ounce of Cam-

Camphire: make them up into little balls with the water of Bettony, and Lather the place with a ſmall quantity of warm Vinegar, and it will effect your deſire. Cake-ſoap, Lemon-Juyce and Roach-Allum will do the like.

To take Pitch, Roſin, Tar or ſoft Wax out of Stuffs or Woollen.

Take Oyl of Turpentine, and ſuffer it to ſoak in a while, then rub the cloth or ſtuff together, and it will crumble out.

To take the Stain of Fruit, Ink, or the like, out of Linnen.

Take Caſtle-ſoap, boil it to a Jelly in Milk, lay it upon the Spot a night, then pour upon it the Juyce of a Lemon; and in doing ſo after a waſhing or two the Spot will diſappear.

To cleanſe Silver or Gold Lace.

Take it off, and dipping a bruſh continually in burnt Allum, rub it gently over and the colour will be reſtored.

An Excellent way to Perfume Gloves is this.

Take of Storax and Calamint, each an ounce; of Benjamine two ounces, the first and the last being to be beaten by themselves; add to them an ounce of the weaker Cinamon-water, and four ounces of the Oyl of sweet Almonds: mingle them with a Muller on a stone; and having first wetted your Gloves with Hysop-water, gently anoint them with the Perfume, and it will smell beyond expectation.

To cleanse all sorts of Plate.

Lay it in Soap lees a night, then with Salt and Vinegar rub out the Spots, after daub it over with Chalk and Vinegar: dry it by the fire, and with a warm Woollen-cloth rub it off, and it will look as bright as new.

Thus have I unravel'd, or at least exposed to some such secrets as are not common; from whence I shall proceed to give the Virtuous Cook-Maid Instructions.

CHAP.

CHAP. XIII.

The Experienced Cook-Maid and Cook, or Directions for the newest and most Excellent way of dressing Flesh, Fish and Fowl of all sorts, and in divers manners; as also making Pyes, Tarts, Custards: Likewise what relates to the under Cook-Maid and Scullery-Maid; with other variety.

SInce the Cook-Maids charge and care is no less than the former, and her labour more, I shall give her what encouragement I can in rendering matters plain and easie: As for her skill, it must chiefly consist in dressing all sorts of Meat, as Flesh, Fish and Fowl, in preparing of bak'd Meats and Pastry, and to be expert in making Sawces, and garnishing proper to the several varieties that must consequently offer. And therefore these things I shall consider, she in the first place considering to have all her Kitchin materials in good order.

A Capon, or Chickens and white Broth being frequently the first dish, dress it after this manner.

Boil the Capon, *&c.* in water and salt, then take three pints of the strongest Broth, adding to to it a quart of White-wine, and a quarter of a pound of Dates: ſtew it in a Pipkin, and add half a pound of white Sugar, and a ſmall quantity of large Mace; the Marrow of three Marrow-bones, and of white Endive a handfull: ſtew 'em leaſurely, and ſtrain the yolk of ten Eggs with part of the Broth before the Capons or Chickens are diſhed up, obſerving that the Eggs curdle not: the Fowls being diſhed up, garniſh the diſh with Dates, Mace, Endive, and preſerved Barberries.

Red or Fallow Deer; how to Roaſt.

Take a Side, or half the Hanch, and parboil it; ſo doing, ſtuff it with all manner of ſweet Herbs, mingled with minced Beef-ſuet, lay the Caul over, and roaſt it in that manner: when it is enough, ſerve it up with Vinegar, Bread, Claret-wine, Ginger and Cloves boiled up with a few ſprigs of Roſemary.

Neats Tongues roaſted.

Take a large Tongue boiled tender, blanched and cold; make a hole at the large end, and take out a great part of the Meat; mince it, and put it in again with ſweet Herbs, hard yolks of Eggs, Pippins, Ginger, Beef-ſuet; all minced ſmall, and ſtop up the hole with a Caul of Veal: Lard it, and being roaſted, ſerve

ſerve it up with Butter, Gravy and Juyce of Oranges, garniſhing the diſh with Barberries and ſlices of Lemon.

Neats Tongue and Udder ; how to boil.

Let both of theſe be fair and young, indifferently ſeaſoned : boil them in water, a little ſeaſoned with Salt and Pepper ; and when you find they are ſufficiently done, blance the Tongue, ſlice it in half, lay it on each ſide the Udder : ſerve 'em up with carved Sipits run over with Butter and Vinegar : garniſh your diſh with Parſley, Barberrys and Marigold-leaves.

How to boil Land or Sea Fowl.

Take the larger ſort, half roaſt 'em, put them after that into a Pipkin with Claret-wine, the Gravy, and as much ſtrong Broth as will cover them ; add Pepper, Cloves, Mace, Ginger, a ſlice or two of Onion, and a little Salt : all being well ſtewed together, ſerve them up with Sipits and green garniſh, as Violet or Marigold-leaves, *&c.*

The ſmaller ſort of wild Fowl, as Black-birds, Plovers, Quails, Rails, Thruſhes, Snites, Larks, cut off the heads and legs, truſs and boil them ; ſcum your boiler, and add White-wine, Currans, Dates, Marrow, Pepper,

Pepper and Salt: being all well boiled or ſtewed, diſh them on carved Sipits; ſawce them with Roſe-water, Sugar and beaten Almonds; garniſh the diſh with Almonds beaten ſmall, Roſe-water and Sugar.

To roaſt a Hare.

Obſerve when ſhe is caſed not to cut off her hinder Legs nor Ears, but thruſt one leg through the ham of the other; and making a ſlit, do the like by the Ears, and ſo roaſt her as you do a Rabit. The proper ſawce is Marjorum, Thyme, Winter-ſavory, Beef-ſuet, hard yolks of Eggs, ſweet Butter, Sugar, Nutmeg, Water and Vinegar: minced and boil up to a ſawce, ſerving your Hare up hole.

To roaſt a Shoulder of Mutton the beſt way.

Take Oyſters parboiled, mince Winter-ſavory, the yolks of hard Eggs, grated Bread: mingle them together, all but the Oyſter, being ſmall, and then making holes in convenient places, ſtuff them in as you ſee convenient, about five or ſix and twenty Oyſters being ſufficient, and the other Oyſters with the like Ingredients put into half a pint of Claret; add three or four ſlices of Onion, and a couple of Anchoveys, to them put the Gravy,

Gravy, with the yolks of two beaten Eggs, and a ſufficient quantity of Nutmeg and ſweet Butter: garniſh your diſh with Lemon-peel and Barberries.

To boil Pigeons with Rice.

Obſerve to ſtuff their bellies with ſweet Herbs, then put them into your boiler with Mutton-broth; boil a ſmall quantity of Rice in Cream, with a blade or two of Mace; which being ſeaſoned with Sugar, lay them in the diſh with their breaſts upward, and lay it thick upon them; ſqueeſe in the Juyce of two Lemons; garniſh the diſh with Marigold-flowers and ſerve it up.

To roaſt an Udder.

Firſt let the Udder be boiled and ſtuck full of Cloves; ſpit it when cold, and baſte it with ſweet Butter; being ſufficiently browned, draw it back: make ſawce of grated Bread, Butter, Vinegar and Cinamon; lay it in the diſh with Sugar as a garniſhment, and ſerve it up.

To Stew a Carp.

Take the largeſt well-trimmed Carp, gut waſh it and lay it in a Pewter-diſh; take half

half a pint of White-wine, with a piece of Butter, Mace, Parsley, Thyme and Winter-savory minced small; put them into the fishes belly, and let it stew a quarter of an hour: mince then the hard yolks of two Eggs; lay it with the Herbs about it, and sprinkling on Sugar, serve it up.

To bake Steaks in the French *fashion.*

With Pepper, Nutmeg and Salt season your Steaks lightly: take the lean part of a Leg of Mutton, mince it small, with some Beef-suet and sweet Herbs, as Thyme, Peneroyal and Marjorum; take grated Bread, yolks of Eggs, Raisins of the Sun, of each a like quantity: work them into rolls, and put them on the Steaks in a deep round Pye; sprinkle them with Verjuice, and close them up, Liquoring it with the Juyce of two or three Oranges.

To boil a fore Loin of Pork the best way.

Season it indifferently, and boil it well. then have in readiness Sorrel stripped a considerable quantity; beat it, and put to it some crumbs of bread and hard yolks of Eggs, with Mustard and Salt, and so serve it up, the dish being garnished with green leaves.

To dress a Leg of Mutton to the best advantage.

In salt and water boil it for the space of an hour, then cut it into thin slices, set it in a dish over the fire, adding a little Salt, grated Nutmeg, Shalot, Thyme and Winter-savory; placing another dish upon it, and stewing it, adding a piece of Butter, serve it up, the dish garnished with pickled Oysters and Barberries.

To boil a Brisket, Surloin, Chine, Rump, Flank, Fillet or Buttock of Beef, to the best advantage.

After a week or ten days powdering it is left to your discretion, whether or not you will stuff them; which if you do, it must be done with such sweet Herbs as are sutable, mingling minced Suet and Nutmeg with it, and thrust them in at convenient places; and being well boiled, serve them in on Bruis, with roots boiled in Milk.

To stew a Leg of Lamb the best way.

Take the Meat, slice it and put it into you stewing-pan, season it well with Salt and Nutmeg; add Butter, Raisins in the Sun, Currans and Gooseberries: it being well stewed, take the yolks of four Eggs, a quarter of a pint of Wine-Vinegar, two ounces of Sugar: beat them well together over a gentle fire, place it in the ſawce, ſtrew Sugar over it and ſerve it up.

To boil a Leg of Veal and Bacon the beſt way.

Take and Lard the former with Bacon, and a ſmall quantity of Lemon-peel; take a convenient piece of Bacon and boil with it, and when your Bacon is boiled, cut it in pieces, and ſeaſon it with dried Sage and Pepper ſmall beaten: lay the Bacon about the Veal, and ſerve it with Sawcers of green ſawce, garniſhed with Marigold-flowers, Barberries and Parſley.

A Rump of Beef to ſtew the beſt way.

Let your Beef be ſeaſoned with Salt, Pepper and Nutmeg; lay the fat ſide downward in an Earthen-pan, then put in an equal portion of Water and Elder-Vinegar to the quantity of three quarts; add two Onions, and half a handfull of the tops of Roſemary, and ſtewing it three hours over a ſoft fire, take it up and diſh it with Sipits, garniſhing with Lemon-peel, and ſawcing with the Gravy, the fat being ſcumed off.

To

To bake a Hare the best way.

Take a large Hare minced, and well seasoned with beaten Mace, Salt and Pepper, making a proportion of the head and shoulders, and lay in a layer of Flesh, and Lard, and Butter above and beneath, and serve it up with Gallentine sawce in Sawcers.

To roast a Rabit with Oysters, the best way.

Take a large fat Rabbit, wash it and dry it, then half a pint of Oysters after the same manner; put them into the belly of the Rabbit with a couple of shread Onions, large Mace, whole Pepper, and sprigs of Thyme; sow 'em up, and when the Rabbit is roasted, mince them with Butter and the yolks of hard Eggs, and dish the Rabbit up, garnishing the dish with red Beet-roots and Orange-peel.

To Carbanado Hens or Pullets, the best way.

Take half a dozen hard yolks of Eggs, half a pint of White-wine and the Gravy; mince the Eggs, and boil them up with Onion or some Shalots; add grated Nutmeg, with a Ladle or two full of drawn Butter; dish your Fowl, pour the sawce on them, garnishing your dish with Lemon-peel and Violet-leaves.

To set off a dish of Marrow, &c.

Take a pound of fine Paste, rowl it very thin, and the Marrow taken whole out of four bones, cleave it in quarters, season it with Pepper, Salt and Dates, all minced, laying one piece in your Paste, framing it pescodwise; and so use the rest, then fry them in Butter and Sugar, and serve them up, garnished with Burrage-flowers.

To stew a Pheasant, the best fashion or way.

Take a large Pheasant, roast him till enough, then boil it gently in Mutton-broth, adding whole Pepper, Mace, the slice or two of an Onion, Pruins, Currans and Vinegar, sufficient to make it sharp, then colour, the broth, with bruised Pruins, and serve up the Pheasant in it.

To Carbanade Mutton, the best way.

Broil a breast or shoulder of Mutton, scotching it with your knife; strow on them minced Thyme, grated Nutmeg, and a little salt, with Claret-wine, Capers, Gravy and a shread Shalot, garnishing with a Lemon-peel.

To roast a Pig.

Take a fat one, cleanſe his belly, put into it minced Sage, Currans, Mace, and grated Nutmeg: roaſt him indifferently by a ſoaking fire, then make up a brisk fire to crackle him, and ſerve him up with Currans, bread, Sage, Butter and Nutmeg made into a thin ſawce with Roſe-water.

To ſtew Veniſon, the beſt way.

Take fat Veniſon, either raw or potted, ſlice it and put it into your ſtewing-pan with Claret-wine, Roſemary-tops, Cloves, Sugar, Vinegar, and grated Bread: being well ſtewed, add grated Nutmeg, and ſerve it up garniſhed with Luke-Olives.

To make a Fricacy of Chickens, the beſt way.

Take four or five Chickens about two months old, ſcald and flea them; put them in Water and White-wine, then take a large Onion, ten or twelve blades of Mace, and the quantity of Nutmeg grated; tye them up in a cloth with a bundle of ſweet Herbs and Salt; put them into an Earthen-pan, and let them ſimper a while, then take three or four Anchoveys, five or ſix Eggs, half

half a pound of the beft Butter diffolved in a pint of Mutton-broth; fhread the Spices fmall with a quarter of a pound of Capers; mix them with the other fawce, and laying the Chickens upon it, ferve them up with Sipits, garnifhed with fliced Lemon. Thus you may drefs and difh up Partridges or Pigeons, with only the abatement of the Eggs.

To ftew a Fillet of Beef, the neweft way.

Take the tendereft, and remove the skin and finews; fteep it in White-wine, fcattering on it a fmall quantity of Pepper and Salt; then covering it with Wine, add more Pepper, and keeping it clofe down with a waight, fuffer it to fteep two nights and a day; when taking it out, put it into an Earthen pot with Beef-broth, cover it on a gentle fire, adding a few Cloves and Mace, and ftanding o're the fire till it is tender, it will be of an admirable tafte, ferve it up with the Broth.

The neweft way to boil a Wild Duck.

The Duck being half roafted, take her off the Spit, put her into a pan with a pint of Claret, and as much Mutton-broth; three Onions cut, and a bundle of fweet Herbs; three or four flices of Bacon and fome whole Pepper:

Pepper: cover the pan with another, and when it is ſtewed or boiled ſufficiently, ſerve it up with the Broth.

To bake a Pig the beſt way.

Take a Pig and dreſs him well as for roaſting, mould him up in a coffin of Clay, buttered a little within; put him into an Oven eight hours, ſo that the clay being dried, the Pig will be very criſp; then ſerve him up with ſawce as for roaſting.

To boil a Pullet, Capon or Chicken, the beſt way.

Truſs them and put them in Mutton-broth, with Mace, Spinage and Endive, Marigold-flowers, Bugloſs, Burrage, Sorrel and Parſley; and when they are enough, garniſh the diſh with Burrage and Marigold-flowers, and ſerve them up in Sipits.

To boil a Capon or Chicken with Sugar-peaſe.

Take the Peaſe when young, and dry them in the cods, taking them from thence to the quantity of two or three handfulls, put them into an Earthen-veſſel with about half a pound of freſh Butter, and near half a pint of fair water; add whole Pepper, Mace and Olive-oyl, of each a ſmall quantity; and your Capon and Chicken being well boiled, ſtrain the Peaſe and other Ingredients, and ſerve them up as ſawce with the yolks of two or three Eggs, and half a quartern of Sack.

To haſh a Capon or Pullet the beſt way.

Take either of them cold, after having been roaſted, take out the brains, and mince them ſmall with the fleſh of the wings; then take off the legs and rump intire, then add ſtrong Broth and Gravy, ſliced Nutmeg, Onion and Salt, and ſtew the divided parts in a large Pipkin; and when they are well ſtewed, add ſome Oyſters, Juyce of Orange, and a yolk of an Egg, and ſerve them up on Sipits, garniſhed with Oranges ſliced and flowers. And thus any Fowl of this or the like kind may be haſhed.

To boil a Pullet or Capon with Aſparagus.

Boil the Fowl in fair water, put bruiſed Mace, chopped Parſley and ſweet Butter into it's belly, tying up the vent; being boiled, take out the Parſley and Mace, garniſhing the diſh with it, in which have Aſparagus ready boiled, place it in good order.

To

To fry a Rabbit with ſweet Sawce.

Cut it in pieces orderly, and waſh it well, then dry it in a cloth, and fry it with ſweet Butter: being half fryed, ſlice ſome of it very ſmall, put it into a quarter of a pint of Cream, the yolks of two Eggs, ſome grated Nutmeg and Salt: when the Rabbit is thoroughly fryed, pour them upon it, and keep 'em ſtirring; adding Verjuice, freſh Butter and Sugar a like quantity, and ſerve them up with ſipits, garniſhing the diſh with any green thing.

To ſtew a Mallard.

Firſt let it be half roaſted, then cut it into ſmall pieces, putting it into a diſh with Gravy, freſh Butter, and a handfull of minced Parſley, with two or three Onions and a hard Lettice: let them ſtand an hour, then add Pepper, Salt and Lemon-juyce, and ſerve it up with ſipits and a garniſh of Lemon-peel.

To fry a Neats-Tongue, the beſt way.

The Tongue being boiled and blanched, cut it, ſeaſon it with Cinamon, grated Nutmeg and Sugar; then add yolks of Eggs and Lemons cut in ſmall pieces, frying them in ſpoonfulls with ſweet Butter ; then heat it hot, pour on your Tongue the ſawce and ſugar, and ſerve it up.

To boil a Haunch of Veniſon in the beſt manner.

Stuff it with ſweet Herbs, Parſley and Beef-ſuet minced ſmall, as likewiſe with the yolk of hard Eggs ; the ſtuffing materials being ſeaſoned with ſalt, Nutmeg and Ginger, and the Veniſon being powdered, boil it in ſtrong Broth, and in another pot two or three Colleflowers, adding to them a quart of new Milk ; and they being taken up, boil in the ſame liquor a handfull or two of Sorrel or Spinage : then part of the Broth being taken away, put in Vinegar, ſweet Butter, grated Bread and Nutmeg ; then lay the Spinage upon ſipits round the diſh, laying the Veniſon in the middle, and Colleflowers in order, garniſhing the diſh with Parſley, Spinage and Marigold-flowers.

To roaſt a Gooſe in the neweſt faſhion.

Draw your Gooſe, and put her on a ſpit, laying her to a gentle fire, which you muſt increaſe by degree : then take nine or ten ſoft [illegible], or Pippins for want of them, boil them in a pint of White-wine, ſweeten them with ſugar, then add a ſmall quantity of Muſtard

Muſtard when they are come to a pulp, and a ſpoonfull of Roſe-water: ſtir them well, and put it in Sawcers apart; though for green Geeſe the ſawce is generally the Juyce of Sorrel, ſcalded Gooſeberries, Butter and Sugar.

To boil a Pike the beſt way.

Waſh and gut it, bring the head and tail together in a circle, ſcotching the back to make it pliable: boil it in Water, Salt and Vinegar, putting it in when the water boils; it being enough, take it out and ſerve it up with Ginger, grated Bread, Butter, White-wine, Oyſters, Dates, and the Juyce of Lemons: garniſhed with green leaves or flowers.

To ſtew a Pike the beſt way.

Waſh out the blood, flat it, and lay it in a diſh, cover it with White-wine; add, when it boils, whole Cinamon, Mace, Salt and ſweet Butter, and diſh it up on ſipits.

To boil a Salmon the beſt way.

Cover it with water, add Roſemary and Thyme-tops, Winter-ſavory and Salt: then add more a pint of Vinegar, and ſerve it up with Butter, the Juyce of Lemons and Anchoveys made into ſawce.

To roaſt an Eel the beſt way.

Take one pretty large Eel, take out the Intrals after it is skinned, then fill the belly with ſweet Herbs and Butter beaten together in a Mortar, after that draw the skin over again and faſten the Eel with ſtrings to the Spit, and moderately roaſt it; then with the Herbs, Anchovey-ſawce and Butter, together with the Gravy, ſerve it up.

To roaſt a Lobſter the beſt way.

Take a large one whilſt alive, bind up the claws, and faſten it to the Spit before a gentle fire; baiſting it firſt with water and ſalt, then with Butter and Claret-wine; and when it is enough, break the ſhell, take out the meat and ſerve it up with Anchovey-ſawce and ſtewed Oyſters.

To roaſt a Pound of Butter.

Lay your Butter in water till it be very ſtiff, then fix it upon a ſmall Sipit; lay it down before a gentle fire; and as ſoon as it begins to drop, dredg Bread on it, and ſo continue to do, adding a little beaten Cinamon and Sugar till the Bread has ſoaked up all the Butter; which done, make the out-ſide brown, and

and ſerve it up in the nature of a Quaking-pudding, with Verjuice, Butter, Roſe-water and Sugar.

To make Sawceages the beſt way.

Take a Leg of Pork, divide the fat from the lean, and chop the latter ſmall, with Marjorum, Peneroyal, Thyme and Winter-ſavory, adding Salt, Pepper, and a little Ginger, together with half the quantity of Meat in Beef-ſuet; and being very ſmall, fill it in Sheeps-guts with a Whalebone-feſcue, and dry them in a Chimley for your uſe.

To dreſs a diſh of Anchoveys the beſt way.

Take the beſt *Legborn* fiſh, about a year old, not being ruſty, waſh them and ſmooth off the white and ſcales; divide them equally in four quarters at length, lay one laying waving in and out, and between them another, ſtrait in the figure of a Star, making of the bones the figure of a Crown, and placing it in the center of the diſh: garniſh it with Lucois, Olives, Sampher, pickled Barberrys, pickled Broom-buds, Muſhroons, Capers, and ſlices of pickle Cucumbers, in what form you pleaſe, adding a ſufficient quantity of Oyl and Vinegar.

How

How to dreſs a diſh of Caveer the beſt way.

Take that which is not ruſty nor over-dryed, ſteep it in the beſt Florence-oyl for the ſpace of an hour, then take it out and work it with a little Vinegar and Pepper into a form or figure as beſt fancies you, and then garniſh it with Olives and Barberrys, ſerving it up with Oyl.

The beſt way to dreſs a diſh of Pickle-Herrings.

Take new Herrings, or the beſt you can get, take off the skins, and take out the bones, ſlice the Herrings, and mince them very ſmall, then ſhread Pickle-Cucumbers, Shalots or Onions, Lemon-peel, Codlings, Pippins or Pome-waters: mix the whole matter with Capers, Barberries and Broom-buds: garniſh the diſh with Olives, French-beans and Muſhrooms: make it into a figure, add Oyl, Vinegar and Pepper, and ſerve it up; or if you pleaſe you may garniſh it with Pickled-oyſters.

To ſet out a diſh of Pickles.

Place in the midſt your Cucumber, then your large Olives, then French-beans at length, and ſmall Olives between them; then Muſhrooms and Capers, and on the edges of of the diſh Pickled Grapes, Pickled Gille-flowers and Broom-buds, and ſo ſerve them up.

How to Pot fowl in order to their keeping by Sea or Land, &c.

Roaſt Ducks, Mallards, Teals, Widgeons, Pigeons or Chickens: drain them from the Gravy, and put into the bellys of them a little Pepper and Salt, with a little bruiſed Mace and ſome Cloves; then take the fat that came from them, preſs them a little flattiſh, and mixing the fat with ſweet Herbs; when you have layed your fowl in order in a glazed Earthen-pot, pour the melted Butter, *&c.* hot on them till they are covered; on that ſtrew ſome Pepper and ſlices of Nutmeg, then cover it with Bay-leaves, and cloſe it up with Leather; and being faſt tied down, rub a little Butter on the Leather to keep it moiſt, and the fowl will keep a twelvemonth.

To dreſs Kid with the colour and taſte of Veniſon.

Take a Haunch well fleſhed, and indifferent fat, pluck away the skin and ſuperfluous fat; open it from the bone, and thruſt in ſome Peter-ſalt, then lay it two hours in water that has been newly heated; after that dry it, and put it on your Spit, or bake it in a Paſty, and it will have the colour and flavour of Veniſon.

An

An Excellent way of Hashing any sort of Meat.

Take your Meat, slice it thin, sprinkle it with a little Salt, Pepper, and shreaded sweet Herbs, put it into your Pan with a piece of fresh Butter and the Juyce of a Lemon; add a few bruised Cloves, Oysters, and an Anchovey: garnish your dish with Parsley and slices of Lemon, and serve it up.

How to roast a Salmon the best way.

Take a Jole or Rand, and divide it into four pieces; season it with Salt and grated Nutmeg: stick on it a few Cloves, and fasten it on a small Spit, putting between it a few Bay-leaves; stick in the out-side little sprigs of Rosemary: baste it with Butter; save the dripping; sawce it with Butter, Verjuice, and Juice of Oranges, garnishing it with some slices.

To fry Salmon the best way.

Take a Chine, Jole or Rand, fry it in the best Butter, and finding it crisp, let your sawce be made of Claret-wine, sweet Butter, grated Nutmeg, Orange-juyce, and the liquor of Pickled-oysters: heat them together, and pour them on the fish; and for a garnish,

garnish, lay Parsley and Sage-leaves fryed in Butter.

How to recover tainted Venison, and make Mutton, Beef or Ram, pass for Venison.

As for the first, wrap it up in a clean cloth a little dampish, dig a hole in the Earth, put it in, and let it lye twenty four hours, and the scent will be gone, the Earth drawing it away.

As for the latter, Take your Mntton, *&c.* and dip it in Pigs blood, or any wholesome warm blood; then parboil it in small Beer and Vinegar, and let it stand all night; then put to it some Turnsole, and bake it, aud it will look and eat like Venison.

To roast a Carp the best way.

Draw and wash him alive, taking out his Intrails, and with Lemon-juyce, Caroways, grated Bread and Nutmeg, Currans, Cream, Almond-paste and Salt make a Pudding, and put it into its belly, insomuch that it may fill it full, the Pudding being put through the gills, and fasten them: and when it is roasted, make sawce with what drops from it; aadding the Juyce of Oranges, Cinamon, Sugar and Butter, and dish it up.

To

To stew a Carp the French *way.*

Take him alive and bleed him, then take out all his Intrals, and scrape the scales from off the back; then take a quart of Claret, Mace, Ginger, Cloves, Nutmegs, sweet Herbs, a large Onion and Salt: Let them boil in the Stew-pan, then put in the Carp with half a pound of sweet Butter; it being enough, lay it in a dish, and make a sawce of grated Bread, Lemon-juyce, beaten Butter, and what remains of the liquid part in the stew-pan, and garnish it with green Spinage and stewed Oysters.

To stew Oysters after the best manner.

Take the largest, parboil them in the water that comes from them, and afterward wash them in warm water; put them into a Pipkin, adding Onion, Mace, Pepper, Nutmeg, and a pint of Wine, with as much Vinegar: If you have two quarts of Oysters, add likewise a pound of sweet Butter, and a spoonfull of salt: then dish them up with sipits, having stewed them, and garnish with Barberries and Lemon-peel.

To

To stew Flounders.

Take the largest, draw and wash them, giving them a scotch or two on the belly; put to them, being in your stewing-pan, small Oysters, Pepper, Ginger, an Onion, sweet Herbs, Salt, suffering them to stew as soon as may be, then dish them up with sipits: and for sawce, take beaten yolks of Eggs, Lemon-juyce, Butter, and a little Ginger; garnishing with Lemon-peel.

To roast an Eel the Dutch *way.*

Strip her, put into her belly grated Bread, sweet Herbs and Butter; then draw the skin over her again, and fasten her to the Spit, basting her with salt and water: being enough, take off the skin by ripping it up, and serve her up with the Herbs made into a sawce with Butter and Juyce of Lemons, and a little Claret-wine.

To stew Breams.

Draw, dry them and let them be well salted; lay them on a Grid-iron over a Charcole fire; suffer them to be brown on both sides: then put half a pint of Claret into a Pewter-dish, set it over the fire to boil, add three

three Anchoveys, two ſliced Onions, a pint of Oyſters, and a little Thyme: when it has boiled, put to it a little melted Butter and Nutmeg, then diſh up the fiſh and pour the ſawce on it with yolks of hard Eggs minced.

To boil a Mullet the beſt way.

Save the Liver and Row, and ſcald him; then put the water on boiling-hot, adding half a pint of Claret and a bunch of ſweet Herbs, Salt, Vinegar, and two Onions, with a ſliced Lemon: take a Nutmeg, quarter it, with Mace and Butter, drawn with Claret, diſſolving in it two or three Anchoveys: ſeaſon the ſawce with ſalt, diſh up your fiſh, and ſerve it up with a garniſh of ſtewed Oyſters and Bay-leaves.

At one and the ſame charge as to the Sawces, you may dreſs a dozen of either of the laſt mentioned fiſh.

How to dreſs a Cods-head the beſt way.

The Head being cut fair, boil it in water and ſalt, adding a pint of Vinegar, that the Head may be a little more then covered; putting into the mouth of it a quart of Oyſters, a bundle of ſweet Herbs and an Onion, binding the Jaws with a thread; when it is well boiled, ſet it a drying over a chaa chafing-dish, then take Oyster liquor, a sliced Onion, and two or three Anchoveys; adding a quarter of a pint of White-wine and a pound of sweet Butter, pour them on the Head, and stick the Oysters where they will enter: scatter over it grated Bread and Nutmeg; garnish the dish with sliced Lemon, and any green thing.

And thus have I given you Instruction as to the Dressing, *&c.* Flesh, Fish and Fowl: And now proceed to the remaining necessary part of Cookery, which is Pastry.

CHAP. XIV.

The Cook-Maids Directions in making Pyes, and managing Pastry to the best and Modish manner and advantage.

AS *Pastry* is the most curious part of Cookery, so it is to be considered even beyond what I have mentioned in other matters, and chiefly in these Observations.

1. Observe your Flower be fine, and free from Bran, or any defect; and having laid it on a smooth Table, or in a Kneading-Trough.

2. Heat

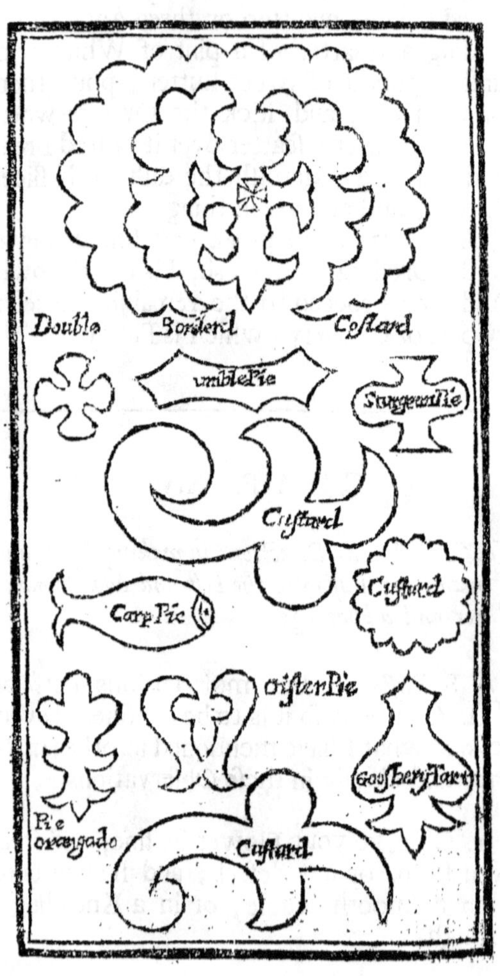
Double
Borderd
Costard
umble Pie
Sturgeon Pie
Custard
Custard
Carp Pie
Oister Pie
Gosbery Tart
Pie
orangado
Custard

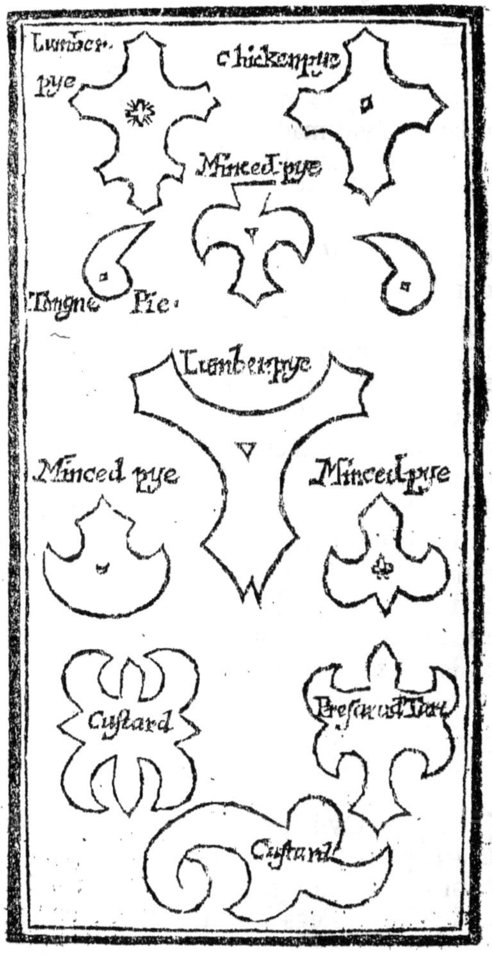
Lumber pye
chicken pye
Minced pye
Tongne Pie
Lumber pye
Minced pye
Minced pye
Custard
Preserued Tart
Custard

2. Heat your Liquor, suffering it to simper, scuming off what arises; and if it be for Tarts, Custards, or the like, let it be fair water with a small Ingredient of Rose-water and Malaga-wine, so that it taste of either: But for larger Pyes made with Meat or the like, add Butter a pound to two quarts of Liquor, and to either of them, in moulding Eggs or new Ale Yest according as you would have your Paste light or solid, which I leave to your discretion.

3. As for those that are to be raised very thin, work them up cold; but those of largeness that will admit a good substance, for the more ease and pliableness, let the Paste be warm, working them into a form with your Hands, Roaler, Nipers, Spur-Iron, Knife and Plate: Mark the Garnishing, or flourish on the lid or sides, I leave likewise to your discretion. But that you may the better understand the form of the most curious thing of this nature, I have caused them to be incerted in the following Pages, and so proceed to the filling them, *&c.*

To make an Oyster-Pye.

LET the Oysters be parboiled in their own Liquor; wash and dry them; season them with Nutmeg, Pepper, Salt, and the hard yolks of Eggs; and the Pye being made Oval,

Oval, put into it Currans and sliced Dates, and on them lay the Oysters: add large Mace, Barberries sliced, Lemon and Butter; and when it is baked, put into it White-wine, Sugar and Butter.

To make a Veal-Pye the best way.

Raise your Paste well, cut a Leg of Veal in slices, season it with salt, Pepper and Nutmeg, adding some large Mace, laying the Meat, with Raisins of the Sun and Currans in the Pye, and fill it with Butter; and when baked, serve it up hot.

The best way to make a Carp-Pye.

Draw, scald and wash a large Carp or two, season him or them with Salt, Pepper and Nutmeg, then fill the Pye with them, good store of Butter, Raisins of the Sun, slices of Orange, and Juyce of Lemon: close it up and bake it.

The best way to make a Chicken-Pye.

Truss your Chickens, and flat the Breast-bones, and having raised your Paste, lay them in order, filling their bodies with Butter, laying above and beneath Raisins, Currans, Pruans, Cinamon, Sugar, Mace and Salt, with a convenient quantity of Butter; and when it is baked, pour in Rose-water, White-wine, beaten Cinamon, Sugar and Verjuice, with the which serve it up, *&c.*

To make a Warden-Pye the best way.

First bake your Wardens gently in a little Water and Claret, adding a pound of Sugar, covering your pot or pan with a lid of dough; and when they are cold, lay them into your Pye with Cloves, Cinamon, Sugar, and a part of the liquor, and bake it gently.

To make a Pye with Sweet-breads and Lamb-stones.

Slit your Lambstones, skin and wash them, take the Liver of a Lamb, shread it small, and slice a Udder-part of a Leg of Veal; which being seasoned with Mace, Cloves, Salt and Nutmeg made small; as also Pepper, shread into it three or four Pippins, and the like quantity of the peels of Candied Lemons and Oranges, five or six Dates cut in the middle and stoned, with Currans, Carraway-seeds, white Sugar, and half a pint of Rose-water and Verjuice; add more a couple of Eggs: make it into balls, and with the Juyce of Sorrel, green it, laying a Sweet-bread and a Lamb-stone till it is near full, covering them with Citron-peel, Dates and slices of Lemon; and being baked enough, pour in Butter, White-

White-wine, Sugar, and the beaten yolks of Eggs, scraping Sugar on the lid to set it off.

To bake a Turky the best way.

When your Turky is parboiled, Lard him, season him with Pepper, Salt, Cloves and Mace: flat the Breast, and put him into your Coffin or Pye, and fill it with Butter when it is baked and cold, and so serve it up.

To make an Artechoak-Pye the best way.

Take the bottoms of half a dozen Artechoaks, boil them tender, season them with Ginger, Mace, Salt and Sugar: lay Marrow at the bottom of your Pye, and them upon it; cover them with Marrow, sliced Dates, Raisins of the Sun; and being half baked, put in a quarter of a pint of Canary, wherein Orange-peel has been boiled, then bake it well.

To make a Marrow-Pudding the best way.

Blanch a pound of Almonds, beat them small with Rose-water, take a pound of fine Sugar, grate a penny white Loaf and a Nutmeg; add a pint of Cream, the Marrow of two or three bones, and a grain or two of Amber-grease: mingle them with a little [illegible]; fill the skin you intend it shall be in, and boil it moderately.

The best way to make a Custard.

Take and boil a quart of Cream with whole Spice; beat the yolks of ten Eggs and five Whites, with a little Cream: put them into the Cream when cold, then put it into Paste, strew Comfits on it, and bake it.

To make an Umble-Pye the best way as has been Approved.

Take Beef-suet, mince it and lay it in your Coffin, or if you please slices of Larded Bacon; then take your Umbles, and cut them into small pieces as big as Hazle-nuts, and your Bacon about the same bigness; then take grated Nutmeg, Pepper and salt, strew them on the top, then lay a laying of Bacon, and on that another of Butter, and so close it up; and being baked, liquor it with striped Thyme, Claret and Butter well beaten together.

A Venison Pasty, the best way to make.

Having well powdered your Haunch or Side, and cleared it from sinews, bones and skin, season it with Pepper and salt, and beat it with your Roaler, making it proportionable for a Pasty; then make your Paste with fine Flower, allowing to a peck three pou[nd] of Butter and twelve Eggs: work it with cold water to a convenient stiffness, suffering it to be as thick as your thumb: then take it upon your Roaler, and open it again upon a couple of sheets, or so much as will serve of cap-paper: and having your White minced, and beaten with water, lay it proportionably upon the Pasty to the breadth and length of the Venison: then in the White lay the Venison, and wash it round with a feather; put on the Border, season the top of the Venison, and turn over the other leaf, and so close your Pasty: then drive out another border for garnishing the Pasty from the sides to the top; the device of which is left to your discretion: then vent it at the top, set it into a well-heated Oven, and suffer it to soak as it ought, *viz.* four or five hours: then draw it, and pour Butter well melted in at the top.

To make an Excellent Minced-Pye.

Take Neats-Tongues, parboil them till they may be peel'd; then mince them with a like quantity of Beef-suet, stoned Raisins and picked Currans: make them in a manner like pap, then mingle a little fine Sugar with a glass or two of old Mallaga; then add slices of candied Citron-peel; and put the whole, being well mingled, into a coffin, the form of which is left to your discretion, and strew on it a few Caraway-comfits, and so bake it moderately.

To make an Eel-Pye the best way.

Take the best silver Eels, indifferent large, strip, gut and wash them: cut them to pieces at about a fingers length; shread a handful of sweet Herbs with some Parsley and an Onion: season them with Pepper, Salt, beaten Cloves, Mace and grated Nutmeg; when the coffin or crust being reared and fashioned to your mind, put them in and strew over them some Currans and a few slices of Lemon over that: put a laying of Butter, and close your coffin with the lid; and when the Pye is baked, put in Butter melted with a little Vinegar, and beaten up with the White of an Egg.

The best way to make a Gooseberry-Tart.

Take your Gooseberries before they are ripe, being well picked, scald them till they will break in a spoon; then strain out the pulp, and beat it up with half a dozen Eggs, and stir them well together on a chafing-dish of Coles, adding Rose-water, and sweetening them with Sugar; and when it is cold you may put it into your coffin, and moderately bake it, or serve it up in Plates without baking.

To make a Pippin or Codling-Tart, or of any such like Fruit.

Take your Pippins gather'd before they are over ripe, pare them, and take the core clear off; strew some Sugar and Rose-water on them, and each Pippin being cut in four quarters, lay them in order between every laying; place thin slices of Quince, then add syrup of Quinces, or of the same fruit; after that strow over the Sugar mixed with a little Cinamon, and closing all up in the coffin, bake them gently that they may be well soaked.

To make a Paste of Marrow, &c.

Take the Marrow of six bones, shread them with a considerable quantity of Apples well pared and cored; then add a sufficient quantity of Sugar, and put them into a Puff-paste; and having fryed them in a Pan with sweet Butter, serve them up with Sugar and Cinamon.

To make a Pye of Calves-feet, the best way.

Having boiled your Calves-feet well, take out the bones and grisles as many as are convenient, shread them as small as you can, and season them with Cloves and Mace; add to them a good quantity of Currans, Raisins and

Dates, the latter well ſtoned, then with a ſufficient quantity of ſweet Butter, put them into your coffin, breaking on them ſome whole Cinamon and ſliced Nutmeg, then ſcatter over them ſome ſalt, and cloſe them up, leaving a vent to pour in when the Pye is baked, a quantity of Verjuice, beaten Cinamon and freſh Butter well beaten together.

To make the beſt Cakes.

Take a ſufficient quantity of fine flower, a quarter the weight of it in picked and waſhed Currans, a pound of Carraway-comfits, half a pound of Marmalade of Oranges, the yolks of a dozen Eggs, half a pint of Malmſey or Mallaga, a quarter of a pint of Roſe-water: Mould them together with a little new Ale Yeſt, and as much Milk as will make them up into Cakes; then Ice them over with Sugar, or waſh them over with Canary, well beat, with the yolk of an Egg, and bake them in a gentle Oven.

To make the beſt Cheeſecakes.

Take new Milk, and put as much Runnet to it as will well bring it to a Curd, then ſtrain out the Whay, in a cloth between two Fatts; which done, beat up the curd with the yolk of Eggs, White-wine, Roſe-water and

and Sugar; after that add as many Currans as you see convenient; then having made your Puff-paste of fine Flower, Eggs, Milk and new Ale Yest, put it into a fashion; and being well knit at the corners, and rowled with a Pastry-spur, put in the curd, and wash it over with the yolk of an Egg, using a feather for that purpose.

CHAP. XV.

How to make several Sawces for Roast or Boiled on all occasions.

AND now since many have been desirous to have an account of Sawces in general, I think it not amiss to place it as an Appendix to *Cookery*; and further, to give the Reader an account of the seasonable Bills of Fare, much observed by the Curious for every Month in the Year: But of these in their order.

The general sawce for green Geese is Gooseberries scalded, and coloured again with the Juyce of Sorrel strewed over with Butter and Sugar, and served up on sipits; and for most Land-fowl, the pulp of stewed Pruins, the Gravy, Cinamon, Ginger and Sugar

gar boiled up to a thickneſs, and ſerved up in Sawcers.

For Roaſted Mutton, the general Sawces are Capers, ſampher the Gravy, a ſliced Shalots and a little Pepper ſtewed together, or Claret-wine, Ginger, the Gravy and an Onion.

For boiled Mutton, Take Verjuice, Butter, Currans, Sugar, and a little Cinamon: mix them well over a fire, and ſerve them up with Sipits or White-broth, made of grated Bread, Currans, Roſe-water and Sugar, with the yolks of two Eggs.

The general ſawce for roaſt Veal is Juyce of Orange, Butter, Verjuice, grated Nutmeg and Claret-wine, or ſweet Herbs chopped ſmall, with the yolks of two or three Eggs boiled hard in Vinegar, Butter and grated Bread, Currans, beaten Cinamon and whole Cloves: For boil'd Veal green ſawce.

For red Deer, ſweet herbs chopped ſmall, the Gravy, with the Juyce of an Orange or Lemon, and grated Bread or Vinegar, Claret-wine, Ginger, Cinamon, Sugar, boiled up with a ſprig of Roſemary, ſome whole Cloves and grated Bread; and if you ſtuff or farce your Veniſon, let it be with whole Cloves, ſweet Herbs and Beef-ſuet, the two latter cut very ſmall.

For roaſt Pork, Apples quartered, boiled in fair water, and the pulp mixed with But-

ter,

ter, Sugar and a little Verjuice, or Sugar, Muſtard, Pepper, and the Gravy: For boiled Pork, chopped Sage, boiled Onions, Pepper, Muſtard and grated bread, or Muſtard Vinegar and Pepper.

For Rabits, Sage, Parſley, Butter, Vinegar and the Gravy, or beaten Butter, Vinegar and Pepper: For a boiled Rabit, Onions, ſweet Herbs, Pepper, grated bread and ſugar ſerved on ſipits.

For Hens roaſted, the Gravy, Claret-wine, Pepper and an Onion, boiled with the head, neck or gizard, or beaten Butter, the Juyce of a Lemon, Pepper, and the yolks of hard Eggs: For a Hen boiled, white Broth and Sipits, with Lemon-peel and the yolk of an Egg minced ſmall.

For roaſt Chickens, Butter, Verjuice, the Gravy or Butter, Vinegar, boiled up with Sugar, and the ſubſtance of an Anchovey, ſerved up on thin ſlices of bread: For boiled Chickens, ſtrong Mutton-broth, grated Bread, chopped Parſly, and the Juyce of a Lemon, with a good piece of Butter well mixed, and ſerved up on ſipits in order.

For roaſt Pigeons, Verjuice, Butter and boiled Parſley, ſhread into it and beaten thick, or Claret-wine, ſtewed Onion, Gravy and Pepper, ſeaſoned a little with Salt. For boiled Pigeons, ſtrong Mutton-broth, the Juyce of Sorrel, the yolks of Eggs beaten in raw,

raw, and a ſprig of Roſemary, or Sprouts and Bacon.

For a Peacock, Turkey, Partridge, Pheaſant, or the like roaſted, boiled Shalots, Pepper, Salt, grated Bread and Gravy, or Onion, grated Nutmeg, Manchet, the yolk of Eggs, Salt, and the Juyce of Oranges boiled up to the thickneſs of Water-grewel: or bruiſe the kernels of ſmall Nuts with grated Bread, Nutmeg, Saffron, Cloves, the Juyce of Oranges and ſtrong Broth: boil them up to a thickneſs.

For a ſtubble Gooſe, ſlice Pomwaters, boil them ſoft; Maſh them in White-wine, and add to the pulp Butter, Sugar, Verjuice and the Gravy.

For a Mallard or Duck roaſted, Take Oyſter-liquor, the Gravy of the Fowl, divided Onions, Nutmeg and an Anchovey: ſtew them together, and ſerve it up in the liquid part, or Vinegar, Cloves and Sugar, a blade of Mace and a Shalot. If boiled, take ſlices of Carriot, ſhread Parſly and Winter-ſavory, Mace, Verjuice and grated Bread.

For any kind of Sea-fowl roaſted, Take grated Bread, Cinamon, Ginger and Sugar, Claret and Wine-Vinegar: boil them with Roſemary and Cloves to a convenient thickneſs: ſtrain them and ſerve them up as a very good ſawce, or Gravy, Claret-wine, an Onion and Pepper, with a ſmall piece of Butter.

For

For roaſt Salmon, Take Oyſter-liquor, ſlice of Nutmeg, the Gravy, the Juyce of Oranges and Butter; beat them up to a thickneſs: or beaten Cloves, the Gravy, grated Nutmeg and grated Bread, beat up with Butter, the yolk of an Egg and Vinegar. For boiled Salmon, Butter, Vinegar, Nutmeg, and the Intrals of the Salmon.

To make excellent green Sawce to ſerve on any occaſion wherein it is requiſite, Take large Sorrel, white Bread, grated, pared and cored Pippins, ſome ſprigs of Mint, a quantity of Verjuice ſufficient to moiſten it; and being ſtamped very ſmall, ſcrape Sugar on it, and mix it well together, and ſo ſerve it up with Pork, Veal, Chickens, Kid, Lamb, Goſling, or the like, they being boiled.

For all ſorts of ſmall Birds roaſted, Take the Gravy, Pepper, Butter, and their Livers and Gizards, minced with Parſley, or the Gravy of a Capon, Ginger and the yolk of an Egg beaten together, with a little Butter and Vinegar. And thus much may ſuffice for Sawces ſo neceſſary to be known by all that pretend to *Cookery*.

CHAP.

CHAP. XVI.

Directions to know what is in season throughout the Twelve Months of the Year; and what ought to be served up as the first and second Courses, &c.

March.

1. NEats-Tongues and Udders. 2. Boiled Chickens. 3. A dish of stewed Oysters with Anchovey-sawce. 4. A dish of young Rabits. 5. A grand Salla'd.

Second Course.

1. A dish of Soles or Smelts. 2. A dish of Marinate Flounders. 3. A Pye of Lamb-stones. 4. Asparagus if to be gotten. 5. A Warden-Pye.

April.

1. Green Geese or Veal and Bacon. 2. A roasted Haunch of Venison. 3. A Lumber-Pye. 4. Rabits. 5. Tarts.

Second Course.

1. Cold Lamb. 2. A cold Neats-Tongue Pye.

Pye. 3. Salmon, Lobſters and Prawns. 4. A diſh of Aſparagus.

May.

1. Boiled Chickens. 2. Roaſt Veal. 3. Roaſt Capons. 4. Roaſt Rabits.

Second Courſe.

1. Artechoak-Pye juſt out of the Oven. 2. Weſtphalia-ham. 3. Tarts. 4. Sturgeon, Salmon, Lobſters. 5. A diſh of Aſparagus. 6. A Tanſey.

June.

1. Boiled Neats-Tongues, or a Leg of Mutton and Colleflowers. 2. A Steak-Pye. 3. A Shoulder of Mutton. 4. A Fore-quarter of Lamb.

Second Courſe.

1. A Sweet-bread Pye. 2. A Capon roaſted. 3. A Gooſeberry-Tart. 4. Strawberries and Cream, or Strawberries, with Roſe-water, White-wine and Sugar.

July.

1. A Weſtphalia-ham and Pigeons. 2. A Loin of Veal. 3. A Veniſon-Paſty. 4. A Capon.

Second

Second Course.

1. Green-peaſe or French-beans. 2. A Codling-Tart. 3. Artechoaks, or an Artechoak-Pye. 4. Roaſted Chickens with Summer-ſawce.

Auguſt.

1. A Calves-head and Bacon. 2. An Olio or grand boiled ſavory Meat. 3. A Haunch of Veniſon. 4. A fat Pig well roaſted with good ſawce.

Second Course.

1. Marinate Smelts. 2. A Pigeon-Pye. 3. A diſh of roaſted Chickens. 4. A Pippin Tart. 5. Codlins and Cream.

September.

1. Boiled Hens and white Broth. 2. Neats-Tongues and Udders roaſted. 3. A powdered Gooſe. 4. A roaſted Turky.

Second Courſe.

1. A Potato-Pye. 2. Roaſted Partridges. 3. A diſh of Larks. 4. A diſh of Cream and ſeaſonable Fruit.

October.

1. A Fillet of Veal. 2. Two roaſted Brand-geeſe. 3. A grand Sallad. 4. A roaſted Capon.

Second

Second Course.

1. Pheasants, Pigeons and Pouts. 2. A dish of Quails and small Birds. 3. A Warden-Pye. 4. Tarts and Custards.

November.

1. A shoulder of Mutton stuffed with Oysters. 2. A Loin of Veal. 3. A roasted Goose. 4. A Venison Pasty.

Second Course.

1. A Larded Hern, and another not Larded. 2. A sowced Tarbet. 3. Two Pheasants, the one Larded, and the other not. 4. A Collar of Beef. 5. A sowced Mullet and Base. 6. Gellys and Tarts of Fruits in season.

December.

1. Stewed broth of Mutton and Marrow-bones. 2. Lambs-head and White-broth. 3. A roasted Chine of Beef. 4. Minced Pyes. 5. A Turky stuck with Cloves, roasted. 6. Two roasted Capons, the one Larded, the other not.

Second Course.

1. A young Kid or Lamb roasted whole. 2. A dish of Partridges. 3. Polonian Sawsages, and a dish of Anchoveys, garnished with Mushrooms. 4. A dish of Caveer and pickled Oysters. 5. A Quince Pye. 6. A dish of Woodcocks.

January.

1. A Collar of Brawn and Mustard. 2. A couple of Pullets boiled with White-broth. 3. A roasted Turky. 4. A hashed shoulder of Mutton. 5. Two Geese. 6. A Surloin of Beef. 7. Minced Pyes. 8. A Loin of Veal. 9. A Venison Pasty. 10. A Marrow Pye. 11. A couple of Capons roasted. 12. A Lamb roasted. 13. Woodcocks, Partridges and small Birds dished up with sawce.

Second Course.

1. A sowsed Pig. 2. A Warden Pye. 3. A cold Neats-Tongue. 4. A sowsed Capon. 5. A dish of Pickled Oysters and Mushroons. 6. A Jole of Sturgeon. 7. A Goose or Turky-Pye.

February.

1. A Bacon-chine. 2. A Loin of Veal or Beef roasted. 3. A Lamb-Pye or Minced-Pye. 4. A couple of wild Ducks roasted. 5. A dish of fryed Oysters. 6. A couple of Rabits roasted. 7. A Skirret-Pye.

Second Course.

1. A Roasted Lamb. 2. A dish of Pigeons. 3. A Pippin-Tart. 4. A Jole of Sturgeon. 5. A cold Turky-Pye.

And

And thus having in all it's Material parts, or what is moſt requiſite, given ſuch Directions to an Ingenious Cook-Maid as may qualifie her, if duly obſerved, for the ſervice of Perſons of Worth. I might ſay likewiſe ſomething of the under Cook-Maid and Scullery-Maid; but they being both dependants upon the former, and their buſineſs conſiſting in helping the Cook-Maid, the greateſt matter beſide is to keep themſelves and the Kitchin Materials neat and clean: And ſo I take my leave of them, and proceed to the Dary-Maid.

CHAP. XVII.

The Accomplished Dairy-Maid, or Directions to make all manner of Junkets and pleasant things, wherein Milk, Cream, &c. *is an Ingredient; the Modish and Experienced way, plain, easie, and exceeding necessary.*

THE Dairy-Maids place and office, though not so universal, is little inferiour to that of the Cook-Maid, in making variety of Junkets; beside which, her chief business is to go neat and cleanly, and to keep all so under her Jurisdiction; observing tho Kine are well fed, and that Butter and Cheese are made of proper Milks, and in their proper season: To make which, few that undertake that business being ignorant, I shall proceed to give Instructions for the making of Junkets, the most curious part of her office, and for which Persons of Quality peculiarly retain such Servants. But to proceed.

To make fresh Cheese of Cream.

Take a Pottle of new Milk warm from the Cow, Almonds blanched half a pound, beat them small, add a pint of Cream, a quarter of a pint of Rose-water, half a pound of Sugar,

gar, half an ounce of beaten Cinamon and Ginger; then add Runnet, bread it up and whey it; press it in a Mould, and serve it up in a dish of Cream.

Cream and Codlings, how to order in the best manner.

Scald your Codlings, take off the skins, and cut the core; mix the pulp with Sugar and Rose-water; add a quarter of a pint of Canary and a quart of Cream, and serve it up.

To make an Excellent Junket.

Take Goats or Ews Milk, put them over a fire; and when they are a little warm, then add Runnet, and let it cool; then strow on it Cinamon and sugar, over that cast Cream, and strew sugar upon the Cream, with Rose-water.

To make a whip'd Sullabub.

Take a pint of Cream, six spoonfulls of Sack, the Whites of two Eggs, two ounces of fine sugar, and with birch-twigs beat it till it froth well; scum it and put it into your Sullabub-pot.

To make Cream of Codlings.

Scald them and peel off the skin, scrape the

the pulp from the core, and ſtrain the pulp, mixed with Sugar and Roſe-water, through a courſe linnen cloth: lay your Codling-pulp in the middle of a diſh, and raw Cream round it; adding more Sugar and Roſe-water.

To make a Cream-Tart.

Take Manchet, chip it and grate it; mix it with good Cream and ſweet Butter; take a dozen yolks of Eggs, beat them well with Cream, adding four ounces of ſugar: boil them altogether till they come to a thickneſs; make two leaves of Paſte as thin as can be raiſed, but very ſhallow: put the Materials before mentioned into it, and cover it with the lid; then bake it, ſtrew ſugar on it, and ſerve it up.

To make Curran-Cream.

Bruiſe red Currans in boiled Cream, ſtrain them through a ſieve, add Sugar and Cinamon, and ſo ſerve it up: And ſo you may by Rasberries or Strawberries.

To make Cream of Eggs.

Take a quart of Cream, and when it is hot, beat into it the Whites of five Eggs, and let it boil, adding two ſpoonfulls of Roſe-water: being enough, let it cool, and add

add a little salt, and scrape on it fine sugar.

To make Curd-Cakes.

Tak a pint of Curds, four Eggs, leaving two of the Whites; add sugar and grated Nutmeg, with a little Flower: mix them well, and drop them like fritters into a Frying pan in which Butter is hot.

To make fresh Cheese.

Take a race of Cinamon, scald it in new Milk or Cream; and taking it off, sweeten it with sugar; then take a spoonfull of Runnet to two quarts of Milk, cover it close, and let it stand till the Cheese comes: strew then upon it Sugar and Cinamon, and serve it up with sipits dipped in Canary or White-wine.

To make Gooseberry-Cream.

Let your Gooseberries be boiled, or for want of green ones, your preserved ones will do; and when your Cream is boiled up, put them in, adding small Cinamon, Mace and Nutmeg; then boil them in the Cream, and strain all through a cloth, and serve it up with Sugar and Rose-water.

To make a Cream Fool.

Heat two quarts of Cream; when it is boiled, add the yolks of twelve Eggs, having firft beat it in the three or four fpoonfulls of cold Cream, ftraining them into the hot, ftir them to prevent burning; when having boiled a pretty while, take them off and let them cool, adding two or three fpoonfulls of Sack, faften fipits to the difh with fyrup of Rasberries: fweeten your Cream, pour it in, and ferve it up.

To make Clouted Cream.

Set new Milk on the fire twelve hours without fuffering it to boil: add fugar and Cinamon, with a third part of Cream, and ferve it up.

To make a Goofeberry Fool.

Pick your Goofeberries not ripe, boil them in clean water to a pulp; take fix yolks of Eggs, a quart of new Milk, Rofe-water and fugar; put the latter in when the former is well boiled, and fuffering them to boil a while, ferve the whole up in a large difh when it is cold.

To make a Tansey.

Take six Eggs, but the Whites only of three; beat them in Cream, then stamp green Wheat-blades, Violets, Spinage, Succory and Strawberry-leaves, of each a handfull, with a few Walnut-tree budds; adding Cream as you beat them: strain out the Juyce, and add it to the Eggs, and more Cream; as also crumbs of Bread, Cinamon, Nutmeg, salt and sweet Butter, the latter being put into the Frying-pan; adding, lastly, the Juyce of Tansey and Sugar: fry them like a Pancake, very thin, and serve it up with Rose-water and sugar.

To make Snow-Cream.

Take the Gleer of half a dozen Eggs and Rose-water, beat them with feathers till they become like Snow; lay it on heaps, and Cream that has been boiled and cooled, with scraped Loaf-sugar: heat it again, and serve it up as as soon as it comes to be cold a second time, upon Rosemary or Bay-branches to thicken; that it may stick the better, add some grated Bread.

To make a pleasant Syllabub.

Take two quarts of Milk come newly from the Cow, half a pint of Verjuice being added, take off the curd, and put to it more, a pint and a half of Cream: beat them together with Sack and Sugar, and put them into your Syllabub-pot for your uſe.

To make a Cream, called Quince-Cream.

Roaſt four or five ripe Quinces, and pare them; cut them from the core in thin ſlices; boil the ſlices in a pint of ſweet Cream, with a root of whole Ginger: when it is boiled to a pulp, ſtrain it; and adding ſugar, ſerve it up cold.

To make the beſt Jumballs.

Take a handfull or two of Wheat-flower, and a pound of white ſugar; mix them well, adding the Whites of two Eggs, and a pound of blanched Almonds well beaten, with half a pound of ſweet Butter, and a ſpoonfull or two of Roſe-water: To theſe add more; half a pint of Cream, mould it till it become a Paſte; rowl it into what ſhape you pleaſe, and dry it a while, then gently bake it: Of this quantity you may make twenty or more.

How to make an Angellet.

Take a pint of Cream, and double the quantity of Milk, putting to them a ſmall quantity of Runnet; and when it thickens, take

take it up with a ſpoon, and put it into a Fat, there let it continue till it is very ſtiff; then ſalt it, and when it is ſo, let it dry, and at the end of three Months eat it.

To make Sage-Cream.

Take a quart of Cream, boil it well, then add a quarter of a pint of the Juyce of red Sage, half as much Roſe-water, and a quarter of a pound of ſugar, and it will be an excellent diſh: And thus you may uſe it with any ſweet Herbs, which will render it pleaſant and healthfull.

Theſe things being exactly performed by thoſe for whoſe ſake they were written, will, no doubt, turn to their credit and advantage.

CHAP. XVIII.

The Judicious Midwives Advice, or Directions relating to the Delivery of Women in case of Natural or Unnatural Births; dead Children, &c. Also how they ought to be used before and after Delivery: with Excellent Receipts and Applications in divers cases, and for Curing distempers incident to the Sex, &c.

AS this undertaking ought to be performed with modesty and caution, so I shall observe both; and though it may seem brief to some, yet it cannot but be necessary and usefull: Wherefore I have placed it as an Appendix to this necessary Book, and in all, consulted the opinion of the Learned.

As for a Midwife, she ought to be well qualified, knowing and expert before she undertakes so great a charge; not too hasty, nor too slow in the performance of her office, and ever have the fear of God before her eyes, as the *Egyptian* Widwives had when they refused to destroy the *Hebrew* Male-children, as regarding their Oaths on Earth, which is, no doubt, bound in Heaven. But not longer to prologue, I shall proceed to the material matter: And first, what ought to be observed upon the lying down of a Woman in Child-

M

If her Travail be hard and tedious, to enliven her ſpirits, and keep her in heart; give her Cordial Eſſence, Syrups or Cordial-waters, ſuch as are ſutable on ſuch occaſions: She may alſo take Chicken-broth, ſeconded by a poached Egg, or ſuch-like matter; not to exceſs, but moderately. As for the poſtures in caſe of Delivery, few are ignorant of them; therefore to avoid abſcenity, I ſhall wave them, and proceed to what is more neceſſary and material.

In caſe of Delivery, the Midwife muſt with patience expect the aſſiſtance of Nature, which on that occaſion wonderfully operates, and not abruptly break the Membrane, leaſt the life of one or the other be endangered, unleſs a great neceſſity require it, but rather ſuffer the Childs head to do it; and when that is done, and the pangs come gently, draw forth the Birth, if it be the right way forward; if not, means muſt be uſed to turn it, as the motion of the Woman, and the diligence of the Midwife. Walking up and down the room, in this caſe, if the Woman be able, is not at all amiſs, nor ſuddain turning her ſelf, whereby ſhe may reduce the Infant to a right poſture, and ſo have an eaſie delivery for Children in the Womb. Lying croſs-ways or ſprawling, not only occaſion danger to the Woman, and hard Labour, but ſometimes, by reaſon of an unskilfull Midwife, Death to the one or the other, the natural Birth being with the head foremoſt ; and when a Child is ſo taken forth, commonly with the face downward, lay it upon it's back for the advantage of reſpiration, and then with an Inſtrument very ſharp let the Midwife cut the Navel ſtring about four Inches from the faſtning, tying that that remains with a piece of ſilk ſtring ; cover then the Childs head and ſtomack, not ſuffering any thing to preſs the face.

The Child being thus ordered, let the Midwife commit it to the Nurſe, or the Woman that aſſiſts, and take care of the Woman in bed, in taking from her the Secondine or After-birth with care and caution, which is eaſieſt done, they being contracted Membranes, by eaſily moving till nature effect the reſt : And if there appear a difficulty therein, many are of the opinion, that the Womans holding Salt in her hand faſt graſped, it is much available in facilitating the buſineſs. Breathing hard, or rather ſtraining when the breath is held, is another expedient, or by ſtraining to vomit; all being helps to nature : But if theſe prove ineffectual, the ſcent of *Aſſa-fœtida* is an Expedient, or drinking the Juyce of Elder, eſpecially if the Woman be troubled with the Wind-Cholick, chafing the Belly is not the leaſt expedient to forward the matter, for thereby the Wind that

that obſtructs is diſperſed or expelled: If theſe fail, the Midwife, by her diſcretion, muſt gently draw them forth.

Many Births there are that are called Unnatural, becauſe they by accident, or the evil ſcituation of the Womb come not forward the right way, ſome lying croſs, others with their feet downward, others ſprawling; ſome with their necks bowing, and others with their arms ſtretched out, ſo that they create great pain and trouble: Therefore of theſe I ſhall ſpeak and give Inſtructions to thoſe of the profeſſion that herein are ignorant.

In many of theſe caſes great caution muſt be uſed to turn the Child, not only by the motion of the Woman, but by fomentations, if occaſion require, and by the hand of the Midwife, either to turn the Child in the Womb the right way, or to contract the Members, that it may be brought forth by delating the Womb, and thereby making ſufficient way to do it, removing what obſtructs the paſſage; and having by degrees brought the Infant into a convenient poſture, if it may be, tenderly move it, the hand being before that attempt anointed with Pomatum, the weakeſt, or what is more convenient, freſh Butter; letting forth the Waters if they are not come down; and whether it lye croſs or ſprawling, feel for the feet; and having gotten them, by degrees draw the Infant gently forth, incouraging the Woman to ftrain, and giving her leave between whiles to breathe; and that in fuch a cafe the hold may not fail, a linnen cloth about the Thigh of the Child will not be amifs; and after the Birth do as in cafe of a Natural birth.

If a dead Child be in the Womb, and Nature be deficient, as in that cafe moftly it is, Art muft be ufed, and the Child, if it cannot be otherwife, muft be drawn forth with an Inftrument hooked and faftned in the Scull by the Eye-hole. This likewife muft be done with caution, and the Woman after it carefully regarded; incouraging her, and not being difmayed at any crofs accident, but rather recollect her fenfes, that fhe may be the better able to perform her office, Wit in the greateft Exegencies being moft needfull: And when fhe is eafed of her burthen, give her for her further comfort a Toaft in Ipocras or Canary: or in cafe fhe cannot be delivered with conveniency, the better to inforce it, let her take the following Drink.

Cut blew Figs fix or feven, Mugwort, the Seeds; of Rue and Fenegreek, of each two drams; Water of Peneroyal and Motherwort, fix ounces: decoct them till half be be confumed; ftrain them, and add of Saffron three grains, and the Trochifes of Myrrh a dram, and a dram of beaten Cinamon: fweeten

ten the liquid part, and ſuffer her to drink it hot.

Reſting a while, let her again try her ſtrength, but not put it out to extremity, leaſt ſhe become too feeble; and then if ſhe be not eaſed of her burthen, it will not be amiſs to make a Suffumation of *Oppoponax*, *Caſtor*, *Sulpher* and *Aſſa-fœtida*, of each a dram beaten to Powder, and wetted to a ſtiffneſs, with the Juyce of Rue burnt on a chafing-diſh of coles, and the ſmoak paſs through the narrow end of a Funnel, ſo as to affect the Matrix only, and ſo wait the good time.

A Woman being delivered either of a natural or croſs Birth, it will be convenient, if ſhe have had hard labour, to wrap her in the skin of a Sheep, the fleſhy ſide being warm towards her, eſpecially to her reins and belly: or for want of it, a Coney or Hares skin newly flea'd and warm, chafing her belly with Oyl of St. *John*'s Wort, and ſwathing her back and belly with fine linnen a quarter of a Yard broad, covering her flanks with a quilt or little pillow, applying a warm cloth to her Nipples; but uſe not preſently ſtriving by any application to drive back the Milk, leaſt it cauſe an Inflamation by the continuing of the evil humour twelve hours at leaſt, being allow'd by Phyſitians for the circulation and ſettlement of the Blood, and what was caſt upon the Lungs by vehement agitation; for in this case Nature is wonderfully out of frame, there not being a Vein nor Artery but what is stretched and moved.

About six hours after delivery, or less, a restorative may be made of the yolks of two Eggs, a pint of White-wine, a quart of Milk, of Oyl of St. *John*'s Wort and Roses, each an ounce; Plantane and Rose-water, of each the like quantity: mix them well, and dip a cloth into them folded; warm it and apply it to the Breasts, and it will much abate the pangs.

To sleep immediately, though the Woman be inclinable, is not at all convenient; four hours after delivery give her Caudles and nourishing Liquids, and let her sleep if she is minded: And in case of a Natural Birth, no more is required, unless some more than ordinary indisposition happen.

But in case of Unnatural Births, or extremity, other things are to be considered; As to observe a temperate diet, which must consist for the first five days of Penados-broths, Jelly of Chickens or Calves-feet, poached Eggs, French Barly-broth, *&c.* And as she strengthens, so let her increase her eating. If no Feaver afflict her, she may, as she sees occasion, drink Wine moderately, Syrup of Roses or Maiden-hair, and such-like astringents: And so the danger being past, Broths of Meat, or Meat it self, will not be amiss,

that

that ſhe may the better recover her ſtrength, the eighth day being the ſooneſt to venture on them, the Womb then for the moſt part purging it ſelf, avoiding as much as may be, ſleep in the day-time: And in caſe of Coſtiveneſs, or the like obſtruction, which too frequently happen, a Cliſter of mollifying Herbs are a preſent removal; and in all ſuch caſes, and many other, what follows is held material.

Marſh and Field-mallows, Peletory of the Wall, Chammomile and Melliot-flowers, of each a handfull: boil them in water wherein a Sheeps head has been boiled; ſtrain them when boiled, and into a quart put an ounce of courſe Sugar, and as much Honey, with an ounce and a half of freſh Butter; and if it opperate not to the purpoſe, half an ounce of *Catholicum* will not be amiſs.

It is uſual for Women to waſh after delivery; and how to make theſe Waſhes, not being vulgarly known, I ſhall give directions.

For the firſt waſh, take a handfull of Chervil, which being boiled in a quart of water; add a ſpoonfull of Honey of Roſes, and waſh with it eight days, and then uſe another, *viz.* Take red Roſes, put them in a linnen bag, boil them in half a pint of water, and as much White-wine; ſtrain the liquid part, and uſe it; ſome require a third, and that may be

made

made of the decoction of Roses, and a pint of Myrrh-water.

To make Astringents usefull on this occasion, Take the seed of Pomgranet, Roach-Allum and Galls, of each two ounces; red Roses and the roots of Knot-grass, of each four ounces; the rinds of Pomgranet and Cassia, of each three ounces; Water-roses, Myrrh and Burnet, of each one ounce; half a quartern of White-wine; and of Smiths-water a quarter of a pint. Take two bags of a quarter long, and half the breadth, boil them in water with the drugs, *&c.* and apply them successively, as is convenient to make an excellent Plaster: Take Venice, Turpentine, *Spermaceti*, Rose and Plantane-water, of each an ounce and a half, with eight ounces of Bees-wax: bruise and melt them, adding an ounce of white Lead; make a Plaster of it, and apply them to the Belly and Nipples, anointing them first with *Spermaceti*, and it will remove the Inflamation, and afford much strength.

Cleansing before rising being convenient, I shall not omit to give directions, as thus:

Take half a pound of bitter Almonds, blanch them and beat them into Paste with Powder of Grise, and the yolk of an Egg; put it into bags of Shammey, and dip it into red Wine, and apply it to the places whence the Cere-cloth was taken, and wash it in the

Wine

Wine wherein Orange-flowers have been ſteeped.

To prevent the curdling of the Milk in the Breaſt, Boil the roots of *Althea* in White-wine Vinegar, ſtrain the liquid part through a Sieve, adding Bean-flower an ounce, Oyl of Maſtick two ounces, Powder of dried Mint and Rue, of each a dram: make them into an Ointment, and anoint the Breaſts.

To dry up the Milk many ways are uſed, but this the beſt, *viz.* Take new Honey, the Juyce of Speremint and Shepherds-purſe, of each an ounce, and put half an ounce into Chicken-broth each morning.

To renew a pain in the Breaſt, Take two ounces of Bees-wax, Oyl of Nutmeg and Rape-oyl, of each half an ounce; make them into an ointment, ſpread them plaſter-wiſe, and apply them to the Breaſt.

In caſe the belly ſwell, which after delivery often happens, Take Barly and Bean-flower finely ſifted, of each four ounces; half a pound of Spaniſh Figs, of the Powder of Brick two ounces, one ounce of Cyprus-nuts: boil them well in the water of a Smiths forge, and apply them as a Linament to the belly.

If an Inflamation of the Breaſt happen, make a Cataplaſm of the leaves of Melliot and Night-ſhade, each a handfull, boiled in Spring-water; adding two ounces of Bean-flower, of Oyl of ſweet Almonds and Oat-meal, each an ounce, and make a timely Application.

To cure a Tumour in the Breast, which proceeds from a thick and unnatural vapour arising from the Menstrual blood, the Woman must be moderate in diet, drinking water wherein Cinamon and Anniseeds have been concocted; as likewise the rind of Cittron, observing evermore to take such things as are proper to provoke the Courses, as the Juyce of Celendine, Groundsel, Chammomile and Ground-ivy boiled in White-wine; and in often so doing you will remove the pain, and render ease to the part.

And thus with modesty (as I well hope) I have performed what I promised; which if rightly considered, and applied to a right end, will undoubtedly turn to the advantage of the Female Sex, and render the ignorant capable, at least of understanding what can be no ways prejudicial to them, but may redound to their profit and advantage.

THE SECOND PART, OR Appendix to the foregoing Work.

Containing Directions for Behaviour as to what relates to the *Female Sex* on all occasions, *&c.*

The Authors Admonition to Parents, or such as have the Tuition of Children, *&c.*

AMong all the Temporal Blessings, God out of the abundance of his Bounty and Goodness, has bestowed upon Mankind, Parents in dutifull and obedient Children, have the greatest: Great indeed it is to have Children, and so it was held and acknowledged by the Fathers and Wise men of old; insomuch that Barrenness was not only looked upon

as

as a Reproach, but a more immediate mark of Heavenly displeasure. Sarah's *heaviness was turned into joy. When* Isaac *was born,* Rachel *was so impatient, that she desired* Jacob *(as not considering they were the immediate gift of the Almighty) to give her Children, or she should dye. The Mother of* Sampson, *when the Angel told her (who had it seems been a long time Barren) that she should conceive a Son, greatly rejoyced.* Hannah *praying before the Lord with an upright heart, and pouring out her supplications to him to take away the Reproach of her Barrenness, had her Petition answered in bringing forth* Samuel. *Great was the joy of* Elizabeth, *the Wife of* Zacharias, *and Mother of* John *the Baptist, when she found she had conceived; insomuch that she cryed as in a Rapture,* Thus hath the Lord dealt with me in the days wherein he looked on me, to take away my Reproach amongst men. *And one of the chief Blessings the Kingly Prophet pronounceth to the just and upright Man is,* That his Children shall be like Olive-branches round his Table. *If the having Children creates such joy, how ought it to multiply in the hearts of Parents, who are appointed by God to watch over them for their good, when through their incouragement and industry they see them arrive, in some measure, to a perfection, in the knowledge and practice of Divine and Moral Virtues, whereby they are rendered not only capable of an Immortal state,*

ſtate, but of gaining a good repute and laſting Memory amongſt Men: The conſideration of which doubtleſs made Solomon *deliver it as a Maxim, That,* A Wiſe Son made a glad Father. *And in this caſe Children are more bound to their Parents for their Education than for their bearing them: Nor is it a Duty leſs incumbent on Parents in the diſcharge of their duty towards God, to ſee to their utmoſt thoſe Children he has intruſted them with as Pledges of his kindneſs, brought up in his fear by a timely ſeaſoning them in the ways of Virtue, than it is on the Childrens to make gratefull returns and acknowledgments for the care and coſt they have beſtowed on them, in nurturing and bringing them up; imagining, that upon the Receiving of every ſuch bleſſing, they hear the Almighty Doner ſpeaking as* Pharoh's *Daughter did to the Mother of* Moſes, Take this Child and Nurſe it for me, &c. *Theſe things rightly weighed and conſidered, may induce thoſe Parents who would be happy in their poſterity, to be more than ordinarily diligent in laying a good foundation for Virtue to build upon, their own good Example being ever the Corner-ſtone of ſuch a Structure; for nothing ſooner makes an impreſſion in tender years, than Precedents infancy, like Wax, taking and retaining the Figure of that Seal which firſt Impreſs'd it, unleſs it be rudely defaced by another, or purpoſely deſtroyed.*

On

On this occasion much more may be ſaid, but Parents naturally inclining to do what may turn to the advantage of their Children, I ſhall in this place preſs it no further, but proceed to lay down Rules and Directions for the Carriage and Conduct of young Gentlewomen, &c. *That climbing by degrees to the Summit of Internal Adornment, they may raiſe themſelves a laſting Monument, ſeeing Virtue ſurvives Time, and ſhakes hands with Eternity.*

Yours to ſerve you,

J. S.

Admo-

CHAP. I.

Admonitions to Young Gentlewomen, in the first place, to observe their Duty towards God.

TO be inflamed with the Love of sacred Things, is undoubtedly a foundation for early Virtue to build on, and is frequently an Introduction to whatever we can justly or truly term good or great: Therefore as you first owe your Duty to God who made you, and on whom depends your Being and Well-being, not only here, but hereafter: You must above all things consider his Glory, and indeavour, as much as in you lyes, to render him tribute of Praise and Thanksgiving, imploring the assistance of his divine Grace to instruct and inable you to supply your defects, and increase your knowledge, and in so, *Remembring your Creator in the days of your youth.* That God who loves the early Sacrifice of the heart, will not be wanting to overshadow you with the Wings of his Providence,

dence; and keep you from falling into thoſe ſnares Satan lays to intrap you.

To induce you to holy deſires, and confirm you in the way of Truth, as you increaſe in ſtrenghth. As ſoon as you are capable to read well, (which ought to be in the ſixth year of your Age at furtheſt, for otherwiſe you or your Parents will be ſubject to a cenſure of knowledge) you muſt apply your ſelf to the reading of good Books; and ſtrive, the more you read, the more to conceive a delight and pleaſure therein; that growing up, you may ſay with Holy *David, From my youth have I loved thy law.* And in ſeriouſly conſidering what you read, it will be very profitable for you to retain in your memory ſuch comfortable Sentences as, being repeated, raiſe in you a holy joy, or more than ordinary deſire to meditate and enter upon a Contemplation of thoſe things that are thereby expreſſed; and theſe muſt be chiefly taken from Holy Writ: But above all things, be not remiſs in the duty of Morning and Evening Prayer; and that you may be the better prepared for ſuch holy Exerciſe, get by heart and retain in your memory the *Pater-Noſter*, or the Lord's Prayer, the *Belief*, or the *Apoſtle's Creed*, and other good Prayers ſutable to your capacity. Get by heart likewiſe the Churches *Catechiſm*, but eſpecially the Ten *Commandments*, that you may the better underſtand the Will of

that

that God that made you, and the World, and be cautious to offend him in breaking any of his Laws by thought, word or deed, considering that from him who is the *searcher of hearts*, nothing can be hid; for to him darkness is as light, and before him all the secrets of our hearts are laid open. Lying above all things must be abhorred, and the Name of God never mentioned but upon pious and lawfull occasions, (and then too, with the profoundest reverence.) The company of naughty Children, whose words and manners may offend or tend to corrupt youth, though your near relations, must not only be reproved by you, but growing incorragible or irreclamable, shun'd and avoided; and as often as stands with your conveniency, especially every day between the Morning and Evening Duties of Prayer, read little or more some portion of Scripture with heed, reverence, and a comely gesture, as co[illegible]ring it is the Word of God, *Written by* [illegible], *inspired for our Learning*. And if it [illegible]vate you read, where none but your [illegible] is present, pause and meditate [illegible] those Sacred Truths as your Heart is most [illegible]able.

As for the Sabbath-day, [illegible] holy set a-part by God, as more pecu[illegible] for his Worship, though it oug[illegible] be omitted. Observe to kee[illegible] greatest strictness, keeping not only

Act

Actions and Words, but, if poſſible, your very Thoughts within compaſs; and ſpend that day eſpecially in Praiſe and Thankſgiving both in private and publick Devotion, with a firm Faith and full relyance on God's mercy and goodneſs for your protection and preſervation in this life, and for his promiſes of a better life in the world to come.

When you are at Church, let not your Eyes by any means wander, nor your Body move in an unſeemly geſture; but in all things ſo behave your ſelf, that you may be an example to others. If at any time you are expoſed to Melancholy or diſcontent, pray to God to remove it; if to mirth, let it be harmleſs and innocent, avoiding leud ſights, or hearing Songs that may tend to corruption aud debauchery; but rather follow on this, as well as the former occaſion; St. *James's* direction or advice, *viz. If any be afflicted, let hi*[illegible]*ay: if merry, let him ſing Pſalms*, c. 5. v. 1[illegible]d in thus doing you will treaſure up ble[illegible]s to your ſelf; for if you carefully perform your du[illegible] in ſerving God as you ought, he will not [illegible]hold from you any thing that is neceſſary [illegible] to thoſe that *ſeek firſt the kingdom o*[illegible]*n and it's Righteouſneſs, all other th*[illegible]*e added.*

A[illegible]uch may briefly ſuffice to in[illegible] you how you ought in duty to behave [illegible] ſelf towards your Maker: From which

I ſhall

I ſhall proceed to the next incumbent, which is your *Duty towards your Parents*, &c.

CHAP. II.

Inſtructions for young Gentlewomen in behaving themſelves Dutifully towards their Parents.

AS our Parents are thoſe from whom, next God, we have our Being, and by whoſe tender care and inſeparable love we are nouriſhed and preſerved from innumerable dangers and hazards; therefore ought we to render them ſutable returns, as far as we are able, and more expreſly in a gratefull acknowledgment by our duty and obſervance. Therefore, young Gentlewomen, take notice that you ſhould no ſoonet arrive at moderate years of underſtanding, but you ought to underſtand your Duty towards your Parents; and that you may not plead ignorance, I will briefly lay down ſuch Rules as may inform you what is neceſſary to be obſerved.

In the firſt place, your Reverence, Love and Obedience is ſtrictly required, not only by the ties of Nature, but by God's holy Word, as ſundry places in Scripture manifeſt; nor can their Infirmities in any-wiſe abſolve

ſolve you, or diſpenſe with your non-performance; but in ſuch a caſe you ought to double your obſervance, that thereby, as much as in you lyes, with *Shem* and *Japhet* you may hide their Weakneſs and defects from the eyes of others, leaſt the Curſe that befell *Cham*, the unnatural diſcoverer of his Fathers nakedneſs, fall upon you; or the more dreadfull threat of the Wiſeman, in *Prov.* 30. 17. *The Eye that mocketh his Father, or deſpiſeth to obey his Mother, the Ravens of the Valley ſhall pluck it out, and the young Eagles ſhall eat it up*: That is, the very fowls of the Air, who are mindfull of thoſe that gave them being, ſhall teſtifie againſt the diſobedient, and become their Enemies. But nearer to the purpoſe.

You muſt obſerve at all times to obey the Will of your Parents (if it be in your power, and not contrary to God's Command) without repining, ſeeming unwilling, or entering into diſpute, performing what you do with chearfulneſs, ſhewing by your willing mind your ready obedience, and by your quick diſpatch demonſtrating the pleaſure you take in the performance, ſhunning all occaſions of giving them any diſquiet, pacifying their anger if it at any time ariſe, with ſubmiſſion either in words or by behaviour, tempering your actions with a moderate ſweetneſs of diſpoſition and ſilence, for too much oſtentation

tation or loquicity is diſpleaſing; when your Parents grieve, be you ſad; when they rejoyce, be you pleaſant, as ſympathizing with them in heavineſs and joy; yet be not over inquiſitive into the cauſe, but if you are deſirous to know it, wait their leaſure to reveal it, or learn it from ſome other hand.

Forget not to pray for your Parents as often as you put up your Vows to Heaven, beſeeching the Almighty to ſhow'r his Bleſſings upon them, that in multiplying they may redound to their advantage and your comfort, which is one great advance by which a Child indeavours to make his Parents reſtitution for their care and tenderneſs; for nothing without calling God to your aſſiance can in that nature be effectual, the difference being otherwiſe ſo vaſt between what has been done for you, and what you can do to deſerve it.

Let not the hopes of Riches, no, nor the ſeverity of your Parents, imprint in your mind a deſire of their death, leaſt the Almighty be offended and ſhorten your days, fruſtrating you not only of what you ſo earneſtly deſired, but of that, which without thoſe unlawfull deſires, you might in his good time have enjoyed.

Shun thoſe that ſpeak ill of your Parents, and would make them ſeem contemptible in your eyes: Nor let their Poverty, ſhould

I you

you be advanced by any means to Riches or Honour, render your Duty and Obedience leſs, for they cannot be but the ſame in all conditions. If they be poor, you ought to relieve them, if it be in your power: If they are weak of underſtanding, you muſt (if you ſee it abſolutely neceſſary, or be required ſo to do) aſſiſt them with your counſel: If they be injured or oppreſſed, you muſt, as much as in you lyes, endeavour to ſuccour and redreſs them, for no years can exempt you from obſerving your Duty to your Parents; nor ought you to diſpoſe of your ſelf in Marriage, nor otherwiſe, without their allowance and conſent, your Perſon being indiſpenſibly theirs in a lawfull way to diſpoſe of, as they for your advantage ſhall think fit. And ſo it was under the Law of *Moſes* in relation to a Virgins vow; the which, though ſhe had made, yet if her Father approved it not, it was void; as in *Numbers*, chap. 30. verſ. 5. *But if her Father diſalow her in the day that he heareth, not any of her vows nor her bonds wherewith ſhe hath bound her Soul ſhall ſtand; and the Lord ſhall forgive her, becauſe her Father diſallowed her.* By this we ſee the great Power that Parents had over their Children, even to a degree of cancelling and rendering of non-effect the obligation of a Vow, which power was given by God himſelf: Nor is it obſervable that thoſe who diſobey their Parents

rents in any thing that is lawfull, or neglect or despise them in their distress or poverty, ever prosper: Or if they flourish for a time, yet are they generally fitted in the same way, for Children cannot fathom the joy and sorrow of their Parents in this kind, till they become Parents themselves; and then, too often, they bewail their remissness. But to conclude as to this Particular.

Certain it is, that no poverty, fault or unkindness of Parents, can dispense with that Duty and Obedience which, by the Law of God and Nature, Children owe their Parents for the tender care, labour and cost, bestowed on them: Nay, though Parents should prove unnatural, and expose them, even in their Infancy, to a desperate fortune of hazard and danger; yet still those Children are bound to perform their duty, and look for their reward from him who is the Author of all Blessing; who for so doing has promised us length of days, and seldom fails to make those days comfortable to us.

CHAP. III.

Instructions for a young Gentlewoman at the Age of Six, or upward, how to behave her ſelf towards her Parents, Superiours, Equals and Inferiours; and upon ſundry other occaſions; as Learning, &c.

HAving briefly diſcourſed the two main Points, I ſhall now proceed to give you a Scheme of decent and comely Behaviour in General, to render you accompliſhed in your Nonage, and introduce you to that which is more materially to be obſerved and practiced.

In all your undertakings let it be obſerved, that you are an Enemy to ſloth, not only by your early riſing, but by your activity; for having neatly dreſſed you, or cauſed ſome other to do it, having proſtrated your ſelf before your Maker, and refreſhed you with what was appointed, fall upon your Knees before your Parents, and receiving their bleſſing, haſten to School, or elſe betake your ſelf to ſuch buſineſs as your Parents or Governeſs (if you are under one) ſhall appoint you at home, doing it with chearfulneſs and reſpect to thoſe that are over you, as well in their abſence, as when they are preſent; and whe-

whether it be Reading, or any curious work, obſerve that your face and hands are clean, and that you handle no dirty or greaſy things; neither preſume to eat before thoſe who are your Inſtructors, whilſt you are at your work or leſſon. If there be more under the ſame Tuterage, as in ſuch caſes is uſual, behave your ſelf kindly towards them; call no unſeemly names, nor make unſeaſonable complaints: Defraud them not, though of trivial things; nor take the leaſt matter by force that is not your own; be courteous and mild; uſe a decent and winning behaviour. If your Miſtreſs or Governeſs be ſharp and ſevere, ſtrive by your diligence to prevent diſpleaſure or correction; and as you approach or return from her, make your Reverence, and the like, to your Parents, when you come into their preſence, or retire; make your obeiſance in the moſt becoming and obliging manner to your Superiours and Equals; nor forget at any any time to be courteous to your Inferiours; beſure your Tongue run not too faſt, but in diſcourſe be moderate; ſpeak with deliberation, and well weigh your words before you utter them; and where you are ſeated, obſerve that you continue till you are called thence, or it is time to leave it.—In reading upon any occaſion, uſe not a Tone, but read diſtinctly, obſerving your ſtops, that you may the better underftand what you read. In Writing, beware that you blot not your Paper, but imitate your Copy in cutting your letters fair and even; let not your Work of any fort be foiled or dirty, and keep what things you ufe in good order, and render your Parents an account of your improvement.

When you are to be at Meat, be not out of the way, but attend the Grace, and then taking the place that is appointed you; after having done your Reverence to your Parents and company, fee that your Napkin be faftned about you, or pinned to fave your cloaths from greafing, and thankfully take what is given you without craving; nor is it feemly for you to fpeak at the Table, unlefs you are asked a queftion, or there be fome great occafion. Cut your Meat handfomely, and be not over defirous of Sawce, nor of another fort of Meat, before you have difpofed of what is on your Plate or Trencher. Put not both your hands to your mouth at once, nor eat too greedily: Let not your mouth or fingers be greafy no more than needs muft; and when you are fatisfied, take your Plate or Trencher with you, or give it to thofe that wait, and retire, but not out of the room till Grace is faid, and the Cloth taken away; at what time making your obeifance, you may depart, unlefs you are defired to ftay: Nor

Nor must you ſit before your Parents, Governeſs or Superiours, unrequired, unleſs you are at your Meat, Needle, Writing, or the like; and obſerve that you attempt not to drink in any company till you have emptied your Mouth, and that you breathe not, nor blubber in the cup or pot. As for your Recreation, when leaſure hours permit, let it be innocent and moderate, never ſtaying late abroad; and above all, be wary in the choice of your Companions; and as you grow up, ſhun the converſation of thoſe that have a report of Lightneſs, leaſt they draw you into a ſnare, or bring a ſcandal cauſleſly upon your good name, but chuſe thoſe whoſe reputations are candid; converſe with thoſe who are modeſt, yet affable; ſtay not at any time where the leaſt occaſion of lightneſs and wantonneſs is adminiſtred; nor lend your Ear to diſcourſe tending to Lewdneſs; and, for the generality, rather chuſe to be ſeen than heard.

For your Carriage in the general, let it be a Medium, not expreſſing too much reſervedneſs, which by ſome is interpreted Pride; nor too much freedom or familiarity, which on the other hand will be looked upon for fondneſs. Be no Makebate between your Parents and their Servants, nor at any time tell a Lye to excuſe a fault, or keep you from the hand of correction. Go to bed in due ſeaſon, without any noiſe, and never be ſeen in unſeemly laughter, nor in pointing with your finger, or nodding with your head, eſpecially in company, or in places of Divine Worſhip, Honour, Age; and pity thoſe that are diſtreſſed by Poverty or any other affliction; ſpeak not at any time ſcornfully, or in a taunting way, but be courteous to all; and in ſo doing you will gain a good repute, and forward your ſelf in thoſe things that will render you Praiſe-worthy.

CHAP. IV.

Inſtructions for a young Gentlewoman how to behave her ſelf towards her Governeſs and Servants, &c.

BEing come to more years of diſcretion, there are many things requiſite to be known that I have not yet mention'd; an account of which, as they offer, I ſhall deliver in their proper places: And in the firſt place I ſhall ſay ſomething of a Governeſs, appointed by Indulgent Parents to inſtruct a young Gentlewoman; as alſo of the Maid-Servant that is to attend her, *&c.*

As for your Governeſs, if diſcreetly choſen, ſhe muſt be a Woman of gravity and diſcretion,

discretion, one that is Learned in curious Arts, such as you are desirous to improve; and although her Age render her reserved, yet must you not censure her as ridged, but comply with her lawfull Commands; and by your mildness and industry move her to gentleness, refraining by all means to make complaints, especially unjust ones; for in disapproving of her, whom your Parents has thought fit to set over you, you tax them with Imbecility in chusing, and by that complaint will either incur their displeasure; or by removing your Governess, perhaps procure a worse; which causing undoubtedly a second complaint, will possess your Parents with a jealousie of your unatractableness and ill disposition.

Some there are that covet to be under a young Governess, with whom they may have the more familiar conversation, though to their small advantage; for it is somewhat improbable that a person who cannot perhaps govern her own youthfull frailties, should discharge so great a trust as she ought; nor is it Morally possible for any person to be a good Governess, unless she has her self been the Mother of Children, and had the bringing them up; for then, and but till then, can she be fully sensible of youthfull frailties, and know what tenderness, and what correction ought to be used:

However, consider with your self, that in being conformable to her, you obey your Parents, who thought fit to commit you to her charge; and that if you do otherwise, you disobey God in abusing or slighting their care and indulgence, who study your advantage: Therefore let not the Servants, nor any other, create a misunderstanding between you and her, but in prudence and charity forget or forgive what ever you conceive to be an injury, as wisely considering you are no competent Judge in your own case.

To the Servants you must be courteous and affable, but not over familiar, least it beget contempt. Tell no tales of them to your Parents, but rather strive to hide their failings, unless they be such as are prejudicial or unseemly; and do them what good you can. If at any time you find occasion to reprove them, let your Reproofs be rather Admonishments than Reproaches: Be not peevish nor froward in your Dressing, or in any other office done you, by the Maid, that more immediately attends you, but by gentle words let her know her error, that she may amend it; which method will oblige and command a constant diligence, which otherways would be but Eye-service; and if your Parents be angry with their Servants, or any of them, do you become their Mediator. And turn not, by any means, your face from the Poor; but

but if it be in your power, without offending your Parents, relieve them; or, as you see occasion, petition on their behalf: by which demeanour you will command Love and Reverence, and gain the character of an humble Spirit. In which you may rest satisfied, that it is better to be Good than Great; and that Humility forcibly commands Love and Service, when Pride on the contrary begets Hatred and Contempt. If Heaven has endowed you with a large Fortune and a noble Birth, let your Virtues shine with the greater lustre; and, above all things, give God the praise, and use what you have to his glory, and your own comfort.

CHAP. V.

Instructions for young Gentlewomen how to behave themselves in all Societies, upon sundry occasions.

WEll to deport and behave your self in company, upon all occasions, requires a sound judgment, and much caution, few being capable of bringing themselves within that compass; yet for your better Instruction, I shall lay down what I think most necessary to be observed.

And

And first, to qualifie your self to understand the quaint, modish and courtly Expressions, it is convenient that you learn the *Latin*, *French* and *Italian* Tongues, not only by Rote, but by Rule and Grammer the better to understand them, since the most refined English has borrowed from these Languages, and without this Knowledge you will be at a loss to understand those that utter high Phrases in the Court-Air, as they term it; nor in this case must you be ignorant in Singing, Dancing and Playing upon such Musick as is sutable to your Sex; though in Exercising your self herein, you must be very modest and moderate, your words on all occasions being but few, yet to the purpose; Discretion, Silence and Modesty being the Ornaments of the Female Sex. And as Society is that which all creatures naturally covet, so, if it be well chosen and managed, it is recreatory to the body and mind; but as bad Society is worse than none, so is it to be avoided.

Wherefore be not easily won to enter into discourse with those you know not, unless some urgent business require it, least you be suspected of Levity and Indiscretion. Always observe to consort your self with your betters or equals, knowing them to be virtuous; and avoid too much familiarity with Inferiours, unless you find them very discreet,

creet, least you fall into contempt, if Female: Or if Male, least you give them encouragement to make their Addresses of Courtship, and by subtil ways to insinuate themselves into your good liking; for Love, that takes the Diadem from Queens, is blind, and Passion distinguishes not Servility from Greatness: by which means, though you are high in Birth and Fortune, you may be brought to a yielding, which may turn to the grief of your Parents, or perhaps to their and your own disgrace. And in this case presume not too much upon your own strength, by interchanging Gloves, Rings, Ribons, or such things which you may term Trifles, least by this kind of familiarity Love, by insensible ways opens a passage to your heart, always considering it imploys weakness, or want of discretion in the besieged to parly with the besiegers.

Be not over desirous of being seen often, for ostentation sake, especially in places of resort, least you expose your self to the assault of the tempter, and purchase that curiosity with the loss of your honour, by giving licentious Amorists liberty to meet you in your Walks, and by powerfull perswasions to listen to their Sireens charms, whilst you are no longer capable of mastering your affections, but let them loose at a venture to your undoing; nor trust too

much

much to Female-Confidents, leaſt for their own advantage they perſwade you to a yielding; and in Speech be not over laviſh to any.

As for your Dreſs, let it be neat, but not gaudy, for Virtue is comely in any dreſs; and be content to appear in your native Beauty. Let your Dreſſing-time be ſhort, and your Recreation moderate; in your Speech or Behaviour ſhun all affectation, and be not over fond of new Faſhions, eſpecially ſuch as are Apiſh or unbeſeeming; and in that caſe let your Dreſs make known you are no friend to Formality. When you enter a Room to pay your reſpects to your Parents, Superiors or Equals, let it be done with a grave and modeſt countenance, making your Curtzies at three approaches, and in the ſame order retire. When you ſit or walk with any, obſerve that you do not rudely take the upper hand, nor expreſs any words that may give offence. Never ſpeak evil of any behind their backs, for thoſe you ſpeak it to may imagine you will do as much by them. Keep your Eyes from wandering. Stare not Men full in the face, nor caſt privates glances. Do not flout, nor be loud in Laughter, leaſt by ſtraining your Mouth wrinkles appear in your Cheeks and Forehead, you thereby become deformed, or appear much older than you are. Wherefore

in

in all things obſerve to behave your ſelf modeſtly and diſcreetly abroad and at home, that you may become an Example to others, and thereby deſerve the Imitation and Applauſe, not only with thoſe you aſſociate, but of ſuch as ſhall have knowledge of your Virtues and good Conduct. And ſo leaving you to conſider of what has been ſaid, I ſhall proceed to Particulars of greater moment.

Inſtructions for a young Gentlewoman to Manage her Gate and Geſture; to Govern her Eyes and Tongue, &c. upon ſundry neceſſary occaſions.

AS there are many other nice matters requiſite for the true Accompliſhment of a young Gentlewoman, I ſhall endeavour to lay down what is material in the moſt eaſie Method: And firſt of the Gate or Geſture that ought to be obſerved upon ſundry occaſions.

And in this caſe obſerve that you walk not careleſly or lightly, ſhouldering as it were your companions, nor ſtrutting or jutting in a proud manner. Keep (in your walk) your Head ſteady, your Countenance not too much elevated, nor too much dejected. Keep your Arms likewiſe ſteady, and throw them

them not about as if you were flying. Let your Feet rather incline a little more inward than outward, least you be censured Splay-footed, for by the motion of the Body the thoughts of the Mind may be discovered; as whether the party be of loose or proud behaviour, or humble and complacient. Do not run or go extream fast in places of Concourse, unless great occasion require it, for in such violent motions it is not always in your power to keep your body steady; nay, by too much haste you may chance to fall, and expose to view what you would conceal. And as the Gesture of the Body is seemly and commendable, so is the Management or Government of the Eye; in which many things are to be observed, and chiefly these.

Keep your Eyes, as we may call it, within compass; that is, let them not be too much fixed upon idle and vain objects, nor drawn away by unseemly sights: Roll them not about in a careless or lacivious manner; nor stare Men in the face as if you were looking Babies in their Eyes. Send not private glances, or look; as they call it, with half a face, turning your head as it were aside. Look not at any time over your shoulder, if you have opportunity to turn you. Open not your Eyes too wide, thereby to distort your countenance; nor keep them

in

in a manner half ſhut. Wink not too often, nor caſt your Eyes aſcance as if you ſquinted, neither keep them too reſerved, nor ſcornfully turn them away when any object offers. Look not too much downward, nor with a more than ordinary elevation. Gaze not often againſt the Sun, nor on the fire, both of them being things that impair the Luſtre of the Eyes. When you diſcourſe with a Woman, look her in the face with as much compoſedneſs as you can; but if with a Man, to look a little downward, for modeſty is commendable, leaſt your earneſt gazing in his face be interpreted in the worſt ſence: But above all things, as often as opportunity will permit, lift up your Eyes to your Redeemer, and with holy *David* implore him, to *turn them away from Vanity*; for the Eyes being the Windows of the Soul, lets in good or evil, according as it fixes, or is intent upon good or bad objects; therefore chuſe the former, and refuſe the latter. And the better to inable you to look up unto him upon all occaſions, God has given Man and Woman five Muſcles to move and guide the Eyes, and the Principal of them to draw it upward without pain; Whereas all irrational Creatures have but four to turn their Eyes about, as being made for no other end than to revert the duſt from whence they ſprung, whilſt the noble rational

nal Creature, endued with an immortal Soul, is capable of thoſe bleſſed Manſions of which he has a proſpect, and towards which he ought to lift his Eyes. But leaving the reſt to your diſcretion, I ſhall paſs on to ſay ſomething of Speech and Complement, *&c.*

In this caſe let all your Diſcourſes be to the purpoſe, and ſuffer not your Complements to be high-flown, extravagant, blunt or nonſenſical; but in all, ſute them with modeſty to the capacity and quality of the perſon to whom you utter them, and ſee they be done upon fit occaſion, and in ſeaſon; beſure not to Congratulate perſons when you ſhould Condole them; uſe in your utterance no hems nor ſtammerings; ſputter not as you ſpeak, nor ſpeak many ſentences between breathings; uſe no Tautologies or affected words or liſpings; neither ſpeak with a Tone, nor too much confidence; gaup not, nor ſtare with your Eyes; point not with your finger, nor expreſs in your diſcourſe thoſe inſipid and inſignificant words of *de-ye ſee, de-ye hear, underſtand-you me, mark-ye me, ſed-ſhe, ſed-he,* or the like; for you can never be an Oratreſs, if you accuſtome your ſelf to 'em; never talk too long, thereby to tire your Auditors, nor broach an unſeaſonable diſcourſe; obſerve that you interrupt not any perſon when he or ſhe is ſpeaking;

ſpeaking; and what you ſpeak, let it be with deliberation. Some there are that affect ſilence, and are little heard in any company. Let me tell you, Ladies, this is an error, and implies the party extreamly reſerved, and not deſirous of Society; or that her underſtanding is ſo weak, ſhe dares not truſt her Tongue to utter the ſence of her Soul, to whom the words of the Philoſopher uttered upon his obſerving one ſit ſilent in a great Aſſembly, may be aptly applied, *viz. If thou art wiſe, thou art a fool: If a fool, wiſe in holding thy peace.* Never ſtrain your words to a pitch of Eloquence, that the ſound is more admired than the ſence; but let a moderate flouriſh rather ſuffice and comprehend much in a few words: Decline to ſpeak much before gravity and multitude of years, unleſs urgent occaſion require it; and beware that you ſpeak not till you are bidden to hold your Tongue; for indeed Womens diſcourſe ſhould not be much, becauſe Modeſty and Moderation is her ornament, and are in themſelves a moving Rhetorick. And when you have opportunity of diſcourſe, let it not taſte of Confidence, Affectation or Conceitedneſs, nor border upon Obſcenity. Theſe things conſidered and practiced, will render your diſcourſe acceptable, and free you from the cenſure of the Wiſe and Judicious. And thus much for

for these Particulars: From whence I shall proceed to speak something of Habit and it's Decency; as also of Fashions commendable and discommendable.

CHAP. VI.

Directions for a young Gentlewoman how she ought to be seen in her Habit or Apparel; and what Garb is most commendable, and otherwise, according to the Quality of the Wearer.

THough God has framed Men and Women beautifull and seemly in every part, yet it is no ways disagreeable to his Will, that Nature should be improved by Art to render a creature he highly regards the more commodious, as appears by his cloathing. Our first Parents with more durable Garments than they themselves had provided to cover their nakedness; nor is it (as some Cinical persons have it) Pride to go neatly attired, for by that the parties discretion is better known than her Fortune, and the Body kept in a due proportion and order.

It matters not, Ladies, of what Stuffs or Silks your Cloathings are made, so they be decent and civil; neither by their ridiculousness discovering the wearer foolish and slovenly, nor by their gaudy and careless putting on to render her suspected of loose or light behaviour, or at least-ways subject her to the censure of the ignorant. Apparel may be rich, and yet decent; and indeed whether it be rich or not, if decent, the matter is not great; though in this case I leave it to the discretion of young Gentlewomen, or those that provide them Apparel, to let it be sutable to their quality or fortune; and will not be of the Morose and Cinical temper of some, who either believe, or spitefully give it as their opinion, that gorgeous or glittering Apparel is the Attire of Sin, and suits with the Pride of the wearers Heart; but am perswaded that the Quality of the Person extenuates the Quality thereof, and renders that opinion vain and frivolous. Since we read that Noble Women, in all Ages, went in sumptuous Attire, nor was it indecent nor unbecoming the character they bore; yet rarely find they were given to covet various fashions, but contented themselves with such Adornments as became their modesty; for indeed what avail they, unless to shew the profuseness of the

the wearer, or should it be to attract the Eyes of Mankind. Know, Gentlewomen, that Men of sence are not taken with glittering Apparel, no, nor External Beauty, so much as with the Internal Adornment of the Mind. And if by these Allurements Half-wits and Idiots should be captivated, your Triumph would not be worth the cost.

Yet I must confess, there is a kind of prividge in Youth to go gay; which should I too severely reprove, I might justly merit your displeasure; yet that gaity may as well be in decency as otherwise, the use of Apparel being to dignifie the wear: Nor does a virtuous demeanour more lively appear, than in Look, Speech, Gesture and Habit, within the compass of Modesty, though Diamonds, Gold, and other pretious things, were made for use, and without being imployed, would be ineffectual; therefore to wear them, in my opinion, is one of the chiefest Ends for which Nature produced them, or Art brought them to a fuller perfection. The Pride in this case being only centered in the Mind, and not in the External Ornaments; which is rather known by the Carrirge and Deportment of the Wearer, than by the Garments. And though to affect Novelty, and run into every fashion be not

not commendable, yet moderation is not amiſs: For two Reaſons. As firſt, ſhould you always keep in a faſhion, though decent, it would be looked upon as a conceited ſingularity; or to continue in any ſtrange garb, after the faſhion is altered, would appear ridiculous, and cauſe laughter, eſpecially amongſt the ruder ſort; as much as a Woman of fourſcore to be habited in the Garb of a Gentlewoman of ſixteen; or to ſee a Dairy-Maid in her Ladies attire: Therefore whatever you wear, let it be proportionably to your Body, and ſutable to your degree.

In a word, Let your Virtue appear in your Geſture by Humility and a modeſt behaviour; In your Looks by a compoſed ſweetneſs; In your Speech by Affability, comprehended within the bounds of Moderation; and in your Habit by decency, and a Regulation ſutable to your Birth and Fortune, whereby you will gain an Eſteem more valuable than whatever you can otherways propoſe to your ſelf on this ſide Eternity.

CHAP.

CHAP. VII.

Instructions for young Gentlewomen how to proceed in their seasonable Recreations; and what is to be observed therein.

SInce moderate Recreation is not unbecoming a young Gentlewoman, I think it not amiss to give my opinion in that case, what is most commendable, and what to be observed therein, as well relating to their Seasonableness, as to the Carriage and Behaviour that ought to be observed therein.

A Ball, amongst other Recreations, is much in esteem with young Gentlewomen, because there they are sure to meet their Compeers in merriment; yet least at such a place a a young Gentlewoman by her folly or unadvisedness expose her self to laughter or contempt, observe, that if you understand the rules of Dancing; yet be not too forward to ingage your self therein, least you intangle your self so far that you are puzled, and at a loss, perhaps for want of understanding the Rules and Formalities practised in that place. And as you ought not to be too forward, so be not too hard to be perswaded,

ſwaded, or abruptly, in a huffing humour, force your hand from any that offers to accommodate you, but rather run the hazard of an error or miſtake in your performance, than let the leaſt pride or rudeneſs appear, or give thoſe that are preſent occaſion to think you are ſubject to either.

In this caſe be not by any means affected, nor when you undertake to Dance, be not tedious, but perform what you undertake with modeſty and moderation, that by a quick diſpatch you may give way to others.

As Dancing is an External Accompliſhment, ſo Vocal Muſick is an Internal one, yet they may indifferently ſerve for either, though the laſt is preferred; therefore if you are expert in your Notes, *&c* and can Sing well; when you are in company, upon the intreaty of a friend, who knows you ſo qualified, be not obſtinate in complying; yet be brief, and let your Song be ſuch as may give no offence; and when you have done, look not as if you expected applauſe, but keeping your ſtation with a compoſed countenance. Give way to another to ſecond you, if any preſent is deſirous, or can be prevailed with to do it; obſerving never to cough nor ſtrain when you enterprize it, nor to ſtop in the middle to crave attention;

and the like obſerve in your playing on Inſtrumental Muſick; not in that Point being teadious in commencing your Harmony; when others do the like, give attention, not interrupting them with diſcourſe. And in this caſe let both your Songs and Tunes be modeſt, ingenious and pleaſant, avoiding by any means what may tend to the corruption of good manners. And as Dancing is the beſt and readieſt way to put the Body upon all occaſions in a gracefull poſture, ſo Muſick is that which tempers the Soul with mildneſs, and diſpoſes it to ſweetneſs.

In Limning or Drawing to the Life, many young Gentlewomen, as well of former as latter times, have exerciſed their Parts, and in that curioſity found much Recreation, it being, in my opinion, an Art ſutable to the accute wit of the Female Sex: Nor is Poetry to be rejected, for by that is the mind inlivened as it were, and tuned to the harmonious Numbers of the Muſes, and furniſhed with lofty Expreſſions.

Next to theſe, Engraving may take place, a thing practiced by many Virtuous Gentlewomen: but amongſt ſolitary Recreations, if they may be ſo termed, Reading of Hiſtory, or ſuch Romances wherein Virtue and Gallantry are lively Portrayed, or ſuch as contain

contain Stories of chast and virtuous Love are to be preferred.

These being allowed, I think it not amiss to advise young Gentlewomen, at leasure hours, to recreate themselves in seeing Stage-plays, wherein many things are represented, that by due construction may redound to their improvement in understanding, though some are so Stoically severe to condemn this kind of Recreation, as altogether tending to the corruption of good manners, yet they can give little reason for it.

These and such-like Recreations being to be preferred, there is something more to be considered, which is the fit time or season, *&c.* The principal thing to be considered in this case is, how you ought to keep within compass, and not run into excess, or any ways give offence, damage, prejudice or scandal to any, or by immoderate pursuing it, impair your Health or Reputation, which too often falls out, besotting a chearfull complection, and overwhelming in a manner the principal Virtue. And if you rightly consider this, and consequently recreate your self with moderation, at seasonable hours, and in proper seasons, it will not only quicken your apprehension, but contribute much to your bodily health, and cannot be any ways offensive to the Almighty, who debars us from

 nothing

nothing innocent and harmless that is for our advantage. So that from hence I may draw a conclusion, that Men and Women may enjoy those pleasures to which they with modesty and moderation incline, with a proviso they launch not out so far as to abuse them.

CHAP. VIII.

Instructions for the Guidance of a young Gentlewomans fancy, in relation to Love; and how she ought to behave her self towards those that seek to gain her in Marriage, &c.

HAving laid down many things highly necessary, and mainly conducing to the Accomplishment of a young Gentlewoman, I shall now proceed to a more difficult and weighty matter than what has hitherto been mentioned; and that is to direct her how to guide her fancy in the Mighty business of Love. A thing, you'l say, somewhat strange to propose: but what cannot the Merits of a Virtuous Woman create in the mind of her Admirer. This indeed, if it proved happy and successfull, will undoubtedly make her amends for her former care and diligence,

gence, and render her an entire felicity on Earth, for Love is the Concord and Harmony of the Universe, nothing subsisting in its proper order without it; nor can there be any happiness when it is wanting; yet there is, as in this case, as in many others, degrees, or rather counterfeits; for Love it self, in it's purity, admits of no Adulteration or mixture, but is essential and unlimited; but many there are that would appear to wear the badge of this sacred Virtue, who only make it an Umbrage to obtain their unlawfull desires and advantage; and though they may indeed for a time express an extraordinary Passion; and not to speak the worst of 'em, entertain a feavorish desire, which is to be known by their earnestly gazing upon the object they at that time perhaps admire; yet it being only a Passion, and not founded upon Virtue, it is not properly Love, nor can it render the expected felicity; but blazing a while in the enjoyment it sought, spends it self; and being spent like a false Star or Comet, expires; or on the other hand, not obtaining its ends, changes into disregard or mortal hatred; and of such a Passion, whether at the time it is proposed, real or feigned, you must beware.

That young Gentlewomen arriving at maturity, are prone to Love and Liking, it would be insignificant for one to relate, seeing it is so well known. The Eye and the Ear being seldom wanting to convey to the Soul what is desirable, the one charming it with beautifull sights, and the other with rhetorical and melodious sounds; yet give not these official members to much scope on this occasion, least they insensibly ruin you by betraying your Affections to what is sordid or inconsiderable, but keep as it were a guard upon your heart to prevent the entrance either of a lawless or disadvantageous Passion. Consider well before you give way, even to imagination in that kind; weigh deliberately each particular, and be seriously intent on what is to come, as well as what is present, not suffering your self, for the present, satisfying your appetite, to be carried away with the Torrent of a Passion, that will unavoidably carry you into the gulf of misery. Man indeed is a noble Creature, and for his sake Woman was made, and therefore ought to be complacient; but being left at liberty to chuse where she thinks fit for her advantage, it is more than common prudence to make such a choice to her humour. The former of which may, but the latter cannot be quickly discovered: But above all, let not a young Gentlewoman for Interest, or by over perswasion, give her

self

felf to one fhe cannot affect, leaft fhe dearly repent at leafure what is paft redreffing, there being nothing more grievous than a loathed bed, for that moft commonly cancels all other earthly felicities; nay, many times fhakes the very foundation of Modefty, and ftruggles with Virtue, till it enters at one door, and drives it out at the other. And this is too often the Parents cruelty to their Daughters, who being paft the youthfull pleafure of a Reciprocal Love, aim rather at their Greatnefs than their Happinefs; though contrary to the opinion of Wife *Themiftocles*, who on the like occafion preferred an honeft Poor Man, before a Rich vicious Man; in thefe words, *viz. That he had rather Marry his Daughter to a Man without Money, than to Money without a Man.* And much to the fame purpofe was the Anfwer of the Magnanimous *Portia*, Daughter to *Cato*, upon her being demanded when fhe would Marry; faid fhe, *When I find one that feeks my Love more than my Riches*; that is, one that fhe could meet with an equal Paffion.

As for your Behaviour in this cafe, it muft be grave and modeft, though not fowre or too much referved, leaft it be interpred for Pride, or want of difcretion. Blufhes upon fundry occafions are very feemly, which, like moving Oratory, let your Lover know the little flames of Love are playing about your heart, and silently betray your Passion.

A kind of pleasing Love there is; which, though it have taken possession of the heart, is either through modesty, or fear of failing if it were proposed, desirous to be concealed; not but that if these Obstacles were removed, they would freely discover it. And this, Gentlewomen, is on your part, who love those that are ignorant of your Passion; yet did they know it, would be more transported than your selves. And this you strive to express by the silent Language of the Eyes, for Lovers Eyes will talk; nor is it always in their power to keep them from wandring. But in this, as in all the mystery of Love, move with deliberation, and let Caution be the scale of your Affection. Consider your happiness, or its contrary depends upon the cast; and that there are many consequent matters or circumstances that a discreet Woman will not only discourse, but discuss, before she enter upon that Honourable, but hazardous, state of Matrimony: And these chiefly are to be taken notice of, *viz.* Disparity in descent: Fortunes and Friends frequently beget distraction in the mind: Disproportionable years create dislike; and loathing obscurity of Descent begets contempt, and unequality of Fortune discontent.

These

These are the hazards to which unconsidering Lovers expose themselves; these the Rocks on which they shipwrack their peace: And yet herein you ought to be contented, if once it is past redress.

As you ought to be slow in entertaining Lovers, so be constant in retaining one that is worthy, that you may thereby gain a greater esteem. Baost not of the multitude of your Suitors; nor be proud that you are admired above others of your rank and quality. Give not those you cannot fancy ground to believe you do or will love them; neither by rudeness, unseemly words or carriage, any affront, but decline, as much as with modesty and civility you may, their company, giving them as little opportunity as may be to find you alone; nor receive any thing from them by way of Presentation, least when they find they are rejected, they exclaim against you as mercenary, or one that gives way to Courtship for your advantage. Be not covetous of Strangers acquaintance on this occasion, nor rely too much upon a Female-confident, least the one prove troublesome, and the other Pick-locks your Breast of those secrets you are not desirous to publish. Whining and sneaking Pretenders are likewise to be avoided; as also such as strive with Tears and Imprecations to possess you with an opinion of their good meaning. But where Manly beauty, bravery of Spirit, Moderation in Speech, and a greater readiness in performance than in promising are centered in one person, who tempers his Actions with discretion, humility and sobriety, you ought to be complacient; and if such a one fall to your share, imagine your Lot is cast in a fair Land; and till you find such an one, let not your Affections loose, if you can possibly restrain 'em; shun temptations; Avoid, above all things, Ease Idleness, the reading of Debauchery in Books, or too much pampering your self with luscious Fare; for these are Incitements to wanton Love.

Ease makes you Love, as that o're comes you wills;
Ease is the food, and cause of all your Ills.

Gentlewomen, Let me intreat you never to be so desirous of Marriage, as desirous to be Married well, for that is the center to which discretion ought to tend; though some more forward than wise think, if they get a Husband they have their ends, though, by sad experience, they are too frequently convinced of that mistake: And before you enter into this Honourable Estate, lay aside all childish behaviour, wanton fancy, and what

what else is inconsistent with Gravity; and so being happily Married, you may promise your selves many days of pleasure and true felicity. And now the better to encourage such as are cold and reserved, or at least have the subtilty to dissemble it with such coyness, as if Nature had benummed them, and rendered in a manner useless the faculties of life, I shall proceed to say something of the Honourable State of Marriage, *&c.*

CHAP. IX.

A brief Discourse of the Honourable State of Matrimony or Marriage, &c.

THat Marriage was ordained and appointed by God himself, is beyond all peradventure; who in his Eternal Wisdom thinking it not fit for Man to be alone, made him an *Internus sensus*, a second self, to be the sweet co-partner of his pleasure, and companion in the easie labour that was first assigned. A Cabinet in which he might repose his inmost secrets, and be delighted with the last best blessing; nor could he be accounted intirely himself, before this Conjunction,

Junction, which made them still but one flesh; the Wife by every virtuous or honest Husband being to be termed as she was by our grand Parent, *Bone of his bone, and flesh of his flesh.* Nor was it less the care of the Almighty, for two causes, to ordain so near a Union: First, for the increase of Posterity; and secondly, to prevent Lawless Lust, by bounding and bridling the inordinate affections and wandring desires. We find it in the Oeconomy of *Zenophon*, That *Matrimonial Conjunction, even by the Appointment of Nature, is not only the pleasantest, but the profitablest kind of life.*

Wherefore seeing the Estate of Matrimony is the most sure, safe and delightfull station, altogther pleasing to the Almighty, it ought not to be declined. Our Blessed Saviour highly commends it, and expressed his Approbation by working his first Miracle at that of *Canaan* in *Gallalee*; and Saint *Paul* styles a Virtuous Woman *the Crown and Ornament of her Husband*; Commanding him to cherish her. And that this strict Union may have greater force upon eithers mind, he makes the most sacred comparison imaginable; affirming, That *the Husband is the Head of the Wife, as Christ is the Head of the Church.*

In

In this caſe there is comfort in Adverſity, as well as pleaſure in Proſperity ; by ſuch a contexture of Souls, if I may ſo term it, an *Elizium* of Happineſs is created, and, in ſome meaſure, Paradiſe reſtored. Where Virtuous Love unites, what can make a ſeparation? Not the Terrors of Death, nor Hells black Legions by temptation nor affrightment can deſtroy it. Great indeed is the Bleſſing, and more than can well be expreſſed ; in the World there is nothing more beautifull or comfortable ; it is a ſweet Society, full of truſt and unſhaken Loyalty ; A fellowſhip not of unruly and diſtempered Love, but of intire and indeared Affection ; the one being as different from the other, as heat from cold, dryneſs from moiſture, as the inflamed diſorder of a Feavor to the temperate and natural heat of a healthfull body. Wherefore I pronounce thoſe that Marry to their content, and are united in the chaſt Indearments of Reciprocal Love to be truly happy ; the Wife being the Joy of the Huſband, and the Husband the Conſolation of the Wife, who takes care to protect her from Violence and Reproach on all occaſions, and is as tender of her Fame, as his Life : And beſide theſe, this happy ſtate produces a happy Off-ſpring, the pledges of chaſt conubial Love, not only as a preſent bleſſing,

bleſſing, but a comfort and ſupport in old Age. So that whatever by looſe and laſcivious perſons, whoſe debauches have corrupted them beyond recovery, may be ſaid of Marriage, it was and is held both by Chriſtians and Heathens, the conſummation of Earthly felicity. From which I ſhall proceed to the Relation of what is requiſite to be obſerved by a Virtuous Wife towards her Husband, *&c.*

CHAP. X.

Inſtructions for a young Gentlewoman when Married, how to carry and behave her ſelf towards her Husband, &c. *as becomes a Virtuous Wife; or Family-Directions in order to a Happy Life,* &c.

AS Marriage is an Honourable Eſtate, ſo are there many weighty things to be obſerved by thoſe that enter upon it; though Love is the ſupreme matter, yet it ought to be attended with prudence, care and diligence, or elſe it will waſte it ſelf, and totter in its Sphere; and above all things, repine not at your lot when it is

fallen

fallen to your ſhare, but weigh your condition in the ſcale of content and diſcretion, and it will be the better ſupported.

Is your Husband very young, and given to Excurſions incident to youthfull frailty? Let your riper experience bring him to a better underſtanding, and your uſage more eaſie than to attempt by extremities to wean him from what he affects, but rather let your good Example, modeſt Reprovements, and the courſe of time work upon his head-ſtrong nature, and either through ſhame, or a reform of Judgment, he will be brought to be himſelf; for doubtleſs Conjugal duty, tempered with ſoftneſs and affability, is of force to conquer the Moroſeſt temper.

If your Husband be much ſuperiour to you in years, ſo that he is not as complyable as Youth, yet let his years beget in you a greater reverence and reſpect, and let his ſage Inſtructions be your rule, and the ſquare of your Actions, keeping in all things his counſel, and not ſuffering ſo much as an unchaſt thought to defile his bed, locking up his Counſels in your breaſt as a ſacred Cabinet of Truſt, and bear with his infirmities, being in his Age a ſtaff to ſupport him, and a hand of help upon all lawfull occaſions.

If your Husband is exalted in the World by Riches or Honour, let not your mind be be puffed up, nor Pride come near your heart, but be affable, humble, courteous and charitable, which will gain you a name not to be purchased with Treasure; and wink not at your Husbands over-lavish profuseness; nor at his over-penurious or covetous inclination, but mildly admonish him of the ill conveniency and danger of either, that so he may be perswaded to reserve a provident care for his own, and avoid Excess; and on the other hand, enjoy what is fitting, and shun baseness.

Though after Marriage you find your self not so happy in the things of this World, as Riches and Honour, *&c.* as you expected. But that on the contrary you are griped with the pinching hand of Poverty, let the poor condition of your Husband add to your Virtue, in furnishing you with Patience and Meekness; for there is not that dangerous want, some imagine, where there wants no content; and in this by any means cross the unadvised Proverb, of *Loves going out at one door, when Poverty comes in at the other.* And so consequently falling into a cold and Aguish distemper, dies unlamented. And let your Affection contemporize in all Affliction, nor be shaken with the Winds of Adversity, seeing no improsperous affair ought to divide you from him to whom you have vowed

vowed your faith, and unto whom you have individually tied your ſelf.

Theſe things reſolved, and well expoſtulated your Chriſtian conſtancy, will make you fortunate in ſpite of oppoſition; nor will the bitter encounter of unſeaſonable or undue repentance ſtruggle with your mind, or ever prevail againſt your reaſon. In this caſe the Example of ſome Women have been famous.

Sulpitia, the Wife of *Lentulus*, though ſhe might have lived at eaſe, ſold all her Poſſeſſions; ſold all ſhe had, and followed her Husband into Baniſhment; nor could any thing reſtrain the Noble *Ipſicrates* from accompanying her vanquiſhed Husband in all extremities.

Theogena, Wife to *Agotholocles*, voluntarily partaking of her Husband's miſeries, and accompanying him when he was forſaken of all others, generouſly declared, *That ſhe had not only betaken her ſelf to be his Companion in Proſperity, but in all Fortunes which poſſibly might befall him.* Many more I might name, but theſe may ſuffice to a Virtuous mind.

The more particular Duties of a Wife, or rather Obligations of Love to him to whom ſacred ties have bound her, are chiefly theſe: *viz.* To eſteem him above all others, not

to

to entertain any mean or low thoughts of him or his Actions, but in all things to give him a due respect; and in due observance of what is lawfull, strive to increase his repute amongst Men, rather than in the least to diminish it, that in so doing you may own him the superiour Virtue, and not by your indiscretion betray his weakness, or rather your own, for so have the wise and virtuous Woman of all Ages done; and those that do otherwise, are highly to be censured of imprudence.

Be peaceable and pleasant towards your Husband, not being angry when he is at any time so, but pacifie him with winning and obliging words; and if you should carelesly or otherwise raise him to a Passion, be not long e're you apply your self to appease it, by shewing a regret or kind relenting for what has occasioned it, or by sound reason let him understand his error; and prepare for him what is necessary in due order, with all imaginable neatness and advantage; shewing, above all things, respect to his Friends and Relations, whether abroad or at home, which must of necessity create in him a greater portion of love and respect for your self.

Suffer, by no means, your Ears to be penetrated with idle and detracting stories of him in whom you ought to delight, but banish, and detest, against such Makebates whom the power

power of Darkness sets on work, to overthrow your Peace, or to move you to a seperation, which is not lawfull; for *those whom God hath joyned together, let no Man put asunder.* Nor is it less expected, that a Curse will fall on those that attempt it.

As for your Children, bring them up in the fear of God, and in duty and obedience to your selves, that it may be well for them and their posterity, for those are the indearing pledges of Conubial Love, that more nearly cement the hearts of Man and Wife, and are the summ of their Earthly felicity.

Observe that what your Husband commits to your management, let it be done chearfully, carefully and with prudence, to the best advantage, and that nothing be wasted and spoiled to his detriment by your self or Servants; but so live, that the springs of Love, if not of prosperity, may ever flow to water your hearts with joy, and render life comfortable; and you thereby be the better inabled to serve your Maker, and support your selves in what condition soever.

CHAP.

CHAP. XI.

Inſtructions for a Gentlewoman Married; how ſhe ought to carry her ſelf towards her Servants, and in the ordering her Houſhold affairs, &c.

AS a Gentlewomans care, next to that of her Husband and Children, ought to be in the well-government of her domeſtick affairs; that cannot conſequently be done without a due regard in her proper per-[illegible], the ill conveniency of too much confidence in ſecond management, being too frequently apparent: And this muſt be done, beſides what you ſet your helping-hand to, by inſpecting the Actions of your Servants, and by behaving your ſelf towards them as you ought, that your good Example may be their guide.

If you find by experience you have a Servant faithfull and ingenious in her ſtation, give her encouragement by letting her know you are not unſenſible of her induſtry; by which, if ſhe be of a ſweet diſpoſition, you will animate her to proceed with alacrity; though ſome there are, that finding themſelves well accepted, will grow proud and con-

conceited, and imagine they by their service lay such obligations on those they serve, that they cannot conveniently be without them. And in this case too much familiarity will beget contempt, though encouragement, where it is deserved, even on this occasion, ought not altogether to be wanting, but be proportioned to a degree of advantage; not by any means disheartening a good Servant in the performance of her duty, by often finding fault, or being continually over them, but rather bear with light faults, if they be not a means to create greater.

If it be your misfortune to have a bad Servant, whose negligence turns to your displeasure or disadvantage, and no gentle Admonitions and convincing Arguments are of force to reform her: Fret not your self, nor be heard unseemly to exclaim, but rather let her upon fair warning, and such as will stand with your conveniency, take her lot in another place, not disparaging your self to retain from her what is her due, nor giving an ill character of her when she is gone; by which she being rejected as an unfit Servant, may, through necessity, be obliged to take evil courses, and thereby be brought to shame and disgrace.

In this case, and any other, avoid Passion, and be not Rixarius, for either of these ill become

come a Gentlewoman; your main business with your Servants being to see they do what is fitting, and that they lavish not out, nor waste that wherewith you intrust them; for this being neglected, the fault will be charged upon your self.

It is an unbecoming thing in Servants to be affected with flaunting fashions, and gaudy attire, above their degree, and indeed not sutable to their station; and to restrain this, a Mistriss ought to concern her self, yet ever allowing them, and encouraging them to go neat, which will redound to both their credits; for a Maid that goes careless and flutternly in her Attire, cannot be cleanly in her Offices of imployment; nor must a Mistriss by any means confine or restrain her Servants from serving God, but rather dispence with business to give them opportunity; nay, exhort them to return tribute of Praise and Thanksgiving to their Maker for all the benefits they have received at his hands; and see that good hours be kept upon all occasions.

Other things necessary to be observed are, that your Cattel and Poultry are fed in due season, and that your Stables and all other Out-places be kept cleanly, especially your Brew-house and Bake-house, and that nothing therein be wasted or squandered away by the

resort

resort of idle people, that too frequently flatter and wheedle your Servants to your disadvantage. In the Kitchen it is requisite that you see no Necessaries are wanting, nor the seasoning of Meats and other things in due time neglected, least by that defect you happen to be disgraced at your own Table. And further, that the Cloth be laid in due season, whereby there may be no excuse for those that spoil what is provided by over-doing.

The Chamber, above all things, must be kept neat, and the Furniture regarded, that it be not injured by dampness, dust or Moths, considering, as occasion requires, to Air them both by the Fire within, and the Sun without, and cleanse them from dust by beating.

The Celler and Pantry too must be regarded, that in frolicks and extravagant merriments great spoil and waste be not made by Servants and their Visitants; and weekly or monthly take an exact account of what is expended, that so your Expences may be proportioned to your Estate or Income; and in all things carry your self prudently, as becomes the Character of a Gentlewoman and a good Housewife.

FINIS.

Advertisement.

AT *Nicholas Boddington's*, at the Sign of the *Golden Ball* in *Duck-lane*, and *Josiah Blare's* at the *Looking-Glass* on *London-Bridge*; Country-Chapmen, and others, may be furnished with All sorts of Bibles, Testaments, Common Prayer-books, Psalters, Primers, School-books, and other Books, by Wholesail or Retail at very Reasonable Rates.

Mary Collier, ‘THE Woman’s Labour’ pp. 5–17 in *THE Woman’s Labour: AN EPISTLE TO Mr. STEPHEN DUCK; In ANSWER to his late Poem, called THE THRESHER’S LABOUR. To which are added, The Three WISE SENTENCES, TAKEN FROM The First Book of ESDRAS. Ch.III. and IV.* (ESTC T52659) is reproduced, by permission, from the British Library copy (shelfmark 1346.f.17). The text block of the original measures 164 × 87 mm.

THE

Woman's Labour:

AN

EPISTLE

TO

Mr. STEPHEN DUCK;

In ANSWER to his late Poem, called
THE THRESHER'S LABOUR.

To which are added,

The Three WISE SENTENCES,

TAKEN FROM

The Firſt Book of ESDRAS, Ch. III. and IV.

By *MARY COLLIER*,

Now a WASHER-WOMAN, at *Peterſfield* in *Hampſhire*.

LONDON,

Printed for the AUTHOR; and ſold by J. ROBERTS, in *Warwick lane*; and at the Pamphlet Shops near the *Royal Exchange*. 1739.

Price Six-Pence.

BRITISH MUSEUM

ADVERTISEMENT.

IT is thought proper to aſſure the Reader, that the following Verſes are the real Productions of the Perſon to whom the Title-Page aſcribes them.

THO' She pretends not to the Genius of Mr. DUCK, nor hopes to be taken Notice of by the Great, yet her Friends are of Opinion that the Novelty of a *Waſher-Woman*'s turning Poeteſs, will procure her ſome Readers.

IF all that follow the ſame Employment would amuſe themſelves, and one another, during the tedious Hours of their Labour, in this, or ſome other Way as innocent, inſtead of toſſing Scandal to and fro, many Reputations would remain unwounded, and the Peace of Families be leſs diſturb'd.

ADVERTISEMENT.

I THINK it no Reproach to the Author, whoſe Life is toilſome, and her Wages inconſiderable, to confeſs honeſtly, that the View of her putting a ſmall Sum of Money in her Pocket, as well as the Reader's Entertainment, had its Share of Influence upon this Publication. And ſhe humbly hopes ſhe ſhall not be abſolutely diſappointed; ſince, tho' ſhe is ready to own that her Performance could by no Means ſtand a critical Examination, yet ſhe flatters herſelf that, with all its Faults and Imperfections, the candid Reader will judge it to be Something conſiderably beyond the common Capacity of thoſe of her own Rank and Occupation.

M. B.

THE Woman's Labour:

TO Mr. *STEPHEN DUCK*.

IMMORTAL Bard! thou Fav'rite of the Nine!
Enrich'd by Peers, advanc'd by CAROLINE!
Deign to look down on One that's poor and low,
Remembring you yourſelf was lately ſo;
Accept theſe Lines: Alas! what can you have
From her, who ever was, and's ſtill a Slave?

No Learning ever was beſtow'd on me;
My Life was always ſpent in Drudgery:
And not alone; alas! with Grief I find,
It is the Portion of poor Woman-kind.
Oft have I thought as on my Bed I lay,
Eas'd from the tireſome Labours of the Day,
Our firſt Extraction from a Maſs refin'd,
Could never be for Slavery deſign'd;
Till Time and Cuſtom by degrees deſtroy'd
That happy State our Sex at firſt enjoy'd.
When Men had us'd their utmoſt Care and Toil,
Their Recompence was but a Female Smile;
When they by Arts or Arms were render'd Great,
They laid their Trophies at a Woman's Feet;
They, in thoſe Days, unto our Sex did bring
Their Hearts, their All, a Free-will Offering;
And as from us their Being they derive,
They back again ſhould all due Homage give.

JOVE once deſcending from the Clouds, did drop
In Show'rs of Gold on lovely *Danae*'s Lap;

The ſweet-tongu'd Poets, in thoſe generous Days,
Unto our Shrine ſtill offer'd up their Lays:
But now, alas! that Golden Age is paſt,
We are the Objects of your Scorn at laſt.
And you, great Duck, upon whoſe happy Brow
The Muſes ſeem to fix the Garland now,
In your late *Poem* boldly did declare
Alcides' Labours can't with your's compare;
And of your annual Task have much to ſay,
Of Threſhing, Reaping, Mowing Corn and Hay;
Boaſting your daily Toil, and nightly Dream,
But can't conclude your never-dying Theme,
And let our hapleſs Sex in Silence lie
Forgotten, and in dark Oblivion die;
But on our abject State you throw your Scorn,
And Women wrong, your Verſes to adorn.
You of Hay-making ſpeak a Word or two,
As if our Sex but little Work could do:
This makes the honeſt Farmer ſmiling ſay,
He'll ſeek for Women ſtill to make his Hay;
For if his Back be turn'd, their Work they mind
As well as Men, as far as he can find.

For my own-Part, I many a *Summer*'s Day
Have ſpent in throwing, turning, making Hay;
But ne'er could ſee, what you have lately found,
Our Wages paid for ſitting on the Ground.
'Tis true, that when our Morning's Work is done,
And all our Graſs expos'd unto the Sun,
While that his ſcorching Beams do on it ſhine,
As well as you, we have a Time to dine:
I hope, that ſince we freely toil and ſweat
To earn our Bread, you'll give us Time to eat.
That over, ſoon we muſt get up again,
And nimbly turn our Hay upon the Plain;
Nay, rake and prow it in, the Caſe is clear;
Or how ſhould Cocks in equal Rows appear?
But if you'd have what you have wrote believ'd,
I find, that you to hear us talk are griev'd:
In this, I hope, you do not ſpeak your Mind,
For none but *Turks*, that ever I could find,
Have Mutes to ſerve them, or did e'er deny
Their Slaves, at Work, to chat it merrily.
Since you have Liberty to ſpeak your Mind,
And are to talk, as well as we, inclin'd,

Why

Why ſhould you thus repine, becauſe that we,
Like you, enjoy that pleaſing Liberty?
What! would you lord it quite, and take away
The only Privilege our Sex enjoy?

WHEN Ev'ning does approach, we homeward hie,
And our domeſtic Toils inceſſant ply:
Againſt your coming Home prepare to get
Our Work all done, our Houſe in order ſet;
Bacon and *Dumpling* in the Pot we boil,
Our Beds we make, our Swine we feed the while;
Then wait at Door to ſee you coming Home,
And ſet the Table out againſt you come:
Early next Morning we on you attend;
Our Children dreſs and feed, their Cloaths we mend;
And in the Field our daily Task renew,
Soon as the riſing Sun has dry'd the Dew.

WHEN Harveſt comes, into the Field we go,
And help to reap the Wheat as well as you;
Or elſe we go the Ears of Corn to glean;
No Labour ſcorning, be it e'er ſo mean;

But

But in the Work we freely bear a Part,
And what we can, perform with all our Heart.
To get a Living we ſo willing are,
Our tender Babes into the Field we bear,
And wrap them in our Cloaths to keep them warm,
While round about we gather up the Corn;
And often unto them our Courſe do bend,
To keep them ſafe, that nothing them offend:
Our Children that are able, bear a Share
In gleaning Corn, ſuch is our frugal Care.
When Night comes on, unto our Home we go,
Our Corn we carry, and our Infant too;
Weary, alas! but 'tis not worth our while
Once to complain, or *reſt at ev'ry Stile*;
We muſt make haſte, for when we Home are come,
Alas! we find our Work but juſt begun;
So many Things for our Attendance call,
Had we ten Hands, we could employ them all.
Our Children put to Bed, with greateſt Care
We all Things for your coming Home prepare:
You ſup, and go to Bed without delay,
And reſt yourſelves till the enſuing Day;

While

While we, alas! but little Sleep can have,
Becaufe our froward Children cry and rave;
Yet, without fail, foon as Day-light doth fpring,
We in the Field again our Work begin,
And there, with all our Strength, our Toil renew,
Till *Titan*'s golden Rays have dry'd the Dew;
Then home we go unto our Children dear,
Drefs, feed, and bring them to the Field with care.
Were this your Cafe, you juftly might complain
That Day nor Night you are fecure from Pain;
Thofe mighty Troubles which perplex your Mind,
(*Thiftles* before, and *Females* come behind)
Would vanifh foon, and quickly difappear,
Were you, like us, encumber'd thus with Care.
What you would have of us we do not know:
We oft' take up the Corn that you do mow;
We cut the Peas, and always ready are
In ev'ry Work to take our proper Share;
And from the Time that Harveft doth begin,
Until the Corn be cut and carry'd in,
Our Toil and Labour's daily fo extreme,
That we have hardly ever *Time to dream.*

THE Harveſt ended, Reſpite none we find;
The hardeſt of our Toil is ſtill behind:
Hard Labour we moſt chearfully purſue,
And out, abroad, a Charing often go:
Of which I now will briefly tell in part,
What fully to declare is paſt my Art;
So many Hardſhips daily we go through,
I boldly ſay, the like *you* never knew.

WHEN bright *Orion* glitters in the Skies
In *Winter* Nights, then early we muſt riſe;
The Weather ne'er ſo bad, Wind, Rain, or Snow,
Our Work appointed, we muſt riſe and go;
While you on eaſy Beds may lie and ſleep,
Till Light does thro' your Chamber-windows peep.
When to the Houſe we come where we ſhould go,
How to get in, alas! we do not know:
The Maid quite tir'd with Work the Day before,
O'ercome with Sleep; we ſtanding at the Door
Oppreſs'd with Cold, and often call in vain,
E're to our Work we can Admittance gain:

But

But when from Wind and Weather we get in,
Briskly with Courage we our Work begin;
Heaps of fine Linen we before us view,
Whereon to lay our Strength and Patience too;
Cambricks and Muſlins, which our Ladies wear,
Laces and Edgings, coſtly, fine, and rare,
Which muſt be waſh'd with utmoſt Skill and Care;
With Holland Shirts, Ruffles and Fringes too,
Faſhions which our Fore-fathers never knew.
For ſeveral Hours here we work and ſlave,
Before we can one Glimpſe of Day-light have;
We labour hard before the Morning's paſt,
Becauſe we fear the Time runs on too faſt.

At length bright *Sol* illuminates the Skies,
And ſummons drowſy Mortals to ariſe;
Then comes our Miſtreſs to us without fail,
And in her Hand, *perhaps*, a Mug of Ale
To cheer our Hearts, and alſo to inform
Herſelf, what Work is done that very Morn;
Lays her Commands upon us, that we mind
Her Linen well, nor *leave the Dirt behind*:

Not this alone, but alſo to take care
We don't her Cambricks nor her Ruffles tear;
And *theſe* moſt ſtrictly does of us require,
To ſave her Soap, and ſparing be of Fire;
Tells us her Charge is great, nay furthermore,
Her Cloaths are fewer than the Time before.
Now we drive on, reſolv'd our Strength to try,
And what we can, we do moſt willingly;
Until with Heat and Work, 'tis often known,
Not only Sweat, but Blood runs trickling down
Our Wriſts and Fingers; ſtill our Work demands
The conſtant Action of our lab'ring Hands.

Now Night comes on, from whence you have Relief,
But that, alas! does but increaſe our Grief;
With heavy Hearts we often view the Sun,
Fearing he'll ſet before our Work is done;
For either in the Morning, or at Night,
We piece the *Summer*'s Day with Candle-light.
Tho' we all Day with Care our Work attend,
Such is our Fate, we know not when 'twill end:

When Ev'ning's come, you Homeward take your Way,
We, till our Work is done, are forc'd to ſtay;
And after all our Toil and Labour paſt,
Six-pence or Eight-pence pays us off at laſt;
For all our Pains, no Proſpect can we ſee
Attend us, but *Old Age* and *Poverty*.

THE *Waſhing* is not all we have to do:
We oft change Work for Work as well as you.
Our Miſtreſs of her Pewter doth complain,
And 'tis our Part to make it clean again.
This Work, tho' very hard and tireſome too,
Is not the worſt we hapleſs Females do:
When Night comes on, and we quite weary are,
We ſcarce can count what falls unto our Share;
Pots, Kettles, Sauce-pans, Skillets, we may ſee,
Skimmers and Ladles, and ſuch Trumpery,
Brought in to make complete our Slavery.
Tho' early in the Morning 'tis begun,
'Tis often very late before we've done;
Alas! our Labours never know an End;
On Braſs and Iron we our Strength muſt ſpend;

Our tender Hands and Fingers ſcratch and tear:
All this, and more, with Patience we muſt bear.
Colour'd with Dirt and Filth we now appear;
Your threſhing *ſooty Peas* will not come near.
All the Perfections Woman once could boaſt,
Are quite obſcur'd, and altogether loſt.

Once more our Miſtreſs ſends to let us know
She wants our Help, becauſe the Beer runs low:
Then in much haſte for Brewing we prepare,
The Veſſels clean, and ſcald with greateſt Care;
Often at Midnight, from our Bed we riſe
At other Times, ev'n *that* will not ſuffice;
Our Work at Ev'ning oft we do begin,
And 'ere we've done, the Night comes on again.
Water we pump, the Copper we muſt fill,
Or tend the Fire; for if we e'er ſtand ſtill,
Like you, when threſhing, we a Watch muſt keep,
Our Wort boils over if we dare to ſleep.

But to rehearſe all Labour is in vain,
Of which we very juſtly might complain:

For

For us, you see, but little Rest is found;
Our Toil increases as the Year runs round.
While you to *Sysiphus* yourselves compare,
With *Danaus' Daughters* we may claim a Share;
For while *he* labours hard against the Hill,
Bottomless Tubs of Water *they* must fill.

So the industrious Bees do hourly strive
To bring their Loads of Honey to the Hive;
Their sordid Owners always reap the Gains,
And poorly recompense their Toil and Pains.

Eliza Fowler Haywood, *A PRESENT FOR A Servant-Maid* (ESTC TI98873) is reproduced by permission from the New York Public Library microfilm (shelfmark *ZZ-16340; the copy of the book [shelfmark VSC (Haywood, E. F. Present for a servant-maid)] is missing from the shelf). The text block of the original measures 160 mm × 85 mm.

Words that are blotted in the original:
19.33: all
19.34: upper
23.22: so ;

A PRESENT FOR A Servant-Maid.

OR, THE

Sure Means of gaining LOVE and ESTEEM.

Under the following Heads:

Obſervance.
Avoiding Sloth.
Sluttiſhneſs.
Staying on Errands.
Telling Family Affairs.
Secrets among Fellow-Servants.
Entring into their Quarrels.
Tale-bearing.
Being an Eye-Servant.
Careleſneſs of Children.
Of Fire, Candle, Thieves.
New Acquaintance.
Fortune-Tellers.
Giving ſaucy Anſwers.
Liquoriſhneſs.
Apeing the Faſhion.
Diſhoneſty.
The Market Penny.
Delaying to give Change.
Giving away Victuals.
Bringing in Chair-women.
Waſting Victuals.
Quarrels with Fellow-Servants.
Behaviour to the Sick.
Hearing Things againſt a Maſter or Miſtreſs.
Being too free with Men-Servants.
Conduct towards Apprentices.
Miſpending Time.
Publick Shews.
Vails.
Giving Advice too freely.
Chaſtity,
Temptations from the Maſter.
If a ſingle Man.
If a married Man.
If from the Maſter's Son.
If from Gentlemen Lodgers.

To which are added,

DIRECTIONS for going to MARKET:

ALSO,

For *Dreſſing* any *Common Diſh*, whether FLESH, FISH or FOWL.

With ſome *Rules* for WASHING, *&c.*

The whole calculated for making both the Miſtreſs *and the* Maid *happy.*

DUBLIN:

Re-printed by and for GEORGE FAULKNER, 1743.

THE NEW YORK
PUBLIC LIBRARY
ASTOR, LENOX AND
TILDEN FOUNDATIONS.
R 1901 L.

PREFACE.

IT is not to be wondered at, that in an Age abounding with Luxury, and over-run with Pride, Servants ſhould be in general ſo bad, that it is become one of our Calamities not to be able to live without them: Corruption, tho' it begins at the Head, ceaſes not its Progreſs till it reaches the moſt inferior Parts, and it is high Time to endeavour a Cure of ſo growing an Evil. I am certain no Undertaking whatever can be more uſeful to the Publick, and I flatter myſelf will meet with greater Encouragement. A due Obſervance of the Rules contained in this little Treatiſe, cannot fail of making every Miſtreſs *of a Family perfectly contented, and every* Servant-Maid *both happy and beloved; and I hope whoever of the latter ſhall read what I have ſet down, will find it ſo much her Intereſt, as well as her Duty, to behave in a contrary Manner from what too many for ſome Years have done; that ſhe will make it her whole Study to avoid the Errors ſhe may ſee in others, and reform ſuch as ſhe has been guilty of herſelf. This is the ſole End propoſed by the Publication of theſe Sheets, and if the Attempt ſucceeds, I ſhall think my Labour well beſtowed.*

CON-

CONTENTS.

A PRESENT FOR A Servant-Maid.

Dear Girls,

Introduction.] I Think there cannot be a greater Service done to the Commonwealth, (of which you are a numerous Body) than to lay down some general Rules for your Behaviour, which, if observed, will make your Condition as happy to yourselves as it is necessary to others. Nothing can be more melancholly, than to hear continual Complaints for Faults which a very little Reflection would render it almost as easy for you to avoid as to commit; most of the Mistakes laid to your Charge proceeding at first only from a certain Indolence and Inactivity of the Mind, but if not rectified in time, become habitual, and difficult to be thrown off.

Caution against bad Houses.] As the first Step therefore towards being happy in Service, you should never enter into a Place, but with a View of *staying in it*; to which End I think it highly necessary, that (as no Mistress worth serving will take you without a Character) you should also make some Enquiry into the Place before you suffer yourself to be hired.

 There

There are ſome Houſes which appear well by *Day*, that it would be little ſafe for a modeſt Maid to ſleep in at *Night*: I do not mean thoſe Coffee-Houſes, Bagnio's, *&c.* which ſome Parts of the Town, particularly *Covent-Garden*, abounds with; for in thoſe the very Aſpect of the Perſons who keep them are ſufficient to ſhew what manner of Trade they follow; but Houſes which have no public Shew of Buſineſs, are richly furniſhed, and where the Miſtreſs has an Air of the ſtricteſt Modeſty, and perhaps affects a double Purity of Behaviour: Yet under ſuch Roofs, and under the Sanction of ſuch Women as I have deſcribed, are too frequently acted ſuch Scenes of Debauchery as would ſtartle even the Owners of ſome common Brothels. Great Regard is therefore to be had to the Character of the Perſons who recommend you, and the manner in which you heard of the Place; for thoſe Sort of People have commonly their Emiſſaries at Inns, watching the coming in of the Waggons, and, if they find any pretty Girls who come to Town to go to Service, preſently hire them in the Name of ſome Perſon of Condition, and by this means the innocent young Creature, while ſhe thanks God for her good Fortune, in being ſo immediately provided for, is enſnared into the Service of the *Devil.* Here Temptations of all Kinds are offered her; ſhe is not treated as a Servant but a Gueſt; her Country Habit is immediately ſtripped off, and a gay modiſh one put on in the Stead; and then the deſigned Victim, willing or unwilling, is expoſed to Sale to the firſt leud Supporter of her Miſtreſs's Grandeur that comes to the Houſe: If ſhe refuſes the ſhameful Buſineſs for which ſhe was hired, and prefers the Preſervation of her Virtue to all the Promiſes can be made her, which way can ſhe eſcape?

She

She is immediately confined, close watched, threatened, and at last forced to Compliance. Then by a continued Prostitution withered in her Bloom, she becomes despised, no longer affords any Advantage to the Wretch who betrayed her, and is turned out to Infamy and Beggary, perhaps too with the most loathsome of all Diseases, which ends her miserable Days in an Hospital or Work-House, in case she can be admitted, tho' some have not had even that Favour, but found their Death-bed on a Dunghill.

Nor are these Artifices confined to Country Girls alone, those cunning wicked ones have their Spies in every Corner of the Town, who lie in wait to intrap the Innocent and Unwary; it behoves you therefore to know very well, for what, and to whom you hire yourself, and be satisfied, at least, that it is for honest Purposes, and that the Persons you serve are People of Reputation.

An honest Service a great Blessing.] Having given you this necessary Caution, I must also remind you, that you ought to rejoice when received into an House, which to be seen in can call no Blush in your Face; and as there is no perfect Happiness in this World, even in the highest Stations, much less ought you to expect to *find* every Thing exactly to your Mind, but to resolve to *make* every thing so, as much as possible; and not say as some of you are apt to do, *There are more Places than Parish Churches*, and on the least Occasion presently give Warning. Those who speak or act in this manner will scarce succeed in any Service; they will be continually roaming from House to House, oftener out of Place than in, without Character, without Money, without Friends or Support, in case of Sickness or any other Exigence, all which, those who have lived any time in a Family have a Right to demand. If therefore you would seriously consider the Miseries that threaten you on the one Hand, and the certain Advantages which offer to you on the other, none of you would have any Disposition to change; but on the contrary, endeavour to avoid doing any thing that might occasion your being turned away.

I know there are People of very odd Humours in the World, but then those Humours have all of them a certain way of being soothed; which if you hit, as a little Attention will teach you how to do, you will find more Kindness from those very Persons, than you might from others of a more even Temper.

Studying to give Content.] Possessed with a strong Desire of pleasing, you will rarely fail of doing it; a good Temper will be charmed with your Readiness, and a bad one disarmed of great Part of its Harshness; and tho' you should be a little awkward in Things you are employed in, when they see it is not occasioned by Obstinacy or Indolence, they will rather instruct you in what they find you ignorant, than be angry that you are so. Whereas if you really perform all the Duties of a Servant with the utmost Exactness, yet if you seem careless whether what you do is agreeable or not, your Services will lose great Part of their Merit. Their manner of doing any thing is as much to be regarded as the thing itself; and because the Humours of People are vastly different, it is your Interest to study by what Sort of Behaviour you can most ingratiate yourself, as the Scripture says, *The Eye of the Handmaid looks up to her Mistress,* so you ought diligently to observe not only what she *says*, but also how she *looks*, in order to give Content. On this you may depend, that if you are fearful of offending, you can scarce offend at all; because that very Timidity is an Indication of your Respect for those you serve, and a real Ambition

bition of deserving their Approbation, than which there is nothing more engaging.

Sloth.] One of the greatest Impediments to the Practice of this Lesson is *Sloth*; which tho' it proceeds at first from a Heaviness in the Blood, and is no more than a Distemper, if indulged grows up into a Vice, and renders you incapable of doing your Duty either to GOD or Man: The *Roman Catholicks* place it among the Number of the deadly Sins, and can really give a better Reason for so doing than for most of their other Tenets; for it is, as I may say, the principal Source of all the Evils a Person in any Station can be guilty of, but more especially in yours. *Sloth* occasions a falling off from every thing that is commendable, and a general Defection of the Animal Spirits; so that you become unable as well as unwilling to perform even what would otherwise be most pleasing to you. Take care, therefore, how you give way to the Love of Idleness, or too much Sleep, both which dull the Spirits, and fill the Body full of gross Humours; you should therefore make use of your utmost Endeavours against these potent Enemies of your Health, your Happiness, your Virtue. There are many *Recipes* in Physic for this Evil, but, believe me, the best Prescription is a willing Mind. Whenever you find yourself inclined to sleep beyond those Hours which Nature requires, rise, tho' it be before the time expected from you: Make Business for yourself if you can find none, and stir nimbly about till the Fit is entirely gone off. This Method frequently practised will wear off in time, whatever Sluggishness you may have from Constitution or Custom, and render you strong and lively.

Temperance in Eating and Drinking.] I must also add, that *Temperance* in Eating and Drinking is very conducive to this End: You should remember you do not *live to eat*, *but eat to live*; and whatever goes down your Throats beyond what is requisite for that Purpose, only engenders Crudities, which naturally occasion *Sloth*: Neither should you sit too long at Meals. It is an old, but very true Saying, *Quick at Meat, quick at Work*, and nothing is more unbecoming in a young Person, especially a Servant, whose Time is not her own, than to indulge herself in this. The Affectation of following your Mistress's Example, has corrupted but too many of you; you imagine it shews a Delicacy, and looks pretty in you, to be able to breakfast on nothing but Tea and Coffee, whereas both these Liquors, especially the former, diminish your Strength, waste your Time, and, for the most part, draw on a more pernicious Consequence, which is Dram-drinking. I have known several who have loathed the very Smell of any spirituous Liquor, become at last to love them to their Ruin, meerly by drinking of Tea, which, by too much cooling and weakening the Stomach, seems to render it necessary to have something warm. You begin with a little, and think you will never exceed a certain Bound, but by degrees increase the Proportion; you crave still for more, till by frequent Use it becomes too habitual to be refrained. The Consequences of these intoxicating Spirits, none of you but have Sense enough to see, if you would give yourselves the Trouble of considering, and the horrible Objects which the Streets every Day afford you, methinks, should make it impossible for you not to do so.

Sluttishness.] The constant Attendant on Sloth is *Sluttishness*: She who gives her Mind to Idleness, can neither be thoroughly clean in her own Person nor the House; and tho' her Pride may sometimes force her to prink herself up when she is to go A-

broad,

broad, or her Fear of being turned away make her keep those Rooms in order, in which her Neglect, if otherwise, would be most conspicuous; yet all her Neatness will be out-side; there will always be some dirty thing about the one, and some unswept Corners in the other. Sloth suggests to you, that *this*, or *that*, will not be taken notice of, and you may sit still and indulge yourself a little, and work the harder for it next Day; but, when the next Day comes, you are as unwilling as before, and by putting off your Business, make it become too heavy for you to go through, even tho' you had the best Inclination; and every thing infallibly shews the Slut, than which there cannot be a more scandalous Character, or that will more effectually disqualify you for any good Service.

But tho' Cleanliness in your own Person, and the Goods committed to your Charge, be highly commendable, yet it is more especially so in dressing of Victuals. To see any thing nasty about what is to go into the Mouth, creates a Loathing, even in those who are the least nice in other Particulars. All the Utensils in the Kitchen, therefore, ought to be kept free from any kind of Dirt, or Rust, and your Hands very well washed, and your Nails close pared, before you touch the Meat: For this Reason it is very odious for Servants to use themselves to the taking of Snuff. The most careful cannot answer that what they are dressing may not be spiced with some of this Powder, which is so fine grounded, especially that which they call *Scotch* or *Spanish*, that in the very opening the Box that contains it, you may see the Dust fly out. As the taking it is nothing but a Custom, and a very bad one too, because it clogs both the Brain and the Passages to the Stomach, soils the Linnen and the Skin, indulges Sloth, and is some Expence, tho' a small one, without any one good Property to attone for all these Inconveniencies, I would advise you by all means to refrain it.

Staying when sent on Errands.] Another very great Fault I have observed in many of you, which, if not proceeding always from downright Sloth, does from something so like it, that the Effect is scarce to be distinguished from the Cause: It shews at least a *Sloth of the Mind*, a Want of Diligence, a Carelesness of pleasing, which, as I have already said, is the Source of almost all the Faults you can be guilty of; and this is staying when you are sent on an Errand; a Croud gathered about a Pick-pocket, a Pedlar, a Mountebank, or a Ballad-singer, has the Power to detain too many of you, tho' when sent on the most important Business to those you serve; and which, perhaps, may greatly suffer by a Moment's Delay. How cruel, therefore, how unjust is it to sacrifice to a little impertinent Curiosity, the Interest of those who give you Bread! But supposing the Affair you go upon is in itself immaterial, it is not so to those who send you: No Body sends for any thing they do not want, nor on any Message which they would not have immediately delivered; and the Suspence they are in while waiting beyond the Time they might expect you back, creates an Uneasiness of Mind which no considerate Person would give to any one, much less to a Master or Mistress. Sometimes, perhaps, you have the Excuse of meeting an Acquaintance, a Friend, or one who knows the Family you lived in before, and has a thousand Things to tell you concerning what happened since you went away, and what is said of yourself; but you ought to remember, that no Intelligence that detains you from your Business can be worth your while to hear, or an Equivalent for disobliging those you

you serve; and that none are truly your Friends that would hold you by the Ears with an idle Story: for while you are in the Condition of a Servant, your Time belongs to those who pay you for it; and all you waste from the Employment they set you about, is a Robbery from them.

Telling the Affairs of the Family.] But infinitely worse is it when you suffer yourselves to be detained in order to discover the Affairs of the Family where you live. The smallest and most trivial Action *there* should never escape your Lips, because you cannot be a Judge what are really such, and what are the contrary. Things that may seem to you Matters of perfect Indifference, may happen to prove of great Importance to those concerned in them, and sometimes a single Word, inadvertently let fall, may so coincide with what has been said by others, as to give room to prying People for Conjectures which you are not aware of. Neither is it sufficient you inviolably preserve what Secrets are intrusted to you, to maintain your Character of Fidelity; if you are found guilty of blabbing small Things, you will be suspected of not being more retentive in greater; so that as what you can say can be of no Service to yourselves, and may be of Prejudice to those you live with, I would advise you to be extremely circumspect how you mention either their Humour, Circumstances, or Behaviour.

Speaking of your Fellow Servants.] It will be likewise prudent in you to be as silent in what relates to your Fellow Servants, if you have any: If they are good, they stand in no Need of any thing you can say; and if bad, it is not your Business to search into their Faults, for Fear of provoking them to be on the Watch for yours, and even laying those to your Charge of which you may be perfectly Innocent: Indeed,

Indeed, if you find them guilty of any flagrant Injustice, such as may touch the Life or Property of your Master or Mistress, to conceal it from them would be no less than to partake of their Crime; but you must be well assured of this before you venture to speak; say nothing on Surmise, for to give even the least Hint of what you cannot prove, will make you be looked upon only as an Incendiary and an envious Person, and excite the Hatred of the whole Family.

Secrets among Fellow-Servants.] Neither would I have you be desirous of being trusted with the Secrets of your Fellow-Servants: You can gain nothing by the Confidence of such as they, and when any two are observed to be continually whispering, it not only raises a Jealousy in the rest, but also is apt to give your Master and Mistress a Suspicion that you are carrying on something to their Detriment.

Entering into their Quarrels.] Nothing can lay you more open to Ill-will than interfering in any Dispute among them; by so doing, you are sure to incur the Displeasure of one Party, and often of *both*, when the Quarrel being made up, it shall be discovered what Hand you had in it.

Tale-bearing.] Much less ought you to report every little Word you hear among them. Many Things, if heard out of the Mouth that first speaks them, would be wholly inoffensive, carry a stronger Meaning when repeated by another: Besides, those who cannot help telling all they hear, are very apt to tell more than they hear; and even tho' they do not, are suspected of it. Neither ought you to meddle with what is not properly your Province. In a Family where there are several Servants, each has her Business assigned, and it is sufficient for you, that you do your own; when others neglect theirs, leave to those to whom it belongs to find out and blame it; by by this Means you will preſerve Peace, and acquire the Love of all of them, without running any Danger of diſobliging your Maſter and Miſtreſs, who, whatever Uſe they may make of the Tales you bring, will not in their Hearts approve ſuch a Propenſity in you.

Being an Eye Servant.] I would alſo warn you againſt being what they call an Eye Servant. To appear diligent in Sight, and be found neglectful when out of it, ſhew you both deceitful and lazy, and when once diſcovered to be ſo, as this is a Fault cannot be long concealed, how irkſome will it be to you to hear the juſt Reproaches made you on this Score, and to be watched and followed in every Thing you do, and how great a Trouble muſt you give your Miſtreſs in forcing her to it! People, who keep Servants, keep them for their Eaſe, not to increaſe their Care; and nothing can be more cruel, as well as more unjuſt, than to diſappoint them in a View they have ſo much Right to expect. The taking any Liberties when your Maſter and Miſtreſs are abroad, which are not allowed you when they are at home, comes alſo under this Head; and however innocent you may think them, or they in Reality may be in themſelves, are ſtill a Breach of Duty which you ought by no means to be guilty of. To avoid all Miſtakes of this Kind, it would be well for you to calculate the firſt Thing you do in the Morning (after having ſaid your Prayers) the Buſineſs of the Day, and contrive it ſo as it may come within as little Compaſs of Time as poſſible, and then go chearfully about it, without taking Notice whether you are obſerved or not. Contrivance is half Work they ſay, and I am certain you will find it ſo; every Thing will go eaſily and ſmoothly on, and no Miſtreſs but will look on ſuch a Servant as a Jewel, when ſhe finds

that

that waking or ſleeping, abroad or at home; ſhe may depend on her Buſineſs being regularly done.

Careleſsneſs of Children.] There is no Negligence you can be guilty of leſs pardonable than that concerning Children committed to your Charge. If you happen to live in a Family where the Miſtreſs either ſuckles, or brings an Infant up by Hand at home, Part of the Duty of a Nurſe will fall to your Share; and to uſe the little Innocent with any Harſhneſs, or omit giving it Food, or any other neceſſary Attendance, is a Barbarity which nothing can excuſe. It was by Diligence and Tenderneſs you yourſelves were reared to what you are; and it is by the ſame Diſpotions you muſt bring up your own Children when you come to have them. Practice, therefore, if it falls in your way, thoſe Leſſons, which it will behove you to be perfect in when you come to be Mothers; but above all Things be careful, whether the Child be yet in Arms, or goes in Leading Strings, that it gets no Falls; and as ſuch Accidents may ſometimes happen in ſpite of the greateſt Caution in the World, never let your Fear of offending prevail on you to conceal it: Do not, becauſe perhaps you may ſee no outward Scarification, aſſure yourſelves there is no Harm done: Internal Damages are of the worſt Conſequence: A Bone may be ſlipt which you do not perceive, and which if not timely rectified, can no way afterwards be ſet to rights. You muſt not defer diſcovering what has happened one Moment; but if your Miſtreſs is abſent, run immediately to ſome ſkilful Perſon, and have the Infant examined. Reflect within yourſelves how great a Shock it would be to you, to find, when it was too late for Remedy, that a Child, committed to your Care, ſhould be lame, crook-back'd, or have any other perſonal Defect entailed on it for Life, merely through your Neglect.

gleƈt. Nature makes few Miſtakes, and I dare anſwer, that of the many unhappy Objeƈts we ſee of this Kind, Ninety nine in a Hundred owe their Miſfortune to the Diſingenuity of thoſe who attended them in their Infancy. The eldeſt Son of an Alderman in the City, with whom I am well acquainted, by a Fall his Nurſe had as ſhe was carrying him down Stairs, had his Back-bone broke at ſix Weeks old: The poor Woman preſently undreſt and examined him according to the beſt of her Judgment; but perceiving nothing appear outwardly, imagined no Hurt had come to him. The Misfortune diſcovered not itſelf till ſome Weeks after, when perceiving that he had no other Strength in his Back than what the Stays afforded him, and that when naked, he fell quite forward, a Surgeon was ſent for, who preſently found the Truth; but there was in Art no Proſpeƈt of Relief: The afflicted Parents ſpared no Coſt for that Purpoſe, but all in vain; and the young Gentleman could never walk without a Crutch under each Arm. I know a Gentleman alſo, whoſe little Daughter of much the ſame Age, and by a Fall of the like Nature, had one Arm and one Leg broke, which, by not being ſet in Time, could never after be repaired; and ſhe has no Uſe, nor ever can have, of either of thoſe Limbs: Another being let fall, had both her Knee-pans ſlipt, and never knew the Pleaſure of walking; but to the Day of her Death (and ſhe lived to be upwards of Twenty) was obliged to be carried wherever ſhe went, in a Footman's Arms. How melancholly a Thing was this, for a fine young Lady to be deprived of all the Pleaſures, all the Advantages of her Rank and Age, and not to be able to taſte in Youth thoſe Satisfaƈtions which Age regrets the Loſs of; yet how much more unhappy would it have been, how would the Misfortune

tune have been doubled, had it befallen a Person whose Parents had it not in their Power to bequeath her a handsome Subsistance. Cripple as she was, she must then have been obliged to the Hospital, or Work-house, for a wretched Support. Consider, therefore, how miserable you must have been, had any such Accident rendered you incapable of getting your Bread; and let no false Modesty, or unseasonable Timidity, make you ashamed or afraid of revealing any thing of this Nature: You may, perhaps, receive a little hasty Word at first, but your Integrity and Good-will for the Child will afterward be praised, and you will besides enjoy the innate Satisfaction of having discharg'd your Duty.

Fire, Candle.] There are also some other Things in which it will become you to be extremely cautious. Most of the dreadful Accidents which have happened through Fire, have been occasioned by the too little Circumspection of Servants: I once lived in a House, which, but by the strangest Providence in the World, must infallibly have been consumed, and probably many others with it, by the Maid taking the Cinders off the Kitchen Fire, and putting them into a Coal Scuttle, which she set under the Dresser, and then went up Stairs to Bed. One of the Family happening to be taken ill in the Night, ran down for some Water, and found the Dresser and Shelves over it in a Blaze: On this timely Discovery an Alarm was given, and proper Methods being immediately taken, the Fire was happily extinguished, which, had it continued but a very small Time longer, wou'd have reach'd the main Beam of the House, all had been in Flames, and the Means perhaps never guess'd at by the unhappy Sufferers. Innumerable have been the Mischiefs that have been done by the Servants letting a Candle burn after they

are

are in Bed, and even by ſnuffing it among Linnen, Paper, or Shavings: A Spark flying off, and happening to fall on ſome very dry thing, has often proved of the moſt dreadful Conſequence, and there cannot be too much Caution uſed in this Particular; and I wou'd recommend it to you to ſee every thing of Fire utterly extinguiſhed before you venture to lie down to ſleep.

Thieves.] Neither is it enough that you are careful in barring all the Doors and Windows to guard againſt the Houſe being robb'd: The Night is not the only Seaſon in which thoſe Invaders of the Properties of others are in Search for Prey. Experience teaches us, that the Day has ſometimes been no leſs favourable to them: The Vizard and the formidable dark Lanthorn they have then indeed no Occaſion for; but by appearing leſs themſelves, are not the leſs dangerous. It is not then their Buſineſs to affright, but to deceive; and ſo many Stratagems they abound with for compaſſing this End, that you cannot be too much warn'd againſt them. Where Lodgings are to be let, they frequently watch an Opportunity of the Family being gone abroad, and under the Pretence of ſeeing ſome Apartment, get Entrance, bind, gag, or perhaps murder the Maid, and plunder the Houſe of every Thing valuable in it. On Sundays, in the Time of Divine Service, when the Family are at Church, it is very dangerous to open the Door to any one that knocks, eſpecially in Squares, or Streets where many People are not continually paſſing, or ſitting at Doors or Windows, as they are apt to do in little Lanes and Courts: I would therefore adviſe you to anſwer all Strangers that ſhall come at that Time, from an upper Window; for ſeveral Houſes have been robb'd by the Inadvertency of a Servant, who, on opening the Door,

Door, has given Admittance to Villains in the Shape of Gentlemen. It would not be only endless, but likewise impossible to recount the various Stratagems they put in Practice; I shall therefore content myself with reminding you, to let no Person, who is not perfectly known to you, into the House, either when you are alone in it, or early in the Morning before the Family is up: They have come sometimes as Footmen, with a Message from some Person, whose Name they make use of as a Sanction: Sometimes as Porters with a Basket from an Inn, with a Present from the Country: Sometimes as a Neighbour's Servant, (especially if you are lately come, and unacquainted) desiring Leave to light a Candle; but whatever their Pretences be, let them wait; better to seem unmannerly, than by your Carelessness expose your Master and Mistress to be robb'd, and yourself murder'd. There are your little Pilferers too, no less impudent nor artful than those who rob by wholesale, who watch the Opportunity of a Sash being up in a Parlour Window, to snatch out any Thing within their Reach; and some of them have long Sticks with Hooks, which will easily bring out a Cloak, Hat, or any other Thing that happens to hang up. Some of these have had the Boldness to knock, and ask to speak with the Mistress of the Family, when they have seen she has been in an upper Room, and on being ask'd to walk into the Parlour, and left alone while the Maid goes up to inform her Mistress, have swept away whatever the Beaufet afforded; so that on no Account, nor at any Time, can you safely give Entrance to one you know not.

New Acquaintance.] To be easily drawn into a Familiarity with Persons who scrape Acquaintance with you, is often of ill Consequence both to your-

selves

ſelves and thoſe you live with. Particularly thoſe you will frequently meet with at Chandler's Shops, and at ſome Markets, where there are always idle People hanging about, who will in a Manner force themſelves upon you, aſk you a Thouſand Queſtions about your Place, tell you that you deſerve a better, and that if you ſhould go away, they can recommend you where you will have more Wages and leſs Work, be very officious in offering to carry any Thing for you, and omit nothing that may make you think they have taken a great Fancy to you, in order that you may aſk them to come to ſee you, when your Maſter and Miſtreſs are abroad. Theſe are a Sort of Sharpers of your own Sex, but not a whit leſs dangerous than thoſe of the other, as many of you, who have been unwarily drawn in by them, have ſadly experienced.

Liſtening to Fortune-tellers.] Telling of Fortunes has been one of the Pretences the Wretches abovementioned have found very ſucceſsful for the bringing about their wicked Deſigns; by no means, therefore, give way to any Inſinuations of that Sort; I know no Path that more readily leads to Deſtruction: Like *Macbeth* in the Play, who, by being told he ſhould be a King, became guilty of all manner of Villainies to make himſelf ſo. There is no Vice whatever, but you may fall an eaſy Prey to, if you are once made to believe it is your *Fate*, and that tho' you ſhould ſtrive againſt it never ſo much, it is unavoidable; and I believe as many Girls have been corrupted by this one Artifice, as by a Thouſand others. But ſuppoſing no Efforts are made on your own Honeſty this Way, nor you ſhould even ſuffer by their Want of it, whom you thus imprudently introduce, you at leaſt miſpend your Time, and have your Head filled with a thouſand vain Imaginations, magınations, which render you thoughtleſs and forgetful of what is really your Intereſt; and if no worſe comes of it, (as is ſeldom the Caſe) that of itſelf is bad enough.

Folly of it.] It muſt be confeſſed a Deſire of prying into future Events is very much ingrafted in human Nature, eſpecially in your Sex; yet ſure nothing can be more ſilly than an Endeavour to penetrate into them by looking into a Cup, as if the Decrees of Heaven were written in the Grounds of Coffee, and intelligible to ſuch poor ignorant Wretches as thoſe who make a Practice of this pretended Art. It is no Excuſe for you, that you ſee your Betters ſometimes guilty of this Weakneſs; you are not to imitate them in their Errors: Beſides, what they do of this Kind is only for Amuſement; they cannot but have more Senſe than to place any Dependance on the abſurd things foretold them by theſe People, nor can run the Hazards you do by bringing them into the Houſe, where, when you happen to be called away, they are often left alone in a Room, and, as I ſaid before, 'tis great Odds if they do not make uſe of that Opportunity to pilfer ſomething, for which afterwards you will have the Blame. Tho' I have only mentioned the Prognoſticators in Coffee-grounds, the Calculators of Nativity, Reſolvers of Horory Queſtions, Palmiſtry, Geomancy-mongers, Card-cutters, Gipſies, and all the other Pretenders to Divination, come under the ſame Head, and are in general to be diſcouraged and avoided by all diſcreet and honeſt Servants.

Lying.] But there is ſcarce any one Thing I would more ſtrenuouſly recommend to you than ſpeaking the exact Truth: If at any Time tax'd with a Fault which you are conſcious of being guilty of, never attempt to ſcreen it with a Lye; For the laſt Fault is an an Addition to the former, and renders it more inexcusable: To acknowledge you have been to blame is the surest Way both to merit and obtain Forgiveness, and establishes an Opinion that you will be careful to avoid the like Trespass for the future. Whereas, if you are once detected in a Lye, you will never after be believed; and though wrongfully accused, all your Protestations of Innocence go for nothing. Some have by Nature so strong a Propensity to this Vice, that they cannot refrain it in the most trivial Concerns, and even where speaking the Truth would be of equal, if not more Advantage. But this is a most dangerous Habitude; for supposing that either through your own artful Manner of delivering what you say, or the easy Credulity of those you impose upon, whatever you alledge for a long time should gain Belief, and repeated Falshoods be looked upon as sacred Truths, the Success might be of worse Consequence to you than the Detection: Emboldened by having never yet been found out, you might be lulled into a fatal Security that you never should be so; and in that Confidence venture to be guilty of Things which no Invention or Dissimulation would have the Power to screen, and an Attempt of that kind only add greater Weight to the Crime, and Shame to the Aggressor. So that to indulge it on any Motive, or in any Shape, is not only base to others, but pernicious to yourselves.

Giving pert or saucy Answers.] It is also very becoming in you to be modest and humble in your Deportment, never pretending to argue the Case, even tho' your Mistress should be angry without a Cause, *A soft Answer puts away Wrath*, says *Solomon*. And if she is a discreet Woman she will reflect after her Passion is over, and use you the more kindly; whereas going about to defend yourself by a saucy Reply,

 gives

gives her a real Occasion of Offence, justifies her ill Humour, and perhaps will be more severely resented by her than the Fault she accused you of would be, had you been guilty of it.

Liquorishness.] As small Errors frequently lead on to greater, there are two things I would advise you not to give way to: The first is a Desire or Craving after Dainties, by which I mean such Things as either are not in the House, or are not allowed to come to your Table: It looks silly and childish in a Servant to be laying out her Money in baubling Cakes, Nuts, and Things which she has no real Occasion for, and can do her no Good; and no less impudent to presume to touch any thing her Mistress has order'd to be set by; who, tho' she may not be of so cruel a Disposition as a certain Lady, who not long since sent her Maid to *Bridewell* for taking a Slice of Pudding, has Reason to be angry at having any thing diminished she reserved for her own eating, or those on whom she intended to bestow it.

Aping the Fashion.] The second of these Errors or Failings, for I think neither of them simply in themselves can be called a Vice, is the Ambition of imitating your Betters in point of Dress, and fancying that tho' you cannot have such rich Cloaths, it becomes you to put them on in the same Manner: Whereas nothing looks so handsome in a Servant as a decent Plainness. Ribbands, Ruffles, Necklaces, Fans, Hoop-Petticoats, and all those Superfluities in Dress, give you but a tawdry Air, and cost you that Money, which, perhaps, you may hereafter have Occasion for. This Folly is indeed so epidemic among you, that few of you but lay out all you get in these imagin'd Ornaments of your Person: The greatest Pleasure you take is in being called *Madam* by such as do not know you; and you fear nothing so much

much as being taken for what you are: I wish you would seriously consider how very preposterous all this is. Enquire of your Mothers and Grandmothers how the Servants of their Times were drest, and you will be told that it was not by laying out their Wages in these Fopperies they got good Husbands, but by the Reputation of their Honesty, Industry and Frugality, in saving what they got in Service. Besides, can you believe any Mistress can be pleased to find, that she no sooner puts on a new thing, than her Maid immediately jumps into something as like it as she can? Do you think it is possible for her to approve, that the Time she pays and feeds her for, and expects should be employ'd in her Business, shall be trifled away in curling her own Hair, pinching her Caps, tying up her Knots, and setting her self forth, as tho' she had no other thing to do, but to prepare for being look'd at? This very Failing, without the Help of any other, I take to be the Cause that so very few of you are able to continue long in a Place, and have so little Money to support yourselves when out. Yet this, my dear Girls, bad as it is, is not the worst; there is an Evil behind that is much more to be dreaded, and may be said to be an almost unavoidable Consequence, and that is, your Honesty is likely to be called in question: People will be apt to examine, how much you gave for such or such a thing, compare your Profits with your Purchases, and if the Calculation of the Expence amounts to a Scruple more than they can account for your receiving, will presently place it to the Score of those you live with, and say, you owe your Finery to your Fraud: If innocent, your Character inevitably suffers; and, if guilty, you pay dearly for the Crime your Vanity has ensnared you into, by a sooner or later sad Remorse.

Dishonesty.] Let not, therefore, any Temptations, much

much leſs thoſe idle ones I have mentioned, prevale upon you to become diſhoneſt. To cheat or defraud any one is baſe and wicked; but where Breach of Truſt is added, the Crime is infinitely enhanc'd: Nor flatter yourſelves, that becauſe you do not actually break Locks, or take any thing out of your Maſter or Miſtreſs's Trunks, you are faithful Servants. There are other kinds of Thieving you may be guilty of, which are of worſe Conſequence to the Loſers, tho' leſs perceptible, and when diſcovered ſhew you refrain from more publick Robberies only for fear of the Penalties of the Law.

The Market Penny.] To purloin or ſecrete any Part of what is put into your Hands in order to be laid out to the beſt Advantage, is as eſſentially a Theft as tho' you took the Money out of the Pockets of thoſe who entruſt you; and in doing this you are guilty of a double Wrong, firſt to your Maſter or Miſtreſs who ſends you to market, by making them pay more than they ought, and to the Tradeſman from whom you buy, by making them appear as guilty of Impoſition in exacting a greater Price than the Commodity is worth. Do not imagine, that by taking pains to find out where you can buy cheapeſt, you are intitled to that Overplus you muſt have given in another Place; for this is no more than your Duty, and the Time it takes to ſearch out the beſt Bargains, is the Property of thoſe to whom you belong. Thoſe among you of any Spirit, methinks, ſhould value the Praiſe of a good Market-woman, far beyond thoſe ſcandalous and pitiful Advantages, which cannot be made without proclaiming you either Fools or Cheats; for depend upon it, you can live with very few who will not examine into the Market-Prices. They will enquire of thoſe who buy for themſelves, and as ſome People have a fooliſh Way of belying their Pockets one way or other, thoſe who pretend to buy the

cheapeſt,

cheapest, will be the most readily believed; so that do the best you can, you will be able to give but bare Satisfaction in this Point. You will, however, have that innate Pleasure in a Consciousness of having discharged your Duty, which not the most secret and advantageous Breach of it could afford. Dishonest Practices, even in the most trivial Matters, fill the Breast with a thousand Apprehensions of Discovery; Every Accident alarms; and a Word sometimes spoke without Design calls a Blush into the guilty Cheek, and is taken as a kind of oblique Accusation. But what Shame, what Confusion, must you be involv'd in, if ever detected in a Crime of this Nature? This puts a final End to all your Hopes; if you are forgiven, you will no more be trusted; no more be recommended, and your Character utterly destroyed: It is a great Chance, if you are not reduced to get your Bread by those infamous Practices by which you lost it; and from petty Frauds proceed to greater, and such as may bring you to the most shameful Death. Dare not, therefore, to harbour the least Thought of converting to your own Use what is the Property of another, much less that which is committed to your Charge. Buy for your Master and Mistress as you would for yourself; and as to what remains, look on it as a Rust that would consume all you have, and get rid of it by returning it to the Owner the Moment you come home.

Delaying to give Change.] A very foolish Custom, to say no worse of it, has been observed in some of you; and that is, when you are sent to buy any thing with a larger Piece of Money than it can possibly cost, you do not immediately give back the Remainder: I once knew a Maid so negligent in this Particular, that whenever her Mistress gave her any Money to change, she

ſhe was obliged to ſtick two Pins acroſs in her Sleeve as a Memorandum to ask for it, without which, ſhe told me, ſhe expected never to have it, and believed ſhe had loſt frequently that way, when the Hurry of Buſineſs had made her forget. You may be ſure, no Miſtreſs would long be under ſuch a Confinement for the ſake of any Servant, the ſilly Girl was turned away at the Month's End, and tho' in other Reſpects I heard ſhe behaved well enough, yet this gave ſo ſtrong a Suſpicion of her Diſhoneſty, that ſhe was truſted with nothing the little Time ſhe ſtaid in that Service, nor could obtain any Recommendation to another.

It is very poſſible, that neither this young Woman, nor many others who may have been guilty of the ſame Folly, had any real Intention of keeping or embezzling this Money; but it ſhews at leaſt a great Careleſsneſs of a Miſtreſs's Concerns, when they can forget to give her an Account of what Money was entruſted with them, which of itſelf is a very great Fault, as I have already fully remonſtrated. But who will believe that a Servant who conſtantly keeps Money in her Hands till it is demanded, can do it with any other View than that of making it her own, in caſe it ſhould happen to be forgotten: By all means, therefore, avoid what gives ſo juſt an Occaſion for Suſpicion; be not only ſtrictly honeſt, but do nothing that may give the leaſt Room to doubt your being ſo. Beſides, 'tis both weak and ſinful to lay yourſelf under a Temptation of this kind. When you have Money of another's in your Pocket, have kept it for ſome Days, and find it is totally forgotten, may not the Devil, who is watchful for ſuch Opportunities of ſeducing the unwary Mind, ſuggeſt to you, that as you want a thouſand Neceſſaries, which the Smallneſs of your Wages will not ſupply you with, there is no Harm in making uſe of a Trifle, which the

the Owner can very well ſpare, and will do you ſo great a Service; and can you be aſſured your Honeſty will be able to hold out againſt the Inſinuations of this ſubtle Fiend? That you will deſpiſe the Bait, and unask'd refund what you imagine you have ſo much Occaſion for, and might preſerve with ſo much Security? Why, therefore, ſhould you voluntarily run into a Danger, which, even if you eſcape, can afford you neither Pleaſure not Profit, or is indeed any Merit in you?

Giving away Victuals.] Giving away any Thing without Conſent or Privity of your Maſter or Miſtreſs, is a Liberty you ought not to take; for tho' Charity and Compaſſion for the Wants of our Fellow-creatures are very amiable Virtues, they are not to be indulged at the Expence of other People's Property, and your own Honeſty: When you find there is any thing to ſpare, and that it is in Danger of being ſpoil'd by being kept too long, it is very commendable in you to ask Leave to diſpoſe of it while it is fit for Chriſtians to eat; if ſuch a Permiſſion is refuſed, the Sin lies at their Doors, you have nothing to anſwer for on that Account: but muſt on no Score beſtow the leaſt Morſel in Contradiction to the Will of thoſe to whom it belongs.

Bringing in Chair-women.] But infinitely more blameable are you, when, unknown to the Maſter or Miſtreſs of the Family, you bring Chair-women into the Houſe, and give them Victuals for helping you in that Work you have undertaken to do alone. This Action is a Complication of Hypocriſy, Deceit, and Injuſtice to thoſe you ſerve, and may be attended with very ill Conſequences to yourſelves: Can you anſwer that nothing of what is committed to your Charge will be pilfer'd? You cannot ſure be without ſome Apprehenſions of this Sort, when you truſt a

Perſon

Person, whose Character and Principles sometimes are little known to you, with Goods, which, if lost, you must not only be blamed for, but obliged to pay for, as far as is in your Power. Does not your Reputation, your Means of getting Bread in the World, and even your Life, depend on the Fidelity of the Person you thus clandestinely introduce? But you'll say, perhaps, that the Person you employ is a very honest tho' poor Woman; that she has been trusted in the best Houses, and where the richest Things have been, and nothing was ever missing. All this may be true, but you ought to remember, that what has not yet happened, a Moment may produce: Scarce can we know our own Hearts beyond the present Moment, much less those of others; and many People who have behaved well for a long Time, have been at last found guilty of what they were least suspected capable of. Far be it from me to impeach the Integrity of these poor Creatures: Doubtless many of them are perfectly honest; but that is still more than you can be ascertain'd of, and it is running a Hazard to take them in, which it would be Prudence in you to avoid; and the more so as you are guilty of an Injustice to those you serve, which deserves some Punishment. You should not undertake more Work than you think you can perform; but if you find yourself mistaken, and that it is heavier than you imagined, or your Strength will enable you to go through, you ought modestly to remonstrate it to your Mistress, and if she insists on it, and will not give Leave for any one to assist you, it is much better to give Warning than to deceive her in this Point: Perhaps this Sincerity may so much win upon her, that she will find some Way to ease you; but if this should not be the Case, she has at least no Fault to lay to your Charge, and cannot refuse giving you a Character.

Wasting

Wasting of Victuals.] To make any Waste of what God has given for the Support of his Creatures, is a Crime of a much deeper Dye, than those imagine who dare be guilty of it; and to say nothing of another World, rarely goes without its Punishment in this, by the severe Want of that which they have so lavishly confounded. What they call the Kitchen-stuff is the usual Appurtenance of the Cook, and I have heard that in large Families, where a great Quantity of every Thing is ordered in, some have been base enough to melt whole Pounds of Butter into Oil, on Purpose to encrease that Perquisite: I should scarce believe this to be Fact, if I did not know that several, who are very far from being of a niggardly Disposition towards their Servants, have denied them the Profits of the Kitchen-stuff merely on this Score. Others also among you have been so dainty, that you could not eat of a Joint of Meat the second Day, especially if your Master and Mistress had any little Thing for their own Table. Suppose a Fricassee, a Fowl, the Remains of which they would be glad to have set by for Supper; but this you cannot allow of, you must have your Share you think, and besides a Bit or two purloined in the Dressing, make sure of all they leave, and then the poor Cat or Dog has the Blame, who, before you were aware, stole all out of the Dish. Indeed there is something very mean and vile in such paltry Pretences, and as they are easily seen through, make you suspected of worse Practices; but, as I have before taken Notice to you, banish *Pride* and *Liquorishness*, and you will have no Occasion for these little Subterfuges. I do not deny but you have the same Appetites with your Superiors, and a good Mistress will doubtless allow her Servants a Taste of every Thing in Season; but then you are not to expect it as often, or in as full Proportion as she has

has it herſelf; that were to deſtroy all Diſparity, and put you too much on a Level with thoſe you ſerve.

This, perhaps, you think a hard Leſſon; but yet were you to know the real Pinches ſome endure who keep you, you would find the Ballance of Happineſs wholly on your Side. The exorbitant Taxes, and other Severities of the Times, have, for ſome Years paſt, reduced our middling Gentry, as well as Tradeſmen, to very great Straits; and the Care of providing for you, and paying your Wages, is much more than an Equivalent for your Care of obliging them, and doing your Duty by them. It often coſts many a bitten Lip and aking Heart, to ſupport the Rank they have been accuſtomed to hold in the World, while you, entirely free from all Incumberances, all Diſtraction of Mind, have only to do your Duty quietly in the Stations God has placed you. Whatever Changes happen in public Affairs, your Circumſtances are unaffected by them. Whether Proviſions are dear or cheap is the ſame Thing to you. Secure of having all your real Neceſſities ſupplied, you riſe without Anxiety, and go to Bed without Danger of having your Repoſe diſturbed. And as to your Labour, if you conſider the Difference of Education, it is no more to you than thoſe Exerciſes which are preſcribed to your Superiors for the Sake of Health.

Methinks, if you would thoroughly weigh the Comforts of your Condition, you could not help having an Affection for thoſe under whoſe Roof and Protection you enjoy them, eſpecially when they behave to you with any tolerable Degree of Affability and Sweetneſs; for then not to love them would be the higheſt Ingratitude: But ſuppoſing they are a little harſh in their Expreſſions, uſe you with Haughtineſs, and keep you at the greateſt Diſtance, yet ſtill you ſhould remember it is their Bed you lie upon, their

their Food that sustains you, and their Money cloaths you.

Hearing any Thing said against your Master or Mistress.] So far from ever speaking against them yourself, you should never listen to any idle Stories to their Prejudice; should always vindicate their Reputation from any open Aspersions, or malicious Insinuations; never mention their Names in a familiar Manner yourself, nor suffer others to treat them disrespectfully; magnify their Virtues, and what Failings they may have, shadow over as much as possibly you can: This, when known, will not only endear you to them, but also gain you the Esteem of those who hear you talk: For tho' many People have the Ill-nature to be pleased with picking out what they can to the Prejudice of their Neighbour, yet none in their Hearts approve of the Person who makes the Report, as we love the Treason but hate the Traytor. Listening, without Contradiction to an ill Thing, is tacitly acknowledging the Truth of it, and is little less base and cruel, than the inventing and telling it yourself. But tho' I would have you defend those you serve by all the Arguments that Truth and Reason will admit, yet I would not advise you to give the least Intimation to themselves of what you have heard; to repeat a rude Thing said of any one, would be rude in you, and gives so great a Shock to the Person concerned in it, as is not easily forgiven: Besides, to recite what Replies you made, would only serve to make you look like a Pickthank, and the Service you have done lose all its Merit, perhaps give Occasion to suspect, that nobody would have taken the Liberty to say such Things to you, if you had not given Room for it by some Complaints of your own. You must therefore be quite silent on this Head; it is better it should be heard from others than

than yourself, and it seldom happens that such Things go no farther than the Mouth which speaks them. Those you have defended will one Time or another be made acquainted with it, and your Discretion and Disinterestedness in concealing it, be reckoned of equal Value with your Fidelity.

Quarrels with Fellow Servants.] Preserve as much as possibly you can the Good-will of your Fellow-Servants; let it not be in the Power of every Trifle to ruffle you, or occasion you to treat them with any grating Reflections, even tho' they should be the first Aggressors; it is better to put up with a small Affront, then by returning it, provoke yet greater, and raise any Disturbance in the Family. When Quarrels in the Kitchen are loud enough to be heard in the Parlour, both Parties are blamed, and it is not always the justest Side finds the most Favour. If injured, the less Passion you discover, the more Advantage you gain over your Adversary; and if you happen to have given the first Ground for Animosity, confessing it in time is the surest Way to have it no more remembered. But of all Things, I would advise you not to throw severe or biting Jests on any one; they sink deeper into the Mind than even foul Names; and tho' you may fancy you shew your Wit in them, and excite the Laughter of the Standers-by, you may excite a Spirit of Revenge in the Person you deride, which may draw many Tears of Repentance from yourself. Any Reflection on personal Defects, as they are obvious, and consequently prove the Truth of your Satire, are the least to be endured, and not only create you an implacable Enemy in the Person you insult, but shew the little Generosity of your own Nature, that can suffer you to reproach what is not a Fault but a Misfortune. Besides, it is impious, instead of thanking God for making you more perfect,

so

to find Fault with his Handy-work in your Fellow-creature.

If you are once discovered to be of a peevish or quarrelsome Disposition, all the good natured Part of the Family will shun all Conversation with you, as much as possible; and those of the same Humour with yourself be continually throwing something in your way to occasion Contention, on Purpose to try your Spirit, and see which of you shall get the better; so that perpetual Wrangling will ensue, all your Business will be neglected, and every Thing in Confusion till the House is rid of the Authors of it. Believe me, there is nothing so engaging as a mild affable Behaviour, especially to People of the same Family; and of all Policies, that is of the most Consequence which teaches us to require the Love and good Wishes of those we converse, or have any Business with.

Behaviour to the Sick.] If any of the Family happen to be sick, let all Animosity, all former Displeasure they may have given you be forgot: Visit, attend, and comfort them all you can, whether you are ordered by your Mistress to do so or not; you have a superior Authority for this Act of Compassion, 'tis a Duty enjoined by God, and owing to Humanity, and which you know not how soon you may stand in need of yourself. If it falls to your Share to administer any Prescription to them, content not yourself with barely giving the Medicines regularly, but add to your Attendance a Softness of Behaviour, which may convince them you are truly concerned for them. A tender Assiduity about a sick Person is half a Cure; it is a Balsam to the Mind, which has a powerful Effect over the Body; it sooths, it composes, it eases the sharpest Pains, and strengthens beyond the richest Cordial: By seeming to feel their Anguish, you relieve it. People never think themselves truly unhappy

happy, while their Sufferings are treated with Pity and Gentleneſs. If good-nature, therefore, be ſo neceſſary to alleviate Misfortunes, and of all Misfortunes Sickneſs is allowed to be the greateſt, how ſhocking, how ſtinging muſt a contrary Behaviour be to a poor Wretch, both incapable and fearful of reſenting any Inſult in a proper Manner. Let no Toil, therefore, you may happen to have about a Perſon in this Circumſtance, weary you out ſo far as to make you anſwer with any Peeviſhneſs; let what you do ſeem a Pleaſure to yourſelf, or it will greatly leſſen the Merit of the Obligation; but to reproach them with any thing is highly ſavage, and what, on their Recovery, they will ſcarce forgive or forget. It is indeed Affliction enough to languiſh under the Chaſtiſement of Heaven; and for a Fellow-creature to add to it by harſh Expreſſions, Sullenneſs, or any other Act of Unkindneſs, ſhews the Perſon guilty of it to have thrown off all Humanity, and to be capable of every Thing that is ill.

Being too free with Men Servants.] If you are in the Houſe of a Perſon of Condition where there are many Men Servants, it requires a great deal of Circumſpection how to behave. As theſe Fellows live high, and have little to do, they are for the moſt Part very pert and ſaucy where they dare, and apt to take Liberties on the leaſt Encouragement; you ought therefore to carry yourſelf at a Diſtance towards them; I do not mean with a proud or prudiſh Air; You are neither to look as if you thought yourſelf above them, or to ſeem as if you imagined every Word they ſpoke to you had a Deſign upon you; No, the one would make them hate and affront you, and the other would be turned into Ridicule: On the contrary, you muſt behave with an extreme Civility mixt with Seriouſneſs, but never be too free. To ſuffer them

them to toy or romp with you, will embolden them, perhaps, to Actions unbecoming Modesty to bear, and the least Rebuff provoke them to use you ill; whereas a cold Reserve at first will prevent both the one and the other. You must also observe an exact Equality in your Deportment; for if you shew the least Distinction in favour of any one, you will not only make him too presuming, but also draw the Resentment of all the others upon you, who will be continually twitting you concerning him, and it may be construe every Thing you do into Meanings very foreign from the Truth.

Conduct toward Apprentices.] With regard to Apprentices a different Conduct is to be observed. If there be more than one, he who has served longest is to be treated with the most Respect, but you ought by no means to use the other in a saucy and imperious Manner; you are to consider that they are Servants only to become Masters, and are often of a better Birth and Education than those they serve, therefore should be treated not only with Kindness, but Civility: It may hereafter lie in their Power to recompence any little Favour you do them, such as mending their Linnen, or other Office of that Kind, when you have a Leisure Hour; but then this good Nature must not proceed too far when they grow up towards Manhood, lest the Vanity of Youth should make them imagine you have other Motives for it, which to prevent, you must behave with the same Reserve I advised to Servants of a different Class. If an Apprentice should be what they call sweet upon you, and make any Overtures of Love, you ought to check the Progress of his Sollicitations in the Beginning; and not think, as some of you have done, to draw him into Marriage, by encouraging his Addresses: Young Men of that Age are incapable of knowing their own Minds; his may alter before his Time is out, and ſhould he marry you before, he forfeits his Indentures; is not perhaps half Maſter of his Trade, his Parents are diſobliged, will do nothing for him, and you both run a very great Riſque of being miſerable for Life. Yet is not this the greateſt Danger: His Deſigns may be of a different Nature from his Pretenſions, and while you imagine he is falling into the Snare you lay for him, may be entangled in one yourſelf to your utter Ruin. So that on all Accounts, and which way ſoever his Paſſion tends, all Engagements with an Apprentice are to be avoided: If he truly loves you, and continues to do ſo when his Years of Servitude are expired, it will then be Time enough to liſten to his Offers, and conſider what Returns you ought to make; if he then marries you, he will value you the more for the Prudence you have ſhewn in his Regard, and make the better Husband.

Tho' I have adviſed you to uſe an Apprentice with a great deal of Good-nature, I do not mean that you ſhould extend it ſo far as to encourage any rakiſh Diſpoſition in him; if you find he ſtays out late, and deſires you to ſit up for him after the Family are in Bed, you may do it for once or twice; but if he continues to make a Practice of it, you ought not only to refuſe, but alſo to threaten him with acquainting your Maſter; and this you muſt not fail to do in reality if he ſtill perſiſts, and gives no Ear to your Admonitions. No Promiſes, no Bribes, ſhould make you countenance ſuch a Behaviour; for as no laudable Buſineſs, nor innocent Recreation, could make him tranſgreſs in this Manner, whatever Wrong he does himſelf or Maſter, or whatever Miſchief may enſue, you are acceſſary to it, by concealing what you know, and thereby preventing any Step being taken

taken to keep him within the Bounds of Duty and Regularity,

Mifpending your own Time.] The Condition of a Servant would be too fevere, were they not allowed fome Time which they may call their own; and it is according to their well or ill employing this Time, that their Difpofitions are to be known. In all well-governed Families a Maid-Servant has the Liberty every *Sunday*, or every other *Sunday* at leaft, in the Afternoon, of going to Church, which if fhe neglects, it difcovers fhe has little Senfe of true Religion, and may well be fufpected of failing in her Duty to an earthly Mafter or Miftrefs, when fhe fails in that to her Maker. And yet, how many of you had rather walk in the Fields, go to drink Tea with an Acquaintance, or even lie down to fleep! Unhappy Choice! and which can never expect to be attended with any Bleffings either here or hereafter. Whatever you do, therefore, never omit divine Worfhip. If you are fo unhappy to live with People who have no Devotion themfelves, and expect you to be always at home, entreat humbly at firft Permiffion to go to Church; if you find that will not prevail, infift upon it as your Right, and rather quit your Place than be refufed. If you lofe *one*, that God, for whofe fake you have left it, will doubtlefs provide another, and perhaps a better for you.

But beware how you make ufe of the facred Name of Religion as a Pretence to cover your going to any other Place. Remember what you are told by the great Oracle of Truth, concerning the Place allotted for Hypocrites in another World; never fay you have been at Church unlefs you have, but if you have gone out with that Intention, and been diverted from it by any Accident or Perfuafions, confefs the Truth, if asked.

There are, however, some Occasions which will render the Omission of this Duty excusable; and that is when you can get Leave on no other Day to shew that Love and Tenderness which ought never to be forgotten by Children to their Parents, as the only Recompence they can make for the Love and Tenderness received from them: If they are good, they will entertain you with such Conversation as may atone for your missing the Precepts delivered from the Pulpit; and if they have not that Consideration for your eternal Welfare, and talk to you only on worldly Matters, you must visit them less often, tho' not totally neglect them: Want of Respect to the Persons of Parents, or Disobedience to their Commands, being one of the first Steps which lead to an abandoned Life; and we rarely find that those who are guilty of it have not a Multiplicity of other Vices also.

But those you live with must be very unreasonable indeed without they have some more than ordinary Motive that requires your continual Attendance) that would not permit you sometimes to see your Friends on other Days than those which ought to be devoted to Heaven alone: Few Servants but are allowed one Holiday at each of the great Festivals of the Year, and in the Time of Fairs, and it is then expected you should go to your Relations, or take what other Recreation you think proper. Innocent Merriment will make you afterward work with the more Alacrity, ought to be sometimes indulged, and is never blameable, but when the Heart is set too much upon it; that is, when your Impatience for the Day makes you unable to think on any thing else, and your Mistress's Business suffers by it.

But this is not all I mean by mispending Time: Some of you who have enough upon your Hands either

either loiter it away at the Door or Windows, or ſit idle at the Fire-ſide, as if it were a Crime to do any more than they were compelled to; but ſhe who would endeavour to oblige her Miſterſs, or prove herſelf a good Houſewife, ſhould, after the common Affairs of the Family are over, aſk if ſhe has any thing to employ her in, and if ſhe anſwers in the Negative, can ſcarce be without ſomewhat to do for herſelf. Induſtry and Frugality are two very amiable Parts of a Woman's Character, and I know no readier Way than attaining them, to procure you the Eſteem of Mankind, and get yourſelves good Huſbands. Conſider, my dear Girls, that you have no Portions, and endeavour to ſupply the Deficiencies of Fortune by Mind. You cannot expect to marry in ſuch a Manner as neither of you ſhall have Occaſion to work, and none but a Fool will take a Wife whoſe Bread muſt be earned ſolely by his Labour, and who will contribute nothing towards it herſelf.

Publick Shews.] But theſe two Virtues ill agree with an immoderate Love of Pleaſure, and this Town at preſent abounds with ſuch Variety of Allurements, that a young Heart cannot be too much upon its Guard: It is thoſe expenſive ones, I mean, which drain your Purſe as well as waſte your Time: Such as Plays, the Wells, and Gardens, and other publick Shews and Entertainments; Places which it becomes nobody to be ſeen often at, and more eſpecially young Women in your Station. All Things that are invented merely for the Gratification of Luxury, and are of no other Service than temporary Delight, ought to be ſhunned by thoſe who have their Bread to get: Nor is it any Excuſe for you that a Friend gives you Tickets, and it coſts you nothing; it coſts you at leaſt what is more precious than

than Money, your Time; not only what you paſs in ſeeing the Entertainments, but what the Idea and Memory of them will take up. They are a kind of delicious Poiſon to the Mind, which pleaſingly intoxicates and deſtroys all Reliſh for any Thing beſides: If you could content yourſelves with one Sight and no more, of any, or even all theſe Shews; or could you anſwer that they would engroſs your Thoughts no longer than while you were Spectators, the Curioſity might be excuſeable; But it rarely happens that you have this Command over yourſelves; the Muſic, the Dances, the gay Clothes, and Scenes make too ſtrong an Impreſſion on the Senſes, not to leave ſuch Traces behind as are entirely inconſiſtent either with good Houſewifery, or the Duties of your Place. Avoid, therefore, ſuch dangerous Amuſements; and that it may be the more eaſy for you to do ſo, refrain the Society of thoſe who either belong to them, or are accuſtomed to frequent them.

Vails.] Never conceal from your Miſtreſs neither the Whole or any Part of what is given you: For as what is beſtowed on you is out of Reſpect to her, it is an inexcuſable Piece of Ingratitude to *her*, as well as to the *Donor*, not to acknowledge the Bounty. And as whatever you receive this Way, be it little or much, is more than you can demand, or could be aſcertained of when you were hired, I would alſo adviſe you to lay it carefully by, (without ſome extraordinary Emergency obliges you to break into it) and never lay out more upon yourſelf than your bare Wages, if ſo much; for as your Wages will be according to the Place you hold in the Family, whether an Upper or Under Servant, ſo ought your Expences in Clothes, and every thing elſe (as I have before obſerved) to be alſo proportioned according to both.

To

To prevent any Temptation from prevailing on you to diminiſh this little Bank, it would be prudent in you to depoſit whatever is given you from Time to Time in your Miſtreſs's Hands: By this Means the Snow-ball will increaſe by Degrees to an Heap, and, if you continue to behave ſo as to deſerve frequent Favours of this Sort, amount to more than you can imagine.

But ſhould your Gains be very ſmall this way, and you receive few Vails, or even none at all, it will be extremely unbecoming in you to murmur at it, to go about your Work diſcontentedly, or throw any Reflections on Perſons who dine and ſup often at the Houſe without remembring the Servant; for this would be affronting your Miſtreſs, who cannot enforce the Liberality of others. She will, however, if ſhe be of a generous Temper herſelf, take Notice of it, and perhaps make up this Deficiency another way, provided ſhe ſees you modeſt and patient, and not in the leaſt wanting in your Obſequiouſneſs to her, for the Neglect of her Friends. But however ſlow ſhe is in her Conſideration, you are ſtill not to grumble. Remember that you have your *Agreement*, and as you can *demand* no more, muſt not only *ſeem contented*, but endeavour to *be ſo*. A ſordid mercenary Diſpoſition is hateful both to God and Man; and to give any Indication of it, will, inſtead of *bettering* your Condition, render it much *worſe*; by depriving you of all that Affection which elſe might, ſooner or later, on ſome Occaſion or other, exert itſelf in your Favour when you leaſt expected it, and perhaps might ſtand in moſt need of it.

Giving your Opinion too freely.] To give your Opinion either of Perſons or Affairs unasked, is ſaucy if directed to your Superiors, and impertinent if to your Equals: I would therefore have you refrain it to both; and even if deſired, nay preſſed to it, to be

very

very cautious how you ſpeak: Such Queſtions are often propoſed to you as a Trap, either to ſound your Inclinations or Sincerity, and may turn to Ill-conſequence to yourſelves. There is an old Saying, that *a cloſe Mouth makes a wiſe Head*, to which I think may alſo be ſubjoined, that *it makes an eaſy Mind*. But you ought chiefly to be upon your Guard, if conſulted in this Manner by your Miſtreſs, (as I have known ſome, who, to gratify their Curioſity, will throw aſide all Diſparity, and ſeem willing to take the Judgment of a Servant.) In ſuch a Caſe it will behove you to reply with all Humility, and excuſe yourſelf from anſwering to the Point with Modeſty, telling her you are utterly incapable of giving any Reaſons either for or againſt the Affair in Queſtion; and if ſhe inſiſts on your ſpeaking, let it be as evaſively as poſſible. This is an innocent Artifice, and the only Medium you can take; for if gueſſing at her Mind, to flatter it, you anſwer contrary to your own, you are guilty of Diſſimulation; and if ignorant of it, you chance to contradict her Sentiments, ſhe will not like you the better for not being of the ſame Opinion with herſelf. Numberleſs Reproaches you may afterwards incur by complying, but can hazard nothing by refuſing; and thoſe, who attempt to ſift you in this Manner, will have the higher Idea of your Diſcretion, by failing in their Deſign upon you.

Chaſtity.] I come now to warn you againſt all thoſe Dangers which may threaten that Branch of Honeſty which concerns your own Perſons, and is diſtinguiſhed by the Name of *Chaſtity*. If you follow the Advice I have already give you, concerning going as frequently as you can to hear Sermons, and reading the Holy Scripture, and other good Books, I need not be at the Pains to inform you how great the Sin is of yielding to any unlawful Sollicitations; but

if

if you even look no farther than this World, you will find enough to deter you from giving the least Encouragement to any Addresses of that Nature, tho' accompanied with the most soothing and flattering Pretences: Every Street affords you Instances of poor unhappy Creatures, who once were innocent, till seduced by the deceitful Promises of their Undoers; and then ungratefully thrown off, they become incapable of getting their Bread in any honest Way, and so by Degrees are abandoned to the lowest Degree of Infamy. The Lessons I have given you concerning the Manner of passing your Time, your Temperance, your Fidelity, the Obligations you lie under to those you serve, if duly observed, will also be no inconsiderable Defence against the Snares laid for you on this Score; but I would have you not only be strictly *virtuous* in rejecting all the Temptations offered you, but likewise prudent in the *Manner* of doing it. There may be some Circumstances in which you will have Occasion to vary your denials, according to the different Characters of the Persons who sollicit you: I shall begin with one which happens but too frequently, and that is, when the Temptation proceeds from your Master.

Temptations from your Master.] Being so much under his Command, and obliged to attend him at any Hour, and at any Place he is pleased to call you, will lay you under Difficulties to avoid his Importunities, which it must be confessed are not easy to surmount; yet a steady Resolution will enable you; and as a vigorous Resistance is less to be expected in your Station, your persevering may, perhaps, in Time, oblige him to desist, and acknowledge you have more Reason than himself: It is a Duty, however, owing to yourself to endeavour it.

Behaviour to him, if a single Man.] If he happens

pens to be a ſingle Man, and is conſequently under leſs Reſtraint, be as careful as you can, Opportunities will not be wanting to proſecute his Aim; and as you cannot avoid hearing what he ſays, muſt humbly, and in the moſt modeſt Terms you can, remonſtrate to him the Sin and Shame he would involve you in; and omit nothing to make him ſenſible how cruel it is to go about to betray a Perſon whom it is his Duty to protect; add that nothing ſhall ever prevail on you to forfeit your Virtue; and take Care that all your Looks and Geſtures correſpond with what you ſay: Let no wanton Smile, or light coquet Air give him room to ſuſpect you are not ſo much diſpleaſed with the Inclination he has for you as you would ſeem; for if he once imagines you deny but for the ſake of Form, it will the more enflame him, and render him more preſſing than ever. Let your Anſwers, therefore, be delivered with the greateſt Sedateneſs; ſhew that you are truly ſorry, and more aſhamed than vain, that he finds any thing in you to like: How great will be your Glory, if, by your Behaviour, you convert the baſe Deſign he had upon you, into an Eſteem for your Virtue! Greater Advantages will accrue to you from the Friendſhip he will afterwards have for you, than you would ever have obtained from the Gratification of his wild Deſires, even tho' he ſhould continue an Affection for you much longer than is common in ſuch Intrigues. But if you fail in this laudable Ambition, if he perſiſts in his Importunities, and you have Reaſon to fear he will make Uſe of other Means than Perſuaſions to ſatisfy his brutal Appetite, (as what may not Luſt ſeconded by Power attempt, and there is no anſwering for the Honour of ſome Men on ſuch Occaſions) you have nothing to do, but, on the firſt Symptom that appears of ſuch a Deſign, to go directly out

out of his Houſe: He will not inſiſt on your forfeiting a Month's Wages for his own Sake, for fear you ſhould declare the Cauſe of your quitting his Service; and if he ſhould be even ſo hardened in Vice, as to have no Regard for his Character in this Point, it is much better you ſhould loſe a Month's Wages, than continue a Moment longer in the Power of ſuch a one.

If a married Man.] Greater Caution is ſtill to be obſerved, if he is a married Man; As ſoon as he gives you the leaſt Intimation of his Deſign, either by Word or Action, you ought to keep as much as poſſible out of his Way, in order to prevent his declaring himſelf more plainly; and if, inſpite of all your Care, he find an Opportunity of telling you his Mind, you muſt remonſtrate the Wrong he would do his Wife, and how much he demeans both himſelf and her by making ſuch an Offer to his own Servant. If this is ineffectual, and he continues to perſecute you ſtill, watching you wherever you go, both abroad and at home, and is ſo troubleſome in his Importunities, that you cannot do your Buſineſs quietly and regularly, your only way then is to give Warning; but be very careful not to let your Miſtreſs know the Motive of it: That is a Point too tender to be touched upon even in the moſt diſtant Manner, much leſs plainly told: Such a Diſcovery would not only give her an infinite Uneaſineſs, (for in ſuch Caſes the Innocent ſuffer for the Crimes of the Guilty) but turn the Inclination your Maſter had for you into the extremeſt Hatred. He may endeavour to clear himſelf by throwing the Odium on you, for thoſe who are unjuſt in one Thing, will be ſo in others; and you cannot expect, that he who does not ſcruple to wrong his Wife, and indeed his own Soul, will make any to take away your Reputation, when he imagines his own will be ſecured by it.

it. He may pretend you threw yourſelf in his Way when he was in Liquor, or that having taken Notice of ſome Indecencies in your Carriage, and ſuſpecting you were a looſe Creature, he had only talked a little idly to you, as a Trial how you would behave; and that it was becauſe he did not perſiſt as you expected, and offer you Money, that you had made the Diſcovery, partly out of Malice, and partly to give yourſelf an Air of Virtue. But tho' he ſhould not be altogether ſo unjuſt and cruel, nor alledge any Thing of this kind againſt you, it would be a Thing which you never ought to forgive yourſelf for, if by any imprudent Hint you gave Occaſion for a Breach of that Amity and Confidence which is the greateſt Bleſſing of the married State, and when once diſſolved, continual Jarring and mutual Diſcontent are the unfailing Conſequences.

Temptations from your Maſter's Son.] But there is yet a greater Trial of your Virtue than theſe I have mentioned, which you may probably meet with; and that is when your young Maſter happens to take a Fancy to you, flatters your Vanity with Praiſes of your Beauty; your Avarice with Preſents; perhaps, if his Circumſtances countenance ſuch a Propoſal, the Offer of a Settlement for Life, and, it may be, even a Promiſe of marrying you as ſoon as he ſhall be at his own Diſpoſal. This laſt Bait has ſeduced ſome who have been Proof againſt all the others: It behoves you therefore to be extremely on your Guard againſt it, and not flatter yourſelves, that becauſe ſuch Matches have ſometimes happened, it will be your Fortune: Examples of this kind are very rare, and as ſeldom happy. Suppoſe he ſhould even keep his Word, which it is much more than a thouſand to one he never intended, what you would ſuffer from the Ill-uſage of his Friends, and 'tis likely from his own Remorſe for what he has done, would make

make you wiſh, in the greateſt Bitterneſs of Heart, that it were poſſible for you to looſe the indiſſoluble Knot, which binds you to a Man who no longer loves you, and return to your firſt humble Station. Such a Diſparity of Birth, of Circumſtances, and Education can produce no laſting Harmony; and where you ſee any ſuch Couples paired, all the Comfort they enjoy are mere outſide Shew; and tho' they may wear a Face of Contentment, to blind the Eyes of the World, and keep them from prying into the Merits of their Choice, their Boſoms are full of Diſquiet and Repining. Suffer not, therefore, your Hearts, much leſs your Innocence, to be tempted with a Proſpect wherein the *beſt* that can arrive is bad enough. What then muſt be the *worſt!* Eternal Ruin; every Miſery you endure rendered more ſevere by the Stings of Diſappointment, and a too late Repentance.

Gentlemen Lodgers.] If it be your Chance to live where they take in Lodgers or Boarders, eſpecially ſuch Gentlemen as do not keep Servants of their own to ſit up for them, you may be ſubjected to ſome Inconvenience, when they ſtay out till after the Family are gone to Bed, come home in Liquor, or without being ſo, take this Opportunity of making Offers to you. If the Attempt goes no farther than Words, get out of their Way as faſt as you can, and ſhew that tho' you are a Servant, you have a Spirit above bargaining for your

your Virtue: But if they once proceed to Rudeneſs, acquaint your Miſtreſs with it, who, if a Woman of Reputation, will reſent it as an Affront to herſelf, and rather loſe her Lodger, than permit any Indecency in her Houſe. But if you give any Ear at firſt to the Sollicitations made you, or accept of any Preſents given on that Score, even tho' you neither make nor intend any Return, you will be accounted a Jilt, uſed ill by the Perſon you impoſe upon, and if it comes to your Miſtreſs's Knowledge, infallibly loſe your Place, with the ſame Diſgrace as tho' you had yielded to the Act of Shame.

Concluſion.] Having thus run through, in as brief a Manner as I could, the ſeveral Obligations you lie under to God, to thoſe you ſerve, and to your ſelves, I ſhall only add a few Words to remind you of the Advantages of living a great while in a Family. Thoſe of you who go young to Service, and continue in one Place eight or ten Years, will be then of a fit Age to marry, and beſides being entitled to the Advice of your Miſtreſs, will be certain of her Aſſiſtance in any Buſineſs you ſhall take up; your Children, if you have any, partake her Favour, perhaps ſome of them be taken into the Family, and both you and yours receive a Succeſſion of good Offices. If your Huſbands behave well to you, they will be encouraged for your Sakes; and if ill, you may depend on Protection from them. An old and tried Servant is looked upon as a Relation, is treated with little leſs Reſpect, and perhaps a more hearty Welcome. This you cannot but be ſenſible of yourſelves; and I ſhall therefore conclude as I began, with exhorting you to make uſe of the Underſtanding God has given you, in a ſerious Conſideration of the Hints I have thrown together, in order to render you both valuable and happy.

DIREC-

DIRECTIONS

FOR

A Young Woman to qualify herſelf for any common Service.

IF you truly deſign to make a good Servant, and to gain the Affection and Eſteem of thoſe you live with, it is abſolutely neceſſary you ſhould endeavour, before you venture out into the World, to have ſome little Skill in thoſe Things you muſt expect to be employed in, and which Practice afterward will make eaſy to you. To this End I have annex'd ſome few Rules, which, if you carefully obſerve, will make you fit for any common Service.

Firſt, For going to MARKET.

How to chuſe FLESH.

Beef.] The right *Ox Beef* is beſt, and that which is ſo has a fine open Grain: If it be *young*, it has a kind of oily Smoothneſs, and if you dent it with your Finger will immediately riſe again; but if *old*, it will be rough and ſpungy, and the Dent remain. Cow Beef is leſs boned than that of the *Ox*, the Fleſh cloſer grain'd, the Lean of it ſomewhat paler, and the Fat whiter; but if young, the Dent you make with your Finger will riſe again. Bull Beef is cloſer grain'd than either, more coarſe, and if you pinch it, feels rough: The Fat is hard and ſkinny, and has a certain Rankneſs in the Scent, tho' it be ever ſo freſh killed.

Mutton.

Mutton.] When Mutton is young, the Flesh will pinch tender, and the Fat part easily from the Lean; but if old, the one will wrinkle and remain so for some Time, and the other not be pull'd off without Difficulty, by reason of a great Number of little Strings: Old Mutton may also be known when the Flesh shrinks from the Bones, and the Skin is loose: In Ewe Mutton the Flesh is of a paler Colour than the Weather, and of a closer Grain. If there happens to be a Rot among the Sheep, the Fat will be inclining to yellow, and the Flesh very pale, loose from the Bone, and if you squeeze it hard, a Dew like Sweat will rise upon it.

Veal.] The Flesh of a Bull Calf is more red, and has a firmer Grain than that of a Cow Calf, and the Fat will be harder. The Butchers about *London* have so many Arts in blowing up their Veal, and keeping it in wet Cloths, that you cannot be too careful in examining the Scent, or what looks beautiful to the Eye may prove musty.

Lamb.] House Lamb, when good, is very fat, the Lean of it looks of a pale pink Colour, and the Fat is exceeding white. Grass Lamb is somewhat of a higher Colour, but the Fat is also white: In a Fore Quarter of either you must observe the Neck Vein; if it looks of a fine light blue, it is fresh killed; but if greenish or yellowish, it is stale. In a Hind Quarter, smell under the Kidney, and try the Knuckle, if it be limber, and you meet with a faint Scent, do not venture to buy it.

Pork.] If it be young and fresh, the Flesh will look of a fine bright Colour, but not too red; the Skin will be thin, and if you nip it with your Nails the Impression will remain; but if the Lean be high colour'd, the Fat flabby, and the Rhind hard, it is old; or if any Part feel clammy, it is stale. If you find

find many ſmall Kernels in the Fat, like Hail-ſhot, it is certainly meazly, and dangerous to be eaten.

Bacon.] Bacon may alſo be known, if young or old, by the Thickneſs or Thinneſs of the Rhind. Always chuſe that, the Fat of which has a reddiſh Caſt; for if it look quite white, like Tallow, or inclin'd to yellowiſh, it is ſtark naught. That Bacon which gives, and becomes flabby in moiſt Weather, has not been well cured, and is either ruſty, or will very ſoon be ſo.

Weſtphalia, or *Engliſh Hams.*] Both theſe are to be tried by putting a Knife under the Bone that ſticks out; and if it comes out in a manner clean, and has a curious Flavour, the Ham is ſweet and good; if, on the contrary, it is much ſmeer'd and ſully'd, and ſmells rank, the Ham was either tainted before it was dried; or grown ruſty afterward.

F I S H.

All Sorts of freſh Fiſh may be judg'd by the Redneſs of their Gills, if no Deceit be uſed; but as there is ſometimes an Impoſition by wetting them with Blood, you muſt obſerve whether they are ſtiff, if their Eyes ſtand out and full, and their Fins and Tails are not ſhrivelled; for if theſe Symptoms do not anſwer, they are ſtale, notwithſtanding the Redneſs of their Gills.

Plaice and Flounders.] As Plaice and Flounders will live a long Time out of the Water, whoever buys them after they are dead, may find them ſweet, but their Subſtance will be ſo far ſpent, that they will almoſt diſſolve in the Water they are boiled in, and afford neither an agreeable Reliſh to the Palate, nor Nouriſhment to the Stomach. To diſtinguiſh Plaice from Flounders, the latter are ſomewhat thicker, are of a darker brown, and have ſmall

Specks of Orange Colour; the Plaice have Spots too, but they are not ſo bright, and of a larger Size. The beſt Sort of both are blueiſh on the Belly.

Whitings.] Theſe are a Fiſh, which if not extremely ſtiff when you buy them, will neither broil nor boil.

Salmon.] To buy this Fiſh you muſt examine the Grain and Colour as you do in Butchers Meat; if the one be fine, and the other high and florid, the Salmon is good; but if coarſe and pale, it is bad: When it is perfectly new, a great Quantity of Blood will iſſue from it when it is cut, and the Liver look very clear, almoſt tranſparent.

POULTRY.

Capon.] If a Capon be young, his Spurs are ſhort, and his Legs ſmooth; if a true Capon, a fat Vein on the Side of the Breaſt, the Comb pale, and a thick Belly and Rump; if new, a cloſe hard Vent; if ſtale, a looſe open one.

A Cock and Hen.] If young, his Spurs are ſhort and dubb'd; but you muſt be careful in taking notice whether they are not pared or ſcraped by the Poulterer, in order to deceive you. You may know if he is new by the Vent, in the ſame Manner as you judge of the Capon, and ſo alſo of a Hen; but if young, her Legs and Comb are ſmooth, if old they are tough.

Cock or Hen Turkey, Turkey Poults.] If the Cock be young, his Legs will be black and ſmooth, and his Spurs ſhort; if old, the contrary: If ſtale, his Eyes will be ſunk, and his Feet hard and dry; and if new, the Eyes will look lively, and the Feet pliable. The like Obſervation you may make of the Hen; and moreover, if ſhe be with Egg, ſhe will have an open Vent, if not, a hard cloſe Vent. Tur-

key

key Poults are known the ſame Way, as to being new or ſtale, and you cannot be deceived in their Age.

Gooſe.] If the Bill of a Gooſe be yellow, and ſhe have but few Hairs, ſhe is young; but if there are many, and the Bill and Feet red, ſhe is old: If new, limber; if ſtale, hard and ſtiff in all her Parts. Never chuſe a Gooſe that is not very fleſhy on the Breaſt, and fat in the Rump.

Duck.] A Duck is every way to be judged in the ſame Manner as a Gooſe.

Chicken.] You cannot well be deceived in Chickens; only take this for a Rule, that the white legg'd are in general the beſt, and taſte the ſweeteſt.

Wild Duck.] A right Wild Duck has a reddiſh Foot, and ſmaller than the tame one; the Marks of being young or old, new or ſtale, are the ſame as with the others.

Woodcock or Snipe.] A Woodcock ought to be thick, fat, and the Fleſh firm; the Noſe dry, and the Throat clear, otherwiſe they are naught. Snipe if young and fat has a full Vein under the Wing, and feels thick in the Vent. As for the reſt like the Woodcock.

Partridge.] When the Bill of a Partridge is white, and the Legs look blueiſh, it ſhews Age; for if young, the Bill is black, and the Legs yellowiſh. To know if new or ſtale, ſmell at their Mouths.

Pidgeons.] Old Pidgeons have generally red Legs, and are blackiſh in ſome Parts: If young and new, the Fleſh looks all of one Colour, and are fat in the Vent.

And thus of grey or green Plover, Fellfare, Blackbirds, Thruſh, Larks, and Wild Fowl in general.

Hare.] A Hare is white and ſtiff when new and clean kill'd; if ſtale, the Fleſh will have a blackiſh Hue. If the Cleft in her Lips ſpread very much, and her Claws are wide and ragged, ſhe is old; the contrary when young.

Leveret.] To know a true Leveret, feel on the fore Leg near the Foot, and if there be a ſmall Bone or Knob, it is right; if not, it is no Leveret but a Hare; and for the reſt of the Marks, you muſt judge as of the Hare.

Rabbit.] The Wild Rabbit is better than the Tame; to diſtinguiſh the one from the other, you muſt obſerve the Head, which is more picked in the Wild than the *Tame*. If it is old, there will be a great deal of yellowiſh Fat about the Kidneys, the Claws will be long, and the Wool rough and mottled with grey Hairs; if young the Reverſe. For being new killed, you muſt judge by the Scent.

Butter.] When you buy freſh Butter, truſt not to the Taſte the Perſon gives you; for they often patch a Piece of good Butter at the End, when the reſt is naught; but run your Knife into the Middle, and if it comes out with a fine ſweet Flavour, the Butter is good. You muſt alſo obſerve that there are no Crumblings ſtick about the Knife; for if ſo, the Butter, tho' it may be well taſted at preſent, has not been well work'd up, and will not keep. As for Salt Butter, having taſted it, and found it to your Palate, make them cut you what Quantity you want out of the Middle; for the Tub is apt to give an ill Flavour to that Part which touches it. If one Cheeſemonger refuſes to do this, go to another; but if you carry ready Money, there is no Danger of his turning you away; but thoſe who go on Credit muſt take up with it.

Cheeſe.

Cheese.] The beſt Cheeſe, whether of *Cheſhire*, *Glouceſter*, or *Warwickſhire*, has generally a rough moiſt Coat, but if too much of the latter, is apt to breed Maggots. Always chuſe that which has a fine yellow Caſt, and is cloſe made.

Eggs.] The beſt Eggs are thoſe which have a clear thin Shell, are of the longeſt Oval, and moſt picked at the Ends. As for the Newneſs of them, hold them before the Light, and if the White is clear, and the Yolk flows regularly in the Midſt, you may depend on their being good, and the contrary when the White looks cloudy, and the Yolk ſinks which way ſoever you hold it.

Now that you may not diſgrace your Marketing, and ſpoil by bad dreſſing what you have well cater'd, take the following Rules, which, without being ordered to the contrary, by thoſe who love their Victuals over much or over little done, you ought not to trangreſs it.

Boiling Butchers Meat.

Beef.] Let your Pot be large enough to contain a ſufficient Quantity of Water for it to have Room to wabble about, and be ſure, before you put it on, to make up a good ſtrong Fire, ſo as it may never ceaſe boiling from the Minute it begins, till it is thoroughly done. As for the Time of boiling, you may allow a Quarter of an Hour to every Pound of Beef, except Briſket, which requires more by Reaſon of its being ſo very fibrous.

Mutton.] Mutton takes not up altogether ſo much Time nor Water, yet it muſt not be cramped in too ſmall a Pot; for if it is, it will be tough, and the Colour ſpoiled. If you make Broth, put in no more Water than will juſt cover it; and after you have taken the Scum off, (which muſt be raiſed by throwing in ſome Salt, and put in what Thickening the Family

Family likes, whether Rice, Barley, or Oatmeal) let it be close stopped till enough.

Veal.] A great Inducement to eating heartily of boiled Veal, is the Whiteness of it: You should therefore not only be particularly careful in taking off the Scum, but also tie the Meat in a Cloth, and the Skin will then look of a delicate Clearness.

Lamb.] The same Care ought to be taken of Lamb, especially *House*; for it being of a more delicate Texture than the *Grass*, is more liable to imbibe any disagreeable Tincture. Both ought to be well boiled, as indeed should all *young* Meat, or it is unwholesome.

Pork.] Pork requires still more boiling, and should never be dressed without salting; for there is a Juice between the Rind and the Fat, which, if not well purged out, breeds bad Humours.

POULTRY.

Turkey.] Three Quarters of an Hour is sufficient for a middling Turkey; but you must always consult the Largeness, and give Time accordingly.

Pullets, Capons, and young Cocks.] Pullets, especially if with Egg, take somewhat more boiling, than either a young Cock or Capon; for the two latter, half an Hour is sufficient, and you must not add to the other above four Minutes. When you boil Fowl and Bacon, you must be sure to scrape the Rind exceeding clean, and pare off the Outside of the Lean, which in the best cured Bacon has an offensive Smell and Taste, and boil the Fowl in a Cloth.

An old Cock.] You can scarce boil an old Cock too much; but as it is seldom used but in Broth, the best Way is to cut it in Pieces.

Chicken.] A Quarter of an Hour is sufficient for a Chicken; if you have Parsley and Butter with it, let

let the Parſley be boiled ſoft, and ſhred very ſmall before you put it into the Butter.

Pidgeon.] When you have well cleaned and truſs'd your Pidgeons, ſtuff their Bellies with Parſley, and be ſure to take off the Scum as often as it riſes. A little more than a quarter of an Hour ſerves to boil them.

Take it for a general Rule, that whatever you boil either of Fleſh or Fowl, ſhould be ſet over a briſk Fire, to the End it may keep conſtantly in Motion; for if it ceaſes, tho' never ſo little a Time, the Gravy drains out into the Water.

F I S H.

Salmon.] Waſh it, and let it bleed well in the Water, then lie a little to drain, after which put it into boiling Water; take out the Liver when about three Parts done, and braid it with Ketchup, which, mingled with the Butter, will make exceeding rich Sauce. This Sort of Fiſh takes almoſt as much boiling as Mutton.

Pike.] Waſh your Pike clean, then truſs it round with the Tail in its Mouth, and its Back ſcotched in three Places; then throw it into boiling Water with a good deal of Salt and Vinegar, three or four Blades of Mace, and the Peel of a whole Lemon: Let it boil faſt at firſt; for that will make the Pike eat firm, but more ſlow afterwards. The Time muſt be proportioned to the Bigneſs of the Fiſh, but half an Hour is enough for a very large one. The beſt Sauce for this is plain Butter, with a few Shrimps and *Seville* Orange.

Freſh Cod.] Mix a great deal of the beſt White-Wine Vinegar with the Water in which you boil Freſh Cod; Lemon Peel, Salt, Mace and Cloves otherwiſe the Fiſh will taſte wateriſh, be very flabby, and liable to break in the Kettle. The Sauce for thir this cannot be too rich, and if you are allowed it, ſpare neither Ketchup, the Body of a Lobſter or Crab, Oyſters and Shrimps; but if you have not all theſe at hand, put in as many of them as you can. You will know when it is enough, as you may all Fiſh, by the dropping out of the Eyes.

Barrel Cod, or any other Salt Fiſh.] All Kinds of Salt Fiſh muſt lie in Water proportionable to its Saltneſs: Truſt not therefore to the Words of thoſe you buy it of, but taſte a Bit of one of the Flakes. This requires more boiling than any Freſh Fiſh. The Sauce for it is Butter, Eggs, Muſtard, and Parſnips, or Potatoes.

Roaſting Butchers Meat.

Beef.] When you roaſt *Beef*, make up a ſtrong laſting Fire, that it may penetrate into the Heart of the Meat, elſe the Inſide will be raw when the Outſide is over-done. When you think it is near enough, make your Fire burn brisker in order to brown it. Rub a good deal of Salt upon it before you lay it down, and while it is roaſting baſte it often with its own Dripping, and flour it well. The Time for roaſting is the ſame with that of boiling, a Quarter of an Hour to every Pound of Meat.

Mutton.] All Joints of *Mutton*, except a Leg, require a briſker Fire than *Beef.* Baſte it with Butter, and flour it often; but, if it be very large, and you ſuſpect it to be Ram *Mutton*, baſte it well on firſt laying it down with Water and Salt, and that will take off the Rankneſs. You muſt abate ſomewhat of a Quarter of an Hour for each Pound, eſpecially when you roaſt a Shoulder or Neck.

Lamb and Veal.] All young Meats, as before obſerved, ought to be thoroughly done; therefore do not take either *Lamb* or *Veal* off the Spit till you ſee they drop white Gravy.

Pork.]

Pork.] *Pork* ſhould lie twelve Hours at leaſt in Salt, before you put it down to roaſt; then flour it well, but a very little baſting will ſerve, except you roaſt it without cutting the Skin, and then you muſt keep it baſting and turning very faſt, as you would do a *Pig*, to preſerve it from bliſtering, or parting from the Fleſh. This is a very luſcious Meat, and requires the ſame Time as Beef, and as ſtrong a Fire, for it will be pernicious if eaten with Gravy in it that has the leaſt Tincture of Redneſs. The moſt common, as well as moſt wholeſome Sauce is Apple-Sauce, and *Muſtard.*

Pig.] Take Sage, ſhred very ſmall, grated Bread, Salt, a little Pepper, and the Yolk of four Eggs, wet them well with White-wine, till they come to a Conſiſtency; then put them into the Belly of the Pig: Sew it up, and after having rubb'd the Skin over with Butter, put it on the Spit: Keep it continually baſting and rubbing with clean Cloths, and turning very faſt, till it is enough. An Hour will roaſt a middling Pig; if large, you muſt allow more Time. When it is done, take the Pudding out of the Belly, mix it with Gravy, and the Brains of the Pig: Sweet Sauce is to be made the ſame way, only add a few *Currants*, ſome Sugar, Nutmeg, and a little White-wine.

POULTRY.

Capon.] Thirty Minutes will roaſt the largeſt *Capon* you can buy, provided your Fire be ſtrong and briſk. Keep it well baſted, and let it turn moderately faſt. The beſt Sauce is a rich Gravy, well reliſh'd with Spice and *Ricamboll* or *Shalotte.*

Pullet with Eggs, or without.] A *Pullet* with *Eggs* will take ſomewhat more roaſting than a Capon: *Egg*-Sauce is moſt proper, and moſt commonly eaten with it. If ſhe be without *Egg* ſhe will take leſs Time in roaſting than the Capon. Gravy Sauce is alſo beſt with this.

Chicken]

Chicken.] A Quarter of an Hour will roaſt a handſome well-grown Chicken. The Sauce is Parſley and Butter, or Gravy.

Tame-Duck.] Shred ſome Sage and Onion very ſmall, mix it with Pepper and Salt, and put it into the Belly of the Duck: when it is enough done, take out the Stuffing, and mingle it with a good deal of Claret and Gravy for Sauce.

Gooſe.] A *Gooſe* requires exactly the ſame Seaſoning as a *Duck:* The Sauce in the Diſh muſt alſo be the ſame, but you muſt add a Plate of Apple-Sauce, and ſet Muſtard and Sugar for thoſe that like it.

Turkey.] A *Turkey* muſt be well floured and baſted, and roaſted with a ſtrong Fire, eſpecially if the Belly be ſtuffed with Oyſters; in that Caſe you muſt take out the Oyſters as ſoon as it comes off the Spit, and put them into melted Butter mix'd with Gravy. If there be no Oyſters leſs Time will roaſt it, and you muſt put no Butter to your Gravy.

Wild-fowl.] When you roaſt a *Wild-Duck* or any other *Wild-fowl*, you ſhould make your Spit very hot before you put them on; otherwiſe the Inſide will be raw, and the Outſide too much done and dry: They muſt all in general be perpetually baſted with Butter and their own Dripping. The Sauce you make for a *Tame-Duck* ſerves for all kind of *Wild-fowl* except a *Patridge*, which muſt be baſted with Butter, and ſtrew'd with grated Bread, and the Sauce made of grated Bread, Yolks of Eggs, White Wine, and Gravy well ſpiced.

Hare.] A Hare is beſt when it is larded, but if this is not thought proper, you muſt at leaſt make a Pudding of grated Bread, the Liver of the *Hare* minced ſmall, Parſley, Thyme, Winter-Savory, Sweet Marjoram, Salt, Pepper, a few Cloves beaten, three Yolks of Eggs, and well wetted with Claret, and

and put it into the Belly, which after you have ſew'd up ſo that none may fall out, put it on the Spit; baſte it with Cream till it is half done, then with its own Dripping; but take Care to keep it always moiſt. Mix half a Pint of Claret with very ſtrong and high ſeaſon'd Gravy for Sauce. It will take an Hour to roaſt.

Rabbits.] Baſte your *Rabbits* well with Butter; about forty Minutes is ſufficient to keep them at the Fire, which ſhould be briſk, but not too ſtrong. The Sauce is only melted Butter with the Liver minc'd ſmall.

Stewing.

Beef.] *Brisket-Beef*, *Thick-flank*, or the *Chuck-Rib* are beſt for ſtewing: Cut it in Pieces of about four or five Ounces each; put it into an *Earthen Pipkin* with a few *Turnips*, one *Carrot*, one whole *Onion*, a little *Thyme*, *Winter-Savory*, *Sweet-Marjoram*, *Parſley*, ſome Corns of *Jamaica Pepper*, *Salt*, and *Black-Pepper*, and three or four *Bay* Leaves; then put as much Water as will a little more than cover them; ſtop it very cloſe to keep any Steam as much as poſſible from going out; and ſet over a ſlow Fire, ſo that it may but juſt ſimmer. If it be Brisket, it will take four Hours to do it right; if any other Part, three will be ſufficient. When it is enough, take out the Bay Leaves, and ſerve up the reſt altogether in a Soup Diſh.

Neck, *Breaſt*, *Knuckle*, *or any other Joint of Veal.*] Whatever Joint of Veal is to be ſtew'd, muſt be put whole into a Stew Pan, with *Parſley*, *Winter-Savory*, *Thyme*, *Sweet-Marjoram*, *Lemon-Peel*, *Mace*, *Nutmeg*, a little *Salt*, and *Pepper*. Mix ſome White-wine with the Water, and put no more than will juſt cover it; then ſtop it cloſe, and put it over a very ſlow Fire; when it is enough, beat up the Yolks of three or four Eggs, and incorporate them with the Gravy that comes from it, and when you have put it in the Diſh ſtrew a few *Muſhrooms*, *Capers*, and a little

little *Samphire* over, and garnish with *Lemon*, or *Seville Orange*. You may also add *Truffles*, *Morelles*, *Coxcombs*, and *Artichoak* Bottoms, if you have them. This is a very delicate and savoury Dish, and pleases most Palates.

Neck, Breast, or any other Joint of Mutton.] Some People like *Mutton* stew'd with *Potatoes*; and if so, you must cut the Mutton in Chops, and slice your Potatoes; put a larger Quantity of Salt and Pepper than you do either with Beef or Veal, and a very little Water; because what comes from the Potatoes, when they have been a little Time on the Fire, will stew the Mutton. You must put in no Herbs, except a Bunch of Thyme, and after covering it close let it just simmer; an Hour and a half will do it thoroughly, provided no Steam evaporates. To stew Mutton without Potatoes, you must also cut it in Chops, or Collops, according as the Part is, and put in two or three Turneps, Thyme, Parsley, Salt, Pepper, a small Onion, and as much Water as will cover it, and when done, strew it over with Capers.

Fricassees.

Of Veal.] Cut your Veal in thin Slices, beat it well with a Rolling-pin; then season it with Pepper, Salt, Nutmeg, Thyme, and Lemon-peel, shred very small; fry it in Butter, and when it is enough, as it will be in Six Minutes, pour away the Butter it is fry'd in, and throw in fresh, with two Eggs well beaten, and two Spoonfuls of Verjuice; shake it up all together, and then serve it.

Of Lamb.] Lamb must also be cut into small Pieces; then season'd with a little Pepper and Salt, fryed first in Water, and, after being well flour'd, in Butter: It requires longer Time than Veal; when enough done, pour off that Butter, and put in fresh, with two Eggs, and a very little Verjuice. Strew it in the Dish with Mushrooms.

Chicken.]

Chicken.] Cut off the Limbs of your Chickens and joint them, and the Breast in thin Slices, and dislocate all the Bones, leaving a very little Flesh on them; fry them in Water, then pour off the Water, and save it, then fry them in Butter till they are of a fine brown: Beat the Yolks of Eggs, a little Pepper, Salt, and enough of pickled Walnut to give it a Flavour; mix all these well with the Water you pour'd off, and put it into the Stew Pan over the Chickens; let it just boil up, and it is ready. If you add Truffles, Morelles, or Coxcombs, they must go in with it. Strew the Fricassee in the Dish with Mushrooms. Rabbits are to be done in the very same Manner.

Puddings.

Plumb-Pudding common.] Take a Quarter of a Peck of the best Wheat-Flour, three Pound of fine Beef Suet, well pick'd from the Skins and Strings, and shred very small; two Pound of Currants, rubb'd in a dry clean Cloth; twelve Eggs, the White of half left out; one Pennyworth of Saffron; a Glass of Brandy and a little beaten Ginger; mix them in as much new Milk as it will require for a moderate Thickness, and stir it well together; then tie it up in a Cloth, and put it into boiling Water. You must take Care to turn it often when it first goes in, that the Currants may not fall to the Bottom, and keep it constantly boiling. It will be five Hours to do it as it ought.

Plain Pudding common.] Plain Pudding is made the same way, and with the same Ingredients, excepting the Currants, and abating one Pound of Suet; it must also boil as long.

Rich Pudding.] To a Quarter of a Peck of Flour, put four Pound of Marrow, four Pound of Currants, the Yolk of twenty-four Eggs, and the White of six, one Pennyworth of Saffron steeped in a Gill of of the beſt Canary, a little beaten Ginger, three Ounces of candy'd Citron, of Lemon and Orange Peel, each an Ounce, cut in thin, ſmall Bits, and well mixed and ſtirred in new Milk.

Quaking Pudding.] Take the Crumb of a Kingſton Loaf, or ſix French Rolls, ſlice them, and put them in an Earthen Pan; put to them a Quart of boiling Milk, cover it, and let it ſtand till it is quite cold; then put in two Ounces of pounded Almonds, a Glaſs of Sack, four Eggs, two Ounces of double-refined Sugar, then tye it in a Cloth, and boil it half an Hour. When you have taken it up pour Butter melted with Sack over it, ſqueeze a Seville Orange, and ſtrew it thick with Sugar; to make it look more beautiful, you may ſtick here and there a Sugar'd Almond.

Tanſey Pudding.] For a Tanſey Pudding you muſt take a Pound of Flour, the ſame Quantity of grated Bread, twelve Eggs, ſix Ounces of double refined Sugar, a Gill of Sack, then preſs out the Juice of Spinage one Spoonful, and of Tanſey half a Spoonful, and mix them well together with Cream. You may either bake it or fry it in a Pan. Squeeze Seville Orange over it, and ſtrew it thick with Sugar.

Common bak'd Puddings are to be made the ſame way with the boil'd.

Pyes.

Beef-ſtake Pye.] Rump-ſtakes are fitteſt for a Pye, becauſe moſt tender. If you uſe any other Part, beat them well with a Rolling-pin. Seaſon them with Pepper and Salt, according to the Palate the Pye is made for. To every Pound of Flour for the Cruſt, you muſt take the ſame Quantity of Butter, but work no more than half up with the Paſte; the other you muſt ſpread over it with your Knife in the Rolling; then fold it, ſpread it again, and ſo on till

till all the Butter is expended. Make your Cruſt thick, and as many times as you roll it, ſo many Flakes it will break in when it is baked, and eat as well as if you did it with Whites of Eggs.

Mutton, Lamb, and Veal Pyes are all to be ſeaſon'd the ſame way, except the two latter are to be made ſweet, for which take the following Rule.

Lamb or Veal Pyes ſweet.] Cut your Lamb or Veal in Collops, then ſeaſon them with Salt, Pepper, Nutmeg, and Lemon-Peel; put to every Pound of Meat a Quarter of a Pound of Currants, and a few ſtoned Raiſins; ſome make a Caudle of Canary and Eggs, and pour it in when the Pye is cut up, but, this is ſuperfluous.

Minc'd Pye.] The beſt Minc'd Pye is made of Neats Tongues or Hearts, which parboil, and then chop very ſmall with an equal Quantity of Beef-Suet nicely picked: Put of Currants and ſtoned Raiſins as many Pound as you have of Meat, and to every Pound add an Apple, the ſharpeſt you can get: Mix a little White-wine or Canary with the Mace, and ſome thin Slices of Citron.

Apple Pye.] With every ſix Apples you put into your Pye, join one Quince: When you have pared them, and taken out the Cores and Bruiſes very clean, cut them in ſmall Bits, and throw in a large Quantity of Sugar; ſo that the Fruit ſhall ſeem buryed; break a Stick of Cinnamon, and ſcatter it, with a few Cloves here and there.

Gooſeberry, Cherry, and *Currant* Pyes, have nothing but Sugar mingled with the Fruit.

Cuſtard.] Take a Quart of Cream and boil it with a little Cinnamon, then beat the Yolk of eight Eggs and four Whites; and when your Cream is almoſt cold, put in your Eggs, ſtir them well together, and ſweeten

ſweeten it with ſix Ounces of Sugar; then pour it into little China Diſhes, and bake it.

Cheeſe-cake.] The common way is to make Cheeſe-cakes of Curd taken from Milk turn'd with Runnet; but the ſureſt way to have them good, is to have it turn'd with White-wine, which if enough is put into the Milk when hot will make a Curd hard enough for your Purpoſe. Boil Cinnamon in it before you pour in the Wine, but ſweeten it afterward when you have taken off the Curd, and preſſed it to a moderate Dryneſs; add more Sugar, and a good Quantity of Currants, mix them well together, then fill your Cruſt, and put five or ſix ſmall Bits of Citron in every Cheeſe-cake, and ſend them to the Oven. I need not tell you that the Paſte muſt be made very rich.

Seed-cake.] Take three Pound of the beſt Flour, wet it with Milk, and put to it the Yolk of twenty-four Eggs, and twelve Whites, one Pound and a half of freſh Butter, half a Pound of Sugar, and two Ounces of Carraway Seeds, a little beaten Ginger and ſome Cinnamon, knead it well and bake it, and it will be a very good Cake. To have it richer you need only double the Quantity of Butter, and ſome ſlic'd Citron and Orange-Peel.

Pancakes.

Flour Pancake.] Take two Pound of the beſt Flour, the Crum of a French Roll grated, the Yolks of ten Eggs, and the Whites of five, well beat; then mix them with a Quart of new Milk, in which a little Bit of Saffron has been infuſed, throw in ſome powdered Ginger and Nutmeg: After ſtirring it till it is very ſmooth, ſo that there is not the leaſt Lump, cover your Batter up, and let it ſtand for two Hours before you put it into the Pan, then pour in ſufficient to make the Pancake of a moderate

Thickneſs:

Thickneſs: Let your Butter be well melted, and your Pan very hot before you put it in; keep it ſhaking round to prevent it from ſticking, till you toſs it; then add more Butter, and when it is fryed criſp, lay it on a Diſh, and ſqueeze Seville Orange over it, and ſtrew it with Sugar.

Clary Pancake.] Beat twenty Eggs, Whites and all, then take as much Clary as, when ſhred exceeding ſmall, will equal the Quantity of the Eggs; mix them together with three Spoonfuls of Flour, and as much Milk as will juſt make it pour; add powder'd Cinnamon, Ginger and Nutmeg; fry it as you do a common Pancake, and when done ſqueeze Seville Orange, and ſtrew Sugar over it.

Fritters.] To every Spoonful of Flour you allow for your Fritters, you muſt take the Yolk of an Egg, and as much Cream, beat all well up together with ſome Ginger, Cinnamon, and Nutmeg finely powdered, then let it ſtand. Pare ſome of the beſt and ſharpeſt Apples you can get, and cut them into ſmall Pieces, but do not put them into your Batter till you are ready to fry it. Let your Pan be half full of Hogs-lard, and as ſoon as it boils up, throw in the Batter by a large Spoonful at a Time, and theſe will be excellent Fritters. When you have taken them up, ſqueeze Seville Orange, and ſtrew Sugar over them.

Bacon Fraiſe.] The Batter for a Bacon Fraiſe muſt be made exactly the ſame as for a Pancake, only of ſomewhat more Conſiſtency. After having pared all the Rind and ruſty Part of the Bacon clean off, cut it in very thin Raſhers, lay it in the Pan with a good deal of Butter, and when it is hot pour the Batter over it. Hold it a good Height above the Fire, that it may not ſcorch before the Heat penetrates quite through it, and keep it ſhaking round to prevent it from ſticking. You cannot toſs a Fraiſe, and muſt be particularly careful in turning it, that it may not crack in thoſe Places where the Bacon lies.

Amlet.] Take the Yolks of twelve Eggs, and the Whites of eight, beat them very well, then ſhred an Handful of young Spinage, Parſley, Winter Savory about half the Quantity each, a little Sweet-Marjoram and Thyme; ſeaſon it well with Pepper and Salt, and a few beaten Cloves; for thoſe that love Onion, you may put in enough juſt to give it a Reliſh. Stir them all well together, and fry it in freſh Butter; but take care not to over-do it, for it will then be tough.

Bacon with Eggs.] Cut all the Rind, and ſo much of Lean as you ſee has a yellowiſh Caſt, clean off your Bacon, then put it into your Pan, and when you have turned it, break in your Eggs, taking Care that the one does not ſtick to the other; when they have lain about half a Minute, turn them one by one with your Slice, let them lie half a Minute more and take them up: Pour Vinegar, and ſhake ſome Pepper over them in the Diſh before you ſerve it up. But the beſt Way of eating Bacon with Eggs is to broil the one, and poach the other, laying one Egg over each Raſher of Bacon, and then pour Vinegar and ſtrew Pepper as you do when they are fryed.

Next to being expert in buying and Dreſſing of Victuals, there is nothing ſo commendable in a Servant as the well and quick waſhing and getting up of Linnen. That you may not therefore be wanting in ſo valuable a Qualification, I have taken the Pains to give you ſome Inſtructions, which I doubt not but will be readily followed by as many of you as are ambitious of acquiring the Reputation of being good Houſe-wives, or wiſh to give Satisfaction to thoſe you ſerve.

Directions

Directions how to manage Linnen for the Wash.

How to wash Linnen.] As soon as any Linnen is left off, look it carefully over, and mend whatever little Cracks or Rents you may find in it, for otherwise they will grow larger when they come into the Water; then fold it up with the same Smoothness you would do if clean, and put it into the foul Bag, that it get no more Soil. Linnen, where bad Housewives have the Manegement of it, is as much worn out by being thrown carelessly about, as by the wearing. If there happen to be any Stains of Ink, Red-Wine, or any Sort of Fruit, you must be sure to get them clean out before you begin to wash.

How to get Spots or Ink out of Linnen.] Take the Linnen and let that Part of it that the Ink has fallen upon, lie all Night in Vinegar and Salt, the next Day rub the Spots well with it, as if you were washing in Water, then put fresh Vinegar and Salt, and let it lie another Night, and the next Day rub it again, and all the Spots will disappear.

How to get the Stains of Fruit out of Linnen.] Rub all the Stains very well with Butter, then put the Linnen into scalding hot Milk; let it lie and steep there till it is cool, and rub the stained Places in the Milk, till you see they are quite out.

Water.] Some People are so inconsiderate as to wash with Water when it first comes in, which being always thick, and very often yellow, gives the Linnen a muddy Cast: Be sure, therefore, to save Water enough for your Washing, that it may stand and settle three or four Days at least before you use it. If it happens to be a harsh Water, take a Chump of Wood, and burn it on the Hearth, then put the Ashes into a Piece of Linnen Rag, tie it close, and throw it into the Water, which will make it as soft as Milk, and save Soap.

Soap.] Be careful in chusing the oldeſt Soap you can; for that which is new-made not only ſpoils the Colour of the Linnen, but alſo does not go ſo far.

Waſhing.] See that your Pot or Copper be nicely clean, that it may not ſoil or greaſe the Water; while it is heating, ſort you Clothes, laying the Small in one Heap, and the Great in another: The Coarſe muſt alſo be ſeparated from thoſe that are finer. When you have done this, rub them all well over with Soap, eſpecially thoſe Places you find moſt dirty, then put the Fine firſt into the Tub, and pour the Water on them of a moderate Heat; for if it be too hot, it ſcalds the Dirt into the Linnen: Paſh it well in the Water before you rub it: In fine Linnen you will not have Occaſion to rub very hard, for without it is more than ordinarily dirty, the Strength of the Lather, and the Motion you give it, will have all the Effect of rubbing, and wear it leſs out. When it is well waſhed, take it out of the Tub, and lay it on your Table or Dreſſer, on a clean Cloth, which you muſt ſpread for that Purpoſe, to prevent any freſh Soil from coming in it; then put in your coarſe Linnen with ſome more hot Water, and rub that with greater Strength than the fine; then lay it on the Dreſſer, and throw away your Suds, without you have any Stair Cloths, Dreſſer Cloths, or ſuch kind of Things to waſh; if you have, you muſt ſave it in another Tub, in order to waſh them when you have done the others. You muſt now ſoap all your Linnen over again, pour Water as before, but ſomething hotter, and waſh it well; if it is not very dirty, two Lathers will ſuffice, but if it has been worn long, you muſt give it three.

Boiling.] Soap it ſlightly when you put it in to boil, and mix a good deal of the beſt Stone Blue with your Water: Paſh it often about while it is boiling, and

and then pour it altogether into your Tub: Let it ſtand till it grows cool enough for your Hands to bear it, and then waſh it well out, taking care that not the leaſt Smear of Soap remains; for if you leave any, it will look like Greaſe when it comes to be dry. Throw every Piece as you waſh it into a Tub full of clean Pump Water well blued, and when you have done, rinſe it thoroughly to take out all the Suds, then hang it directly on Lines, which you muſt be careful to keep nicely clean. As ſoon as it is moderately dry, take it down, fold it ſmooth, clap it, and let it lie till you iron it, which ought to be as ſoon as poſſible, for Linnen is apt to turn yellow by lying damp.

Ironing.] Whether you make uſe of Box, or Flat-Irons, let them be kept very bright and ſmooth: If the latter, they muſt be well rubbed on a Piece of Matt, and afterward on Flannel every Time they are taken from the Fire. Uſe them as hot as you can without Danger of ſingeing; to prevent which, always try them firſt on a Rag. If the Linnen happens to be too dry, ſprinkle it with a little fair Water, fold it again, and let it lie together clap'd down, that it may be all over of an equal Dampneſs. Fine Linnen ſhould be ironed ſomewhat more damp than the coarſe, in order to make it ſtiff, and look like new.

Starching.] Muſlin, and very thin or old Cambrick and Lawn require ſtarching, or they will look like Rags, and not laſt clean a Moment. Uſe nothing but the beſt *Poland* Starch, make it very thin, and mix a ſmall Quantity of Powder-blue with it, and when it is boiled almoſt enough, put in a little Piece of Iſinglaſs to clear it; then dip your Muſlins, &c. into it, juſt warm, and clap them between your Hands till they are dry enough to iron: To prevent them from shining, take a Piece of white Paper, and lay over them, and rub your Iron over that. You must always take this way with Laces or Edgings, or any thing that is flourished or spotted, to keep the Work from being too much flatted.

How to wash Silk Stockings.] Make a strong Lather with Soap, and pretty hot, then lay the Stockings on a Table, and take a Piece of very coarse rough Cloth, roll it up, and rub them with it as hard as you can, turning them several times from one side to the other, till they have passed through three Lathers; then rinse them in three or four Waters, till not the least Tincture of the Soap remains; and when you find them quite clear, hang them up to dry without ringing, wrong side outwards. When they are about half dry, take them down and pull them out with your Hands into Shape, let them lye a while, and then smooth them with your Iron on the wrong Side.

Having now (with great Care and Pains) completed what I at first intended, I have nothing more to add, than, once more, strongly to recommend to you, a strict Observance of the several Particulars contained in this small Treatise, which will be the only Means of entitling you to the Blessing of God, the Love and Esteem of the Families in which you live, and procuring to yourselves a never-failing Source of Comfort and Satisfaction.

FINIS.

Just published by George Faulkner, Printer hereof, most beautifully printed in Octavo, on a fine Genoa Paper, Price 5 s. bound, and 4 s. 4 d. stitcht in blue Paper.

LETTERS to and from the Rev. Dr. JONATHAN SWIFT, D. S. P. D. From the Year 1714 to 1738.

At the same Place may be had,

The above Author's Works in Six Volumes Octavo (printed the same Size of the Letters) Price 1 l. 10 s. viz.

Vol. I. The Authors Miscellanies in Prose.

Vol. II. His Poems.

Vol. III. The Travels of Captain Lemuel Gulliver to several remote Nations.

Vol. IV. Papers relating to Ireland.

Vol. V. The Conduct of the Allies, and the Examiners.

Vol. VI. The Publick Spirit of the Whigs, and other Pieces of Political Writings, with Polite Conversation, &c.

Those Ladies and Gentlemen who have had the four first Volumes, may have the fifth and sixth to match them, or the Poems alone.

Just published,

The above Works in Six neat Pocket Volumes, printed on a fine Dutch Paper and Elziver Type. Price 16 s. 3 d.

Also lately published by the Printer hereof.

Pope's Works, 3 Vols. 12mo.		6	6
Ditto Letters 2 Vols.		4	4
Miscellaneous Works of his Excellency Matthew Prior, Esq; in 2 Vols. Vol. I. containing the History of his own Time. Compiled from his own Manuscripts. Revised and signed by himself. Vol. II. containing a new Collection of Poems, consisting of Epistles, Tales, Satyrs, Epigrams, &c. Never before published.		5	5
The Memoirs of Signior Gaudentio di Lucca. Taken from his Confession and Examination before the Fathers of the Inquisition.		2	8
Voltaire's Letters concerning the English Nation		2	2
The Turkish Spy, 8 Vols.		17	0
Thoughts on Religion, and other various Subjects. By M. Pascal, 8vo.		4	4
Gordon's Geographical Grammar.		5	0
The Pantheon		2	6
Father Paul on Ecclesiastical Benefices and Tythes, with an Account of his Life, 8vo.		4	6
Chambers's Dictionary	4	11	0
The Plain Dealer		2	2
The Winter Evening Tales, containing 17 delightful Novels		2	2
The Ascent of Cyrus the Younger, with the Retreat of Ten Thousand Greeks from Babylon. Translated by Mr. J. Hawkey, A. B.	0	5	5
Rollin's Method of teaching and studying the Belle's Letters, 4 Vols.		11	4
The Third Edition of the History of Peter I. Emperor of Russia, By John Motley, Esq; embellished with curious Frontispieces, an accurate Map of the Russian Empire, and several other Copper-Plates, representing a Prospect of the City of Moscow, a Plan of the City of Petersburgh, the Fortress of Cronslot and the different Habits and Customs of the several Nations subject to that Empire, &c.	9	9	[illegible]
The Batchelor of Salamanca, or the Memoirs of Don Cherubim de la Ronda; containing many delightful Novels, 2 Vols. By Mr. Le Sage, Author of Gil-Blas, and the Devil upon Two Sticks.		4	4
Wolfius's Algebra		5	5

This Day is published, by the Printer hereof, Price 13 d

THE MODERN HUSBANDMAN; or the PRACTICE of FARMING. As it is carried on by the most Accurate Farmers in several Counties of England. For the Month of *NOVEMBER*: Containing the following Particulars, viz.

I. Several curious Cases, relating to Plowing and Sowing Wheat in this Month. *To chuse a right Seed for any Soil; the best Sort for late Sowing; the Benefit and Loss of Sowing Wheat late. Why more Seed must be sown in wet than dry Weather. The Value of a good Ploughman, and the Loss necessarily sustained by a bad one. To know good from bad Wheat Seed, &c.*

II. Of Plowings preparatory for sowing Lent Crops of Grain, &c. in the Hill Country. *Calculation of the Profit of a Crop of Clover, &c.*

III. Of Plowings for Barley and Oats in one Part of Buckinghamshire.

IV. Of Plowings for Lent Grain in Middlesex.

V. Of Plowing Land in Vales preparatory to Sowing of Lent Grain.

VI. Of Dungs and Manures proper for Corn and Grass Grounds in this Month. *The several ways of saving and improving Horse, Swine, and other Dungs; and the great Losses shewn that Farmers sustain by their ill Management.*

VII. Of the different Management of Turnep Crops. *Method of preserving them good through the Winter and Spring, &c.*

VIII. Of Carrots. *Method of preserving them for Winter Use. How a Person made sixty Pounds of one Acre of Carrots. The great Profit of feeding Hogs, &c. with Carrots.*

IX. Of Beech-Maste, Acorns, &c. *The great Profit Farmers make by feeding Swine with them.*

X. Of Stubble or Wheat Haulm.

XI. Of Sheep. *To know the Value of a Sheep by weighing it alive.*

XII. Of the Management of Lambs, to be kept for Store Sheep.

XIII. Of knitting Rams.

XIV. Of the Management of Horses for Plough and Cart. *Dr. Bracken's Directions to a Groom, for preventing Scratches, or Grease, in a Horse.*

XV. Of Banking Meadow Grounds. *The Necessity of cutting up Ant Hills. Description of new-invented Ploughs for destroying Ant Hills expeditiously.*

XVI. Of Planting Trees. *The right Time of Planting several kinds; the proper Soil, Situation, &c.*

XVII. *How to lay down Ground with Artificial Grasses for Meadow. The Quantity of Seeds necessary for sowing an Acre; their Prices, &c.*

And speedily will be published,

The MODERN HUSBANDMAN, for the Month of *December*.

At the same Place may be had,

The MODERN HUSBANDMAN, for the Months of

MAY,	JULY,	SEPTEMBER, and
JUNE,	AUGUST,	OCTOBER.

Just published, by the Printer hereof,

Price 13 d. stitched, or 1 s. 8d. bound,

THE Third and Last Volume of *The Life of Marianne*, which finishes the Nun's Story, and compleats the whole Work.——It is needless to say any thing in Favour of this Story, as it is written by the celebrated M. Marivaux, and is universally allowed to be superior to any thing of the kind ever yet published.——Such Persons as have had the former Volumes, and are willing to have this, are desired to send Pattern Books, to match their Binding.

Also, Just published, by the Printer hereof, Price 2s. 8d.

THE SATIRES of *JUVENAL* translated: With explanatory and critical Notes, relating to the Laws and Customs of the Greeks and Romans.

These Satyrs are so well translated, that they have met with universal Approbation, and are allowed by the best Judges to be the best Performance of that kind; and therefore proper to be in the Hands of Gentlemen of Learning, as well as English Readers.

Jonathan Swift, *DIRECTIONS TO SERVANTS IN GENERAL; And in particular to The BUTLER, COOK, FOOTMAN, COACHMAN, GROOM, HOUSE-STEWARD, and LAND-STEWARD, PORTER, DAIRY-MAID, CHAMBER-MAID, NURSE, LAUNDRESS, HOUSE-KEEPER, TUTORESS, or GOVERNESS* (ESTC T69637) is reproduced, by permission, from the British Library copy (shelfmark 1077.1.45). The text block of the original measures 165 × 83 mm.

Words that are faint in the original:
36.1: and
36.2: a Present

DIRECTIONS
TO
SERVANTS
IN GENERAL;

And in particular to

The BUTLER,	PORTER,
COOK,	DAIRY-MAID,
FOOTMAN,	CHAMBER-MAID,
COACHMAN,	NURSE,
GROOM,	LAUNDRESS,
HOUSE-STEWARD,	HOUSE-KEEPER,
and	TUTORESS, or
LAND-STEWARD,	GOVERNESS.

By the Reverend Dr. SWIFT, D. S. P. D.

I have a Thing in the Press, begun above twenty-eight Years ago, and almost finish'd: It will make a Four Shilling Volume; and is such a PERFECTION OF FOLLY, *that you shall never hear of it, till it is printed, and then you shall be left to guess. Nay, I have* ANOTHER OF THE SAME AGE, *which will require a long Time to perfect, and is worse than the former, in which I will serve you the same Way.* Letters to and from Dr. Swift, &c. Lett. LXI. alluding to POLITE CONVERSATION and DIRECTIONS TO SERVANTS.

LONDON:

Printed for R. DODSLEY, in *Pall-Mall*, and M. COOPER, in *Pater-Noster-Row*,

MDCCXLV.

[Price One Shilling and Six-Pence.]

RULES

THAT CONCERN

All SERVANTS in general.

WHEN your Maſter or Lady call a Servant by Name, if that Servant be not in the Way, none of you are to anſwer, for then there will be no End of your Drudgery: And Maſters themſelves allow, that if a Servant comes when he is called, it is ſufficient.

When you have done a Fault, be always pert and inſolent, and behave your ſelf as if you were the injured Perſon; this will immediately put your Maſter or Lady off their Mettle.

If you ſee your Maſter wronged by any of your Fellow-ſervants, be ſure to conceal it, for fear of being called a Tell-tale: However, there is one Exception, in caſe of a favourite Servant, who is juſtly hated by the whole Family; who therefore are bound in Prudence to lay all the Faults you can upon the Favourite.

The Cook, the Butler, the Groom, the Market-man, and every other Servant who is concerned in the Expences of the Family, ſhould act as if his Maſter's whole Eſtate ought to be applied to that Servant's particular Buſineſs. For Inſtance, if the Cook computes his Maſter's Eſtate to be a thouſand Pounds a Year, he reaſonably concludes that a thouſand Pounds a Year will afford Meat enough, and therefore, he need not be ſparing; the Butler makes the ſame Judgment, ſo may the Groom and the Coachman, and thus every Branch of Expence will be filled to your Maſter's Honour.

When you are chid before Company, (which with Submiſſion to our Maſters and Ladies is an unmannerly Practice) it often happens that ſome Stranger will have the Good-nature to drop a Word in your Excuſe; in ſuch a Caſe, you will have a good Title to juſtify yourſelf, and may rightly conclude, that whenever

ever he chides you afterwards on other Occaſions, he may be in the wrong; in which Opinion you will be the better confirmed by ſtating the Caſe to your Fellow-ſervants in your own Way, who will certainly decide in your Favour: Therefore, as I have ſaid before, whenever you are chidden, complain as if you were injured.

It often happens that Servants ſent on Meſſages, are apt to ſtay out ſomewhat longer than the Meſſage requires, perhaps, two, four, ſix, or eight Hours, or ſome ſuch Trifle, for the Temptation to be ſure was great, and Fleſh and Blood cannot always reſiſt: When you return, the Maſter ſtorms, the Lady ſcolds; ſtripping, cudgelling, and turning off, is the Word: But here you ought to be provided with a Set of Excuſes, enough to ſerve on all Occaſions: For Inſtance, your Uncle came fourſcore Miles to Town this Morning, on purpoſe to ſee you, and goes back by Break of Day To-morrow: A Brother-Servant that borrowed Money of you when he was out of Place, was running away to *Ireland:* You were taking Leave of an old Fellow-Servant, who was ſhipping for *Barbados:* Your Father ſent a Cow to you to ſell, and you could not get a Chapman till Nine at Night: You were taking Leave of a dear Couſin who is to be hanged next *Saturday:* You wrencht your Foot againſt a Stone, and were forced to ſtay three Hours in a Shop, before you could ſtir a Step: Some Naſtineſs was thrown on you out of a Garret Window, and you were aſhamed to come Home before you were cleaned, and the Smell went off: You were preſſed for the Sea-ſervice, and carried before a Juſtice of Peace, who kept you three Hours before he examined you, and you got off with much a-do: A Bailiff by miſtake ſeized you for a Debtor, and kept you the whole Evening in a Spunging-houſe: You were told your Maſter had gone to a Tavern, and came to ſome Miſchance, aud your Grief was ſo great that you inquired for his Honour in a hundred Taverns

Taverns between *Pall-mall* and *Temple-bar*.

Take all Tradeſmens Parts againſt your Maſter, and when you are ſent to buy any Thing, never offer to cheapen it, but generouſly pay the full Demand. This is highly to your Maſter's Honour; and may be ſome Shillings in your Pocket; and you are to conſider, if your Maſter hath paid too much, he can better afford the Loſs than a poor Tradeſman.

Never ſubmit to ſtir a Finger in any Buſineſs but that for which you were particularly hired. For Example, if the Groom be drunk or abſent, and the Butler be ordered to ſhut the Stable Door, the Anſwer is ready, An pleaſe your Honour, I don't underſtand Horſes: If a Corner of the Hanging wants a ſingle Nail to faſten it, and the Footman be directed to tack it up, he may ſay, he doth not underſtand that Sort of Work; but his Honour may ſend for the Upholſterer.

Maſters and Ladies are uſually quarrelling with the Servants for not ſhutting the Doors after them: But neither Maſters nor Ladies conſider that thoſe Doors muſt be open before they can be ſhut, and that the Labour is double to open and ſhut the Doors; therefore the beſt and ſhorteſt, and eaſieſt Way is to do neither. But if you are ſo often teized to ſhut the Door, that you cannot eaſily forget it, then give the Door ſuch a Clap as you go out, as will ſhake the whole Room, and make every Thing rattle in it, to put your Maſter and Lady in Mind that you obſerve their Directions.

If you find yourſelf to grow into Favour with your Maſter or Lady, take ſome Opportunity, in a very mild Way, to give them Warning, and when they aſk the Reaſon, and ſeem loth to part with you, anſwer that you would rather live with them, than any Body elſe, but a poor Servant is not to be blamed if he ſtrives to better himſelf; that Service is no Inheritance, that your Work is great, and your Wages very

ſmall:

ſmall: Upon which, if your Maſter hath any Generoſity, he will add five or ten Shillings a Quarter rather than let you go: But, if you are baulked, and have no Mind to go off, get ſome Fellow-ſervant to tell your Maſter, that he had prevailed upon you to ſtay.

Whatever good Bits you can pilfer in the Day, ſave them to junket with your Fellow-ſervants at Night, and take in the Butler, provided he will give you Drink.

Write your own Name and your Sweet-heart's with the Smoak of a Candle on the Roof of the Kitchen, or the Servants Hall, to ſhew your Learning.

If you are a young ſightly Fellow, whenever you whiſper your Miſtreſs at the Table, run your Noſe full in her Cheek, or if your Breath be good, breathe full in her Face; this I have known to have had very good Conſequences in ſome Families.

Never come till you have been called three or four Times; for none but Dogs will come at the firſt Whiſtle:

And when the Maſter calls [*Who's there?*] no Servant is bound to come; for [*Who's there*] is no Body's Name.

When you have broken all your earthen Drinking Veſſels below Stairs (which is uſually done in a Week) the Copper Pot will do as well; it can boil Milk, heat Porridge, hold Small-Beer, or in Caſe of Neceſſity ſerve for a Jordan; therefore apply it indifferently to all theſe Uſes; but never waſh or ſcour it, for Fear of taking off the Tin.

Although you are allow'd Knives for the Servants Hall, at Meals, yet you ought to ſpare them, and make Uſe only of your Maſter's.

Let it be a conſtant Rule, that no Chair, Stool or Table in the Servants Hall, or the Kitchen, ſhall have above three Legs which hath been the antient, and conſtant Practice in all the Families I ever knew, and is ſaid to be founded upon two Reaſons; firſt to ſhew that Servants are ever in a tottering Condition; ſecondly, it was thought

thought a Point of Humility, that the Servants Chairs and Tables ſhould have at leaſt one Leg fewer than thoſe of their Maſters. I grant there hath been an Exception to this Rule, with regard to the Cook, who by old Cuſtom was allowed an eaſy Chair to ſleep in after Dinner; and yet I have ſeldom ſeen them with above three Legs. Now this epidemical Lameneſs of Servants Chairs is by Philoſophers imputed to two Cauſes, which are obſerved to make the greateſt Revolutions in States and Empires; I mean Love and War. A Stool, a Chair or a Table is the firſt Weapon taken up in a general Romping or Skirmiſh; and after a Peace, the Chairs if they be not very ſtrong, are apt to ſuffer in the Conduct of an Amour, the Cook being uſually fat and heavy, and the Butler a little in Drink.

I could never endure to ſee Maid-Servants ſo ungenteel as to walk the Streets with their Pettycoats pinned up; it is a fooliſh Excuſe to alledge, their Pettycoats will be dirty, when they have

have ſo eaſy a Remedy as to walk three or four times down a clean Pair of Stairs after they come home.

When you ſtop to tattle with ſome crony Servant in the ſame Street, leave your own Street-Door open, that you may get in without knocking, when you come back; otherwiſe your Miſtreſs may know you are gone out, and you muſt be chidden.

I do moſt earneſtly exhort you all to Unanimity and Concord. But miſtake me not: You may quarrel with each other as much as you pleaſe, only bear in Mind that you have a common Enemy, which is your Maſter and Lady, and you have a common Cauſe to defend. Believe an old Practitioner; whoever out of Malice to a Fellow-Servant, carries a Tale to his Maſter, ſhall be ruined by a general Confederacy againſt him.

The general Place of Redezvous for all the Servants, both in Winter and Summer, is the Kitchen; there the grand Affairs of the Family ought to be be conſulted; whether they concern the Stable, the Dairy, the Pantry, the Laundry, the Cellar, the Nurſery, the Dining-room, or my Lady's Chamber: There, as in your own proper Element, you can laugh, and ſquall, and romp, in full Security.

When any Servant comes home drunk, and cannot appear, you muſt all join in telling your Maſter, that he is gone to Bed very ſick; upon which your Lady will be ſo good-natured, as to order ſome comfortable Thing for the poor Man, or Maid.

When your Maſter and Lady go abroad together, to Dinner, or on a Viſit for the Evening, you need leave only one Servant in the Houſe, unleſs you have a Black-guard-boy to anſwer at the Door, and attend the Children, if there be any. Who is to ſtay at home is to be determined by ſhort and long Cuts, and the Stayer at home may be comforted by a Viſit from a Sweet-heart, without Danger of being caught together. Theſe Opportuni-

ties

ties muſt never be miſſed, becauſe they come but ſometimes; and you are always ſafe enongh while there is a Servant in the Houſe.

When your Maſter or Lady comes home, and wants a Servants who happens to be abroad, your Anſwer muſt be, that he but juſt that Minute ſtept out, being ſent for by a Couſin who was dying.

If your Maſter calls you by Name, and you happen to anſwer at the fourth Call, you need not hurry yourſelf, and if you be chidden for ſtaying, you may lawfully ſay, you came no ſooner, becauſe you did not know what you were called for.

When you are chidden for a Fault, as you go out of the Room, and down Stairs, mutter loud enough to be plainly heard; this will make him believe you are innocent.

Whoever comes to viſit your Maſter or Lady when they are abroad, never burthen your Memory with the Perſon's Name, for indeed you have too many other

other Things to remember. Befides, it is a Porter's Bufinefs, and your Maf-ter's Fault he doth not keep one, and who can remember Names; and you will certainly miftake them, and you can neither write nor read.

If it be poffible, never tell a Lye to your Mafter or Lady, unlefs you have fome Hopes that they cannot find it out in lefs than half an Hour. When a Servant is turned off, all his Faults muft be told, although moft of them were never known by his Mafter or Lady; and all Mifchiefs done by others, charge to him. [Inftance them.] And when they afk any of you, why you never acquainted them before? The Anfwer is, Sir, or Madam, really I was afraid it would make you angry; and befides perhaps you might think it was Malice in me. Where there are little Mafters and Miffes in a Houfe, they are ufually great Impediments to the Diverfions of the Servants; the only Remedy is to bribe them with Goody Goodyes, that they may not tell Tales to Papa and Mamma. I ad-

I advise you of the Servants, whose Master lives in the Country, and who expect Vales, always to stand Rank and File when a Stranger is taking his Leave; so that he must of Necessity pass between you; and he must have more Confidence, or less Money than usual, if any of you let him escape, and according as he behaves himself, remember to treat him the next Time he comes.

If you are sent with ready Money to buy any Thing at a Shop, and happen at that Time to be out of Pocket, sink the Money and take up the Goods on your Master's Account. This is for the Honour of your Master and yourself; for he becomes a Man of Credit at your Recommendation.

When your Lady sends for you up to her Chamber, to give you any Orders, be sure to stand at the Door, and keep it open fidling with the Lock all the while she is talking to you, and keep the Button in your Hand for fear you should forget to shut the Door after you.

If your Master or Lady happen once in

in their Lives to accuſe you wrongfully, you are a happy Servant, for you have nothing more to do, than for every Fault you commit while you are in their Service, to put them in Mind of that falſe Accuſation, and proteſt yourſelf equally innocent in the preſent Caſe.

When you have a Mind to leave your Maſter, and are too baſhful to break the Matter for fear of offending him, the beſt way is to grow rude and ſaucy of a ſudden, and beyond your uſual Behaviour, till he finds it neceſſary to turn you off, and when you are gone, to revenge yourſelf, give him and his Lady ſuch a Character to all your Brother-ſervants, who are out of Place, that none will venture to offer their Service.

Some nice Ladies who are afraid of catching Cold, having obſerved that the Maids and Fellows below Stairs, often forget to ſhut the Door after them as they come in or go out into the back Yards, have contrived that a Pulley and a Rope with a large Piece of Lead at the End, ſhould be ſo fixt as to make the Door ſhut of itſelf, and require a ſtrong Hand to open it, which is an immenſe Toil to Servants, whoſe Buſineſs may force them to go in and out fifty Times in a Morning: But Ingenuity can do much, for prudent Servants have found out an effectual Remedy againſt this inſupportable Grievance, by tying up the Pully in ſuch a Manner, that the Weight of the Lead ſhall have no Effect; however, as to my own Part, I would rather chuſe to keep the Door always open, by laying a heavy Stone at the Bottom of it.

The Servants Candleſticks are generally broken, for nothing can laſt for ever. But, you may find out many Expedients; You may conveniently ſtick your Candle in a Bottle, or with a Lump of Butter againſt the Wainſcot, in a Powder-horn, or in an old Shoe, or in a cleft Stick, or in the Barrel of a Piſtol, or upon its own Greaſe on a Table, in a Coffee Cup or a Drinking Glaſs, a Horn Can, a Tea Pot, a twiſted Napkin, a Muſtard Pot, an Inkhorn,

horn, a Marrowbone, a Piece of Dough, or you may cut a Hole in the Loaf, and ſtick it there.

When you invite the neighbouring Servants to junket with you at home in an Evening, teach them a peculiar way of tapping or ſcraping at the Kitchen Window, which you may hear, but not your Maſter or Lady, whom you muſt take Care not to diſturb or frighten at ſuch unſeaſonable Hours.

Lay all Faults upon a Lap-Dog or favourite Cat, a Monkey, a Parrot, a Child, or on the Servant who was laſt turned off: By this Rule you will excuſe yourſelf, do no Hurt to any Body elſe, and ſave your Maſter or Lady from the Trouble and Vexation of chiding.

When you want proper Inſtruments for any Work you are about, uſe all Expedients you can invent, rather than leave your Work undone. For Inſtance, if the Poker be out of the Way or broken, ſtir up the Fire with the Tongs;

if the Tongs be not at Hand, ufe the Muzzle of the Bellows, the wrong End of the Fire Shovel, the Handle of the Fire Brufh, the End of a Mop, or your Mafter's Cane. If you want Paper to finge a Fowl, tear the firft Book you fee about the Houfe. Wipe your Shoes, for want of a Clout, with the Bottom of a Curtain, or a Damafk Napkin. Strip your Livery Lace for Garters. If the Butler wants a Jordan, he may ufe the great Silver Cup.

There are feveral Ways of putting out Candles, and you ought to be inftructed in them all: you may run the Candle End againft the Wainfcot, which puts the Snuff out immediately: You may lay it on the Ground, and tread the Snuff out with your Foot: You may hold it upfide down until it is choaked with its own Greafe; or cram it into the Socket of the Candleftick: You may whirl it round in your Hand till it goes out: When you go to Bed, after you have made Water, you may dip

dip the Candle End into the Chamber Pot: You may ſpit on your Finger and Thumb, and pinch the Snuff until it goes out: The Cook may run the Candle's Noſe into the Meal Tub, or the Groom into a Veſſel of Oats, or a Lock of Hay, or a Heap of Litter: The Houſe-maid may put out her Candle by running it againſt a Looking-glaſs, which nothing cleans ſo well as Candle Snuff: But the quickeſt and beſt of all Methods, is to blow it out with your Breath, which leaves the Candle clear and readier to be lighted.

There is nothing ſo pernicious in a Family as a Tell-Tale, againſt whom it muſt be the principal Buſineſs of you all to unite: Whatever Office he ſerves in, take all Opportunities to ſpoil the Buſineſs he is about, and to croſs him in every Thing. For Inſtance, if the Butler be the Tell-Tale, break his Glaſſes whenever he leaves the Pantry Door open; or lock the Cat or the Maſtiff in it, who will do as well: Miſlay a Fork or a Spoon ſo as he may never find it. If it be the Cook, whenever ſhe turns her Back, throw a Lump of Soot, or a Handful of Salt in the Pot, or ſmoaking Coals into the Dripping-Pan, or daub the roaſt Meat with the Back of the Chimney, or hide the Key of the Jack. If a Footman be ſuſpected, let the Cook daub the Back of his new Livery; or when he is going up with a Diſh of Soup, let her follow him ſoftly with a Ladle-full, and dribble it all the Way up Stairs to the Dining-room, and then let the Houſe-maid make ſuch a Noiſe, that her Lady may hear it: The Waiting-maid is very likely to be guilty of this Fault, in hopes to ingratiate herſelf. In this Caſe, the Laundreſs muſt be ſure to tear her Smocks in the waſhing, and yet waſh them but half; and, when ſhe complains, tell all the Houſe that ſhe ſweats ſo much, and her Fleſh is ſo naſty, that ſhe fouls a Smock more in one Hour than the Kitchen-maid doth in a Week.

DIREC-

DIRECTIONS TO SERVANTS.

CHAP. I.

Directions to the BUTLER.

IN my Directions to Servants, I find from my long Obſervation, that you, Butler, are the principal Perſon concerned.

Your Buſineſs being of the greateſt Variety, and requiring the greateſt Exactneſs, I ſhall, as well as I can recollect, run thro' the ſeveral Branches of your Office, and order my Inſtructions accordingly.

In waiting at the Side-board, take all poſſible Care to ſave your own Trouble, and your Maſter's Drinking Glaſſes: Therefore, firſt, ſince thoſe who dine at the ſame Table are ſuppoſed to be Friends, let them all drink out of the ſame Glaſs, without waſhing, which will ſave you much Pains, as well as the Hazard of breaking them; give no Perſon any

Liquor

Liquor until he hath called for it thrice at leaſt; by which means, ſome out of Modeſty, and others out of Forgetfulneſs, will call the ſeldomer, and thus your Maſter's Liquor be ſaved.

If any one deſires a Glaſs of Bottled-Ale, firſt ſhake the Bottle, to ſee whether any thing be in it, then taſte it, to ſee what Liquor it is, that you may not be miſtaken; and laſtly, wipe the Mouth of the Bottle with the Palm of your Hand, to ſhew your Cleanlineſs.

Be more careful to have the Cork in the Belly of the Bottle than in the Mouth; and, if the Cork be muſty, or White Fryers in your Liquor, your Maſter will ſave the more.

If an humble Companion, a Chaplain, a Tutor, or a dependent Couſin happen to be at Table, whom you find to be little regarded by the Maſter, and the Company, which nobody is readier to diſcover and obſerve than we Servants, it muſt be the Buſineſs of you and the Footman, to follow the Example of your Betters, by treating him many degrees worſe than any of the reſt, and you cannot pleaſe your Maſter better, or at leaſt your Lady.

If any one calls for Small-beer towards the End of Dinner, do not give yourſelf the Pains of going down to the Cellar, but gather the Droppings and Leavings out of the ſeveral Cups, and Glaſſes and Salvers into one; but turn your Back to the Company, for fear of being obſerved: On the contrary, when any

one

one calls for Ale towards the End of Dinner, fill the largeſt Tankard-cup top-full, by which you will have the greateſt Part left to oblige your Fellow-Servants, without the Sin of ſtealing from your Maſter.

There is likewiſe a Perquiſite full as honeſt, by which you have a chance of getting every Day the beſt Part of a Bottle of Wine for your ſelf; for, you are to ſuppoſe that Gentlefolks will not care for the Remainder of a Bottle; therefore, always ſet a freſh one before them after Dinner, although there hath not been above a Glaſs drank of the other.

Take ſpecial Care that your Bottles be not muſty before you fill them, in order to which, blow ſtrongly into the Mouth of every Bottle, and then if you ſmell nothing but your own Breath, immediately fill it.

If you are ſent down in haſte to draw any Drink, and find it will not run, do not be at the Trouble of opening a Vent, but blow ſtrongly into the Foſſet, and you will find it immediately pour into your Mouth; or take out the Vent, but do not ſtay to put it in again, for fear your Maſter ſhould want you.

If you are curious to taſte ſome of your Maſter's choice Bottles, empty as many of them juſt below the Neck as will make the Quantity you want; but then take care to fill them up again with clean Water, that you may not leſſen your Maſter's Liquor.

There is an excellent Invention found out of late Years in the Management of Ale and Small-beer at the Side-board: For Inſtance, a Gentleman calls for a Glaſs of Ale, and drinks but half; another calls for Small-beer, you immediately teem out the Remainder of the Ale into the Tankard, and fill the Glaſs with Small-beer, and ſo backwards and forwards as long as Dinner laſts; by which you anſwer three great Ends: Firſt, you ſave your ſelf the Trouble of waſhing, and conſequently the Danger of breaking your Glaſſes: Secondly, you are ſure not to be miſtaken in giving Gentlemen the Liquor they call for: And laſtly, by this Method you are certain that nothing is loſt.

Becauſe Butlers are apt to forget to bring up their Ale and Beer time enough, be ſure you remember to have up yours two Hours before Dinner; and place them in the ſunny Part of the Room, to let People ſee that you have not been negligent.

Some Butlers have a Way of decanting (as they call it) bottled Ale, by which they loſe a good Part of the Bottom: Let your Method be to turn the Bottle directly upſide down, which will make the Liquor appear double the Quantity; by this means, you will be ſure not to loſe one Drop, and the Froth will conceal the Muddineſs.

Clean your Plate, wipe your Knives, and rub the dirty Tables, with the Napkins and Table-

Table-cloths used that Day; for, it is but one washing, and besides it will save you wearing out the coarse Rubbers; and in Reward of such good Husbandry, my Judgment is, that you may lawfully make use of the finest Damask Napkins for Night-caps for yourself.

When you clean your Plate, leave the Whiting plainly to be seen in all the Chinks, for fear your Lady should not believe you had cleaned it.

There is nothing wherein the Skill of a Butler more appears, than in the Management of Candles, whereof, although some Part may fall to the Share of the other Servants, yet you being the principal Person concerned, I shall direct my Instructions upon this Article to you only, leaving to your Fellow-servants to apply them upon Occasion.

First, to avoid burning Day-light, and to save your Master's Candles, never bring them up till Half an Hour after it be dark, altho' they are called for never so often.

Let your Sockets be full of Grease to the Brim, with the old Snuff at the Top; and then stick on your fresh Candles. It is true, this may endanger their falling, but the Candles will appear so much the longer and handsomer before Company. At other Times, for Variety, put your Candles loose in the Sockets, to shew they are clean to the Bottom.

When your Candle is too big for the Socket, melt it to a right Size in the Fire; and to hide the

the Smoke, wrap it in Paper half way up.

You cannot but obſerve of late Years the great Extravagancy among the Gentry upon the Articles of Candles, which a good Butler ought by all means to diſcourage, both to ſave his own Pains and his Maſter's Money: This may be contrived ſeveral Ways: As when you are ordered to put Candles into the Sconces.

Sconces are great Waſters of Candles, and you who are always to conſider the Advantage of your Maſter, ſhould do your utmoſt to diſcourage them: Therefore, your Buſineſs muſt be to preſs the Candle with both your Hands into the Socket, ſo as to make it lean in ſuch a manner, that the Greaſe may drop all upon the Floor, if ſome Lady's Head-dreſs or Gentleman's Perriwig be not ready to intercept it: You may likewiſe ſtick the Candle ſo looſe, that it will fall upon the Glaſs of the Sconce, and break it into Shatters; this will ſave your Maſter many a fair Penny in the Year, both in Candles, and to the Glaſs-man, and your ſelf much Labour; for the Sconces ſpoiled cannot be uſed.

Never let the Candles burn too low, but give them, as a lawful Perquiſite, to your Friend the Cook, to increaſe her Kitchen-ſtuff; or if this be not allowed in your Houſe, give them in Charity to the poor Neighbours, who often run on your Errands.

When you cut Bread for a Toaſt, do not ſtand idly watching it, but lay it on the Coals,

and

and mind your other Bufinefs; then come back, and if you find it toafted quite through, fcrape off the burned Side, and ferve it up.

When you drefs up your Side-board, fet the beft Glaffes as near the Edge of the Table as you can; by which means they will caft a double Luftre, and make a much finer Figure; and the Confequence can be at moft, but the breaking half a Dozen, which is a Trifle in your Mafter's Pocket.

Wafh the Glaffes with your own Water, to fave your Mafter's Salt.

When any Salt is fpilt on the Table, do not let it be loft, but when Dinner is done, fold up the Table-cloth with the Salt in it, then fhake the Salt out into the Salt-celler to ferve next Day: But the fhorteft and fureft Way is, when you remove the Cloth, to wrap the Knives, Forks, Spoons, Salt-cellars, broken Bread, and Scraps of Meat all together in the Table-cloth, by which you will be fure to lofe nothing, unlefs you think it better to fhake them out of the Window amongft the Beggars, that they may with more Convenience eat the Scraps.

Leave the Dregs of Wine, Ale, and other Liquors in the Bottles: To rince them is but Lofs of Time, fince all will be done at once in a general wafhing; and you will have a better Excufe for breaking them.

If your Mafter hath many mufty, or very foul and crufted Bottles, I advife you, in point of of Confcience, that thofe may be the firft you truck at the next Ale-houfe for Ale or Brandy.

When a Meffage is fent to your Mafter, be kind to your Brother-fervant who brings it; give him the beft Liquor in your keeping, for your Mafter's Honour; and with the firft Opportunity he will do the fame to you.

After Supper, if it be dark, carry your Plate and China together in the fame Bafket, to fave Candle-light, for you know your Pantry well enough to put them up in the Dark.

When Company is expected at Dinner or in the Evenings, be fure to be abroad that nothing may be got which is under your Key, by which your Mafter will fave his Liquor, and not wear out his Plate.

I come now to a moft important Part of your Oeconomy, the bottling of a Hogfhead of Wine, wherein I recommend three Virtues, Cleanlinefs, Frugality, and brotherly Love. Let your Corks be of the longeft Kind you can get; which will fave fome Wine in the Neck of every Bottle: As to your Bottles chufe the fmalleft you can find, which will increafe the Number of Dozens, and pleafe your Mafter; for a Bottle of Wine is always a Bottle of Wine, whether it hold more or lefs; and if your Mafter hath his proper Number of Dozens, he cannot complain.

Every Bottle muft be firft rinced with Wine, for fear of any Moifture left in the Wafhing; fome, out of miftaken Thrift, will rince a Do-

zen

zen Bottles with the ſame Wine; but I would adviſe you, for more Caution, to change the Wine at every ſecond Bottle; a Jill may be enough. Have Bottles ready by to ſave it; and it will be a good Perquiſite, either to ſell or drink with the Cook.

Never draw your Hogſhead too low; nor tilt it for fear of diſturbing your Liquor. When it begins to run ſlow, and before the Wine grows cloudy, ſhake the Hogſhead, and carry a Glaſs of it to your Maſter, who will praiſe you for your Diſcretion, and give you all the reſt as a Perquiſite of your Place: You may tilt the Hogſhead the next Day, and in a Fortnight get a Dozen or two of good clear Wine, to diſpoſe of as you pleaſe.

In bottling Wine, fill your Mouth full of Corks, together with a large Plug of Tobacco, which will give to the Wine the true Taſte of the Weed, ſo delightful to all good Judges in drinking.

When you are ordered to decant a ſuſpicious Bottle, if a Pint be out, give your Hand a dexterous Shake, and ſhew it in a Glaſs, that it begins to be muddy.

When a Hogſhead of Wine or any other Liquor is to be bottled off, waſh your Bottles immediately before you begin; but, be ſure not to drain them, by which good Management you Maſter will ſave ſome Gallons in every Hogſhead.

This

This is the Time that in Honour to your Maſter, you ought to ſhew your Kindneſs to your Fellow-ſervants, and eſpecially to the Cook; for what ſignifies a few Flagons out of a whole Hogſhead? But make them drunk in your Preſence, for fear they ſhould be given to other Folks, and ſo your Maſter be wronged: But adviſe them, if they get drunk, to go to Bed, and leave Word they are ſick, which laſt Caution I would have all the Servants obſerve, both Male and Female.

If your Maſter finds the Hogſhead to fall ſhort of his Expectation, what is plainer, than that the Veſſel leaked: That the Wine-Cooper had not filled it in proper Time: That the Merchant cheated him with a Hogſhead below the common Meaſure?

When you are to get Water on for Tea after Dinner (which in many Families is Part of your Office) to ſave Firing, and to make more Haſte, pour it into the Tea-pot, from the Pot where Cabbage or Fiſh have been boyling, which will make it much wholſomer, by curing the acid and corroding Quality of the Tea.

Be ſaving of your Candles, and let thoſe in the Sconces of the Hall, the Stairs, and in the Lanthorn, burn down into the Sockets, until they go out of themſelves, for which your Maſter and Lady will commend your Thriftineſs, as ſoon as they ſhall ſmell the Snuff.

If a Gentleman leaves a Snuff-box or Pick-tooth-caſe on the Table after Dinner, and goeth away, look upon it as Part of your Vails; for ſo it is allowed by all Servants, and you do no Wrong to your Maſter or Lady.

If you ſerve a Country 'Squire, when Gentlemen and Ladies come to dine at your Houſe, never fail to make their Servants drunk, and eſpecially the Coachman, for the Honour of your Maſter: to which, in all your Actions, you muſt have a ſpecial Regard, as being the beſt Judge: For the Honour of every Family, is depoſited in the Hands of the Cook, the Butler, and the Groom, as I ſhall hereafter demonſtrate.

Snuff the Candles at Supper as they ſtand on the Table, which is much the ſecureſt Way; becauſe, if the burning Snuff happens to get out of the Snuffers, you have a Chance that it may fall into a Diſh of Soup, Sack-poſſet, Rice-milk, or the like, where it will be immediately extinguiſhed with very little Stink.

When you have ſnuffed the Candle, always leave the Snuffers open, for the Snuff will of itſelf burn away to Aſhes, and cannot fall out and dirty the Table, when you ſnuff the Candles again.

That the Salt may lie ſmooth in the Salt-celler, preſs it down with your moiſt Palm.

When a Gentleman is going away after dining with your Maſter, be ſure to ſtand full in View

View, and follow him to the Door, and as you have Opportunity look full in his Face, perhaps it may bring you a Shilling; but, if the Gentleman hath lain there a Night, get the Cook, the Houſe-maid, the Stable-men, the Scullion, and the Gardiner, to accompany you, and to ſtand in his Way to the Hall in a Line on each Side him: If the Gentleman performs handſomely, it will do him Honour, and coſt your Maſter nothing.

You need not wipe your Knife to cut Bread for the Table, becauſe, in cutting a Slice or two it will wipe it ſelf.

Put your Finger into every Bottle, to feel whether it be full, which is the ſureſt Way, for feeling hath no fellow.

When you go down to the Cellar to draw Ale or Small-beer, take care to obſerve directly the following Method: Hold the Veſſel between the Finger and Thumb of your Right Hand, with the Palm upwards, then hold the Candle between your Fingers, but a little leaning towards the Mouth of the Veſſel, then take out the Spiggot with your Left Hand, and clap the Point of it in your Mouth, and keep your Left Hand to watch Accidents; when the Veſſel is full withdraw the Spiggot with your Mouth well wetted with Spittle, which being of a ſlimy Conſiſtence, will make it ſtick faſter in the Foſſet: If any Tallow drops into the Veſſel you may eaſily (if you think of it) remove it with a Spoon, or rather with your Finger.

Always

Always lock up a Cat in the Closet where you keep your *China* Plates, for fear the Mice may steal in and break them.

A good Butler always breaks off the Point of his Bottle-screw in two Days, by trying which is hardest, the Point of the Screw, or the Neck of the Bottle: In this Case, to supply the Want of a Screw, after the Stump hath torn the Cork in Pieces, make use of a Silver Fork, and when the Scraps of the Cork are almost drawn out, flirt the Mouth of the Bottle into the Cistern until you quite clear it.

If a Gentleman dines often with your Master, and gives you nothing when he goes away, you may use several Methods to shew him some Marks of your Displeasure, and quicken his Memory: If he calls for Bread or Drink, you may pretend not to hear, or send it to another who called after him: If he asks for Wine, let him stay a while, and then send him Small-beer; give him always foul Glasses; send him a Spoon when he wants a Knife; wink at the Footman to leave him without a Plate; By these, and the like Expedients, you may probably be a better Man by Half a Crown before he leaves the House, provided you watch an Opportunity of standing by when he is going.

If your Lady loves Play, your Fortune is fixed for ever: Moderate Gaming will be a Perquisite of ten Shillings a Week; and in such a Family I would rather chuse to be Butler than Chaplain, or even rather than be Steward: It is all ready Money and got without Labour, unleſs your Lady happens to be one of thoſe, who either obligeth you to find Wax-Candles, or forceth you to divide it with ſome favourite Servants; but at worſt, the old Cards are your own; and, if the Gameſters play deep or grow peeviſh, they will change the Cards ſo often, that the old ones will be a conſiderable Advantage by ſelling to Coffee-Houſes, or Families who love Play, but cannot afford better than Cards at ſecond Hand: When you attend at the Service, be ſure to leave new Packs within the Reach of the Gameſters, which, thoſe who have ill Luck will readily take to change their Fortune; and now and then an old Pack mingled with the reſt will eaſily paſs. Be ſure to be very officious on Play Nights, and ready with your Candles to light out your Company, and have Salvers of Wine at Hand to give them when they call; but manage ſo with the Cook, that there be no Supper, becauſe it will be ſo much ſaved in your Maſter's Family; and, becauſe a Supper will conſiderably leſſen your Gains.

Next to Cards there is nothing ſo profitable to you as Bottles, in which Perquiſite you have no Competitors, except the Footmen, who are apt to ſteal and vend them for Pots of Beer; But you are bound to prevent any ſuch Abuſes in your Maſter's Family: The Footmen are not to anſwer for what are broken at a general

Bottling;

Bottling; and those may be as many as your Discretion will make them.

The Profit of Glasses is so very inconsiderable, that it is hardly worth mentioning: It consists only in a small Present made by the Glassman, and about four Shillings in the Pound added to the Prices for your Trouble and Skill in chusing them. If your Master hath a large Stock of Glasses, and you or your Fellow-servants happen to break any of them without your Master's Knowledge, keep it a Secret till there are not enough left to serve the Table, then tell your Master that the Glasses are gone; this will be but one Vexation to him, which is much better than fretting once or twice a Week; and it is the Office of a good Servant to discompose his Master and his Lady as seldom as he can; and here the Cat and Dog will be of great Use to take the Blame from you. *Note*, That Bottles missing are supposed to be half stolen by Stragglers and other Servants, and the other half broken by Accident, and a general Washing.

Whet the Backs of your Knives until they are as sharp as the Edge, which will have this Advantage, that when Gentlemen find them blunt on one Side, they may try the other; and to shew you spare no Pains in sharpening the Knives, whet them so long, till you wear out a good Part of the Iron, and even the Bottom of the Silver Handle. This doth Credit to your Master, for it shews good House-keeping, and the Goldſmith may one Day make you a Preſent.

Your Lady when ſhe finds the Small-beer or Ale dead, will blame you for not remembring to put the Peg into the Vent-hole. This is a great Miſtake, nothing being plainer, than that the Peg keeps the Air in the Veſſel, which ſpoils the Drink, and therefore ought to be let out; but if ſhe inſiſts upon it, to prevent the Trouble of pulling out the Vent, and putting it in a Dozen Times a Day, which is not to be born by a good Servant, leave the Spiggot half out at Night, and you will find with only the Loſs of two or three Quarts of Liquor, the Veſſel will run freely.

When you prepare your Candles, wrap them up in a Piece of brown Paper, and ſo ſtick them into the Socket: Let the Paper come half way up the Candle, which looks handſome, if any body ſhould come in.

Do all in the Dark to ſave your Maſter's Candles.

CHAP. II.

Directions to the COOK.

ALTHO' I am not ignorant that it hath been a long Time, ſince the Cuſtom began among People of Quality to keep Men Cooks, and generally of the *French* Nation; yet

yet because my Treatise is chiefly calculated for the general Run of Knights, 'Squires, and Gentlemen both in Town and Country, I shall therefore apply myself to you, Mrs. Cook, as a Woman: However, a great Part of what I intend may serve for either Sex; and your Part naturally follows the former, because the Butler and you are join'd in Interest; your Vails are generally equal, and paid when others are disappointed: You can junket together at Nights upon your own Progue, when the rest of the House are abed; and have it in your Power to make every Fellow-servant your Friend; you can give a good Bit or a good Sup to the little Masters and Misses, and gain their Affections: A Quarrel between you is very dangerous to you both, and will probably end in one of you being turned off; in which fatal Case, perhaps, it will not be so easy in some Time to cotton with another. And now Mrs. Cook, I proceed to give you my Instructions, which I desire you will get some Fellow-servant in the Family to read to you constantly one Night in every Week when you are going to Bed, whether you serve in Town or Country, for my Lessons shall be fitted for both.

If your Lady forgets at Supper that there is any cold Meat in the House, do not you be so officious as to put her in Mind; it is plain she did not want it; and if she recollects it the next Day, say she gave you no Orders, and it is spent; therefore, for fear of telling a Lye, dispose of it with the Butler, or any other Crony, before you go to Bed.

Never send up a Leg of a Fowl at Supper, while there is a Cat or a Dog in the House that can be accused of running away with it: But, if there happen to be neither, you must lay it upon the Rats, or a strange Greyhound.

It is ill Housewifry to foul your Kitchen Rubbers with wiping the Bottom of the Dishes you send up, since the Table-cloth will do as well, and is changed every Meal.

Never clean your Spits after they have been used; for the Grease left upon them by Meat, is the best thing to preserve them from Rust; and when you make use of them again, the same Grease will keep the Inside of the Meat moist.

If you live in a Rich Family, roasting and boiling are below the Dignity of your Office, and which it becomes you to be ignorant of; therefore leave that Work wholly to the Kitchen Wench, for fear of disgracing the Family you live in.

If you are employed in Marketing, buy your Meat as cheap as you can; but when you bring in your Accounts, be tender of your Master's Honour, and set down the highest Rate; which besides is but Justice, for no body can afford to sell at the same Rate that he buys, and I am confident that you may charge safely; swear that you gave no more than what the Butcher and Poulterer asked. If your

Lady

Lady orders you to ſet up a Piece of Meat for Supper, you are not to underſtand that you muſt ſet it up all, therefore you may give half to yourſelf and the Butler.

Good Cooks cannot abide what they juſtly call fidling Work, where Abundance of Time is ſpent and little done: Such, for Inſtance, is the dreſſing ſmall Birds, requiring a World of Cookery and Clutter, and a ſecond or third Spit, which by the way is abſolutely needleſs; for it will be a very ridiculous Thing indeed, if a Spit which is ſtrong enough to turn a Surloyn of Beef, ſhould not be able to turn a Lark; however, if your Lady be nice, and is afraid that a large Spit will tear them, place them handſomely in the Dripping-pan, where the Fat of roaſted Mutton or Beef falling on the Birds, will ſerve to baſte them, and ſo ſave both Time and Butter: for what Cook of any Spirit would loſe her Time in picking Larks, Wheatears, and other ſmall Birds; therefore if you cannot get the Maids, or the young Miſſes to aſſiſt you, e'en make ſhort Work, and either ſinge or flay them; there is no great Loſs in the Skins, and the Fleſh is juſt the ſame.

If you are employed in Market, do not accept a Treat of a Beef Stake and Pot of Ale from the Butcher, which I think in Conſcience is no better than wronging your Maſter, but do you always take that Perquiſite in Money, if you do not go in Truſt, or in Poundage when you pay the Bills.

The Kitchen Bellows being uſually out of Order with ſtirring the Fire with the Muzzle to ſave the Tongs and Poker, borrow the Bellows out of your Lady's Bed-chamber, which being leaſt uſed, are commonly the beſt in the Houſe; and if you happen to damage or greaſe them, you have a Chance to have them left entirely for your own Uſe.

Let a Blackguard Boy be always about the Houſe to ſend on your Errands, and go to Market for you in rainy Days, which will ſave your Cloaths, and make you appear more creditable to your Miſtreſs.

If your Miſtreſs allows you the Kitchen-ſtuff, in return of her Generoſity, take care to boil and roaſt your Meat ſufficient. If ſhe keeps it for her own Profit, do her Juſtice, and rather than let a good Fire be wanting, enliven it now and then with the Dripping and the Butter that happens to turn to Oil.

Send up your Meat well ſtuck with Scewers, to make it look round and plump; and an Iron Scewer rightly employed now and then, will make it look handſomer.

When you roaſt a long Joint of Meat, be careful only about the Middle, and leave the two extreme Parts raw, which may ſerve another Time, and will alſo ſave Firing.

When you ſcour your Plates and Diſhes, bend the Brim inward, ſo as to make them hold the more.

Always

Always keep a large Fire in the Kitchen when there is a ſmall Dinner, or the Family dines abroad, that the Neighbours ſeeing the Smoak, may commend your Maſter's Houſe-keeping: But, when much Company is invited, then be as ſparing as poſſible of your Coals, becauſe a great deal of the Meat being half raw will be ſaved, and ſerve next Day.

Boil your Meat conſtantly in Pump Water, becauſe you muſt ſometimes want River or Pipe Water, and then your Miſtreſs obſerving your Meat of a different Colour, will chide you when you are not in Fault.

When you have Plenty of Fowl in the Larder, leave the Door open, in Pity to the poor Cat, if ſhe be a good Mouſer.

If you find it neceſſary to market in a wet Day, take out your Miſtreſs's Riding-hood and Cloak to ſave your Cloaths.

Get three or four Char-women to attend you conſtantly in the Kitchen, whom you pay at ſmall Charges, only with the broken Meat, a few Coals, and all the Cinders.

To keep troubleſome Servants out of the Kitchen, always leave the Winder ſticking on the Jack to fall on their Heads.

If a Lump of Soot falls into the Soup, and you cannot conveniently get it out, ſtir it well in, and it will give the Soup a high *French* Taſte.

If you melt your Butter to Oil, be under no Concern, but ſend it up; for Oil is a genteeler Sauce than Butter.

Scrape

Scrape the Bottoms of your Pots and Kettles with a Silver Spoon, for fear of giving them a Tafte of Copper.

When you fend up Butter for Sauce, be fo thrifty as to let it be half Water; which is alfo much wholefomer.

If your Butter, when it is melted, taftes of Brafs, it is your Mafter's Fault, who will not allow you a Silver Sauce-pan; befides, the lefs of it will go further, and new tinning is very chargeable: If you have a Silver Sauce-pan, and the Butter fmells of Smoak, lay the Fault upon the Coals.

Never make ufe of a Spoon in any thing that you can do with your Hands, for fear of wearing out your Mafter's Plate.

When you find that you cannot get Dinner ready at the Time appointed, put the Clock back, and then it may be ready to a Minute.

Let a red hot Coal now and then fall into the Dripping Pan, that the Smoak of the Dripping may afcend, and give the roaft Meat a high Tafte.

You are to look upon your Kitchen as your Dreffing-room; but, you are not to wafh your Hands till you have gone to the Neceffary-houfe, and fpitted your Meat, truffed your Fowl, picked your Sallad; nor indeed till after you have fent up your fecond Courfe; for your Hands will be ten times fouler with the many things you are forced to handle; but when your Work is over, one Wafhing will ferve for all.

There

There is but one Part of your Dreſſing that I would admit while the Victuals are boiling, toaſting, or ſtewing, I mean the combing your Head, which loſeth no Time, becauſe you can ſtand over your Cookery, and watch it with one Hand, while you are uſing your Comb in the other.

If any of the Combings happen to be ſent up with the Victuals, you may ſafely lay the Fault upon any of the Footmen that hath vexed you: As thoſe Gentlemen are ſometimes apt to be malicious, if you refuſe them a Sop in the Pan, or a Slice from the Spit, much more when you diſcharge a Ladle-full of hot Porridge on their Legs, or ſend them up to their Maſters with a Diſhclout pinned at their Tails.

In roaſting and boiling, order the Kitchen-maid to bring none but the large Coals, and ſave the ſmall ones for the Fires above Stairs; the firſt are propereſt for dreſſing Meat, and when they are out, if you happen to miſcarry in any Diſh, you may lay the Fault upon want of Coals: Beſides, the Cinder-pickers will be ſure to ſpeak ill of your Maſter's Houſekeeping, where they do not find Plenty of large Cinders mixt with freſh large Coals: Thus you may dreſs your Meat with Credit, do an Act of Charity, raiſe the Honour of your Maſter, and ſometimes get a Share of a Pot of Ale for your Bounty to the Cinder-woman.

As ſoon as you have ſent up the ſecond Courſe, you have nothing to do in a great Family until

Supper;

Supper: Therefore ſcoure your Hands and Face, put on your Hood and Scarf, and take your Pleaſure among your Cronies, till Nine or Ten at Night——But dine firſt.

Let there be always a ſtrict Friendſhip between you and the Butler, for it is both your Intereſts to be united: The Butler often wants a comfortable Tit-bit, and you much oftener a cool Cup of good Liquor. However, be cautious of him, for he is ſometimes an inconſtant Lover, becauſe he hath great Advantage to allure the Maids with a Glaſs of Sack, or White Wine and Sugar.

When you roaſt a Breaſt of Veal, remember your Sweet-heart the Butler loves a Sweet-bread; therefore ſet it aſide till Evening: You can ſay, the Cat or the Dog has run away with it, or you found it tainted, or fly-blown; and beſides, it looks as well at the Table without it as with it.

When you make the Company wait long for Dinner and the Meat be overdone, which is generally the Caſe, you may lawfully lay the Fault upon your Lady, who hurried you ſo to ſend up Dinner, that you was forced to ſend it up too much boiled and roaſted.

If your Dinner miſcarries in almoſt every Diſh, how could you help it? You were teized by the Footmen coming into the Kitchen; and, to prove it true, take Occaſion to be angry, and throw a Ladle-full of Broth on one or two of their Liveries; beſides, *Friday* and *Childer-*

Childermas-day are too croſs Days in the Week, and it is impoſſible to have good Luck on either of them; therefore on thoſe two Days you have a lawful Excuſe.

When you are in haſte to take down your Diſhes, tip them in ſuch a manner, that a Dozen will fall together upon the Dreſſer, juſt ready for your Hand.

To ſave Time and Trouble, cut your Apples and Onions with the ſame Knife; and well-bred Gentry love the Taſte of an Onion in every thing they eat.

Lump three or four Pounds of Butter together with your Hands, then daſh it againſt the Wall juſt over the Dreſſer, ſo as to have it ready to pull by Pieces as you have occaſion for it.

If you have a Silver Saucepan for the Kitchen Uſe, let me adviſe you to batter it well, and keep it always black; this will be for your Maſter's Honour, for it ſhews there has been conſtant good Houſekeeping: And make room for the Saucepan by wriggling it on the Coals, &c.

In the ſame Manner, if you are allowed a large Silver Spoon for the Kitchen, let half the Bole of it be worn out with continual ſcraping and ſtirring and often ſay merrily, This Spoon owes my Maſter no Service.

When you ſend up a Meſs of Broth, Water-gruel, or the like, to your Maſter in a Morning, do not forget with your Thumb and two Fingers

Fingers to put Salt on the Side of the Plate; for if you make uſe of a Spoon, or the End of a Knife, there may be Danger that the Salt would fall, and that will be a Sign of ill Luck. Only remember to lick your Thumb and Fingers clean, before you offer to touch the Salt.

CHAP. III.

Directions to the FOOTMAN.

YOUR Employment being of a mixt Nature, extends to a great Variety of Buſineſs, and you ſtand in a fair way of being the Favourite of your Maſter or Miſtreſs, or of the young Maſters and Miſſes; you are the fine Gentleman of the Family, with whom all the Maids are in Love. You are ſometimes a Pattern of Dreſs to your Maſter, and ſometimes he is ſo to you. You wait at Table in all Companies, and conſequently have the Opportunity to ſee and know the World, and to underſtand Men and Manners; I confeſs your Vails are but few, unleſs you are ſent with a Preſent, or attend the Tea in the Country; but you are called Mr. in the Neighbourhood, and ſometimes pick up a Fortune, perhaps your Maſter's Daughter; and I have known many of your Tribe to have good Commands in the Army. In Town you have a Seat reſerved for you in the Play-Houſe, where you have an Opportutunity of becoming Wits and Criticks: You have no profeſt Enemy except the Rabble, and my Lady's Waiting-woman, who are ſometimes apt to call you Skipkennel. I have a true Veneration for your Office, becauſe I had once the Honour to be one of your Order, which I fooliſhly left by demeaning myſelf with accepting an Employment in the Cuſtom-Houſe.— But that you, my Brethren, may come to better Fortunes, I ſhall here deliver my Inſtructions, which have been the Fruits of much Thought and Obſervation, as well as of ſeven Years Experience.

In order to learn the Secrets of other Families, tell them thoſe of your Maſter's; thus you will grow a Favourite both at home and abroad, and regarded as a Perſon of Importance.

Never be ſeen in the Streets with a Baſket or Bundle in your Hands, and carry nothing but what you can hide in your Pocket, otherwiſe you will diſgrace your Calling: to prevent which, always retain a Black-guard Boy to carry your Loads; and if you want Farthings, pay him with a good Slice of Bread or Scrap of Meat.

Let a Shoe-boy clean your own Shoes firſt, for fear of fouling the Chamber, then let him clean your Maſter's; keep him on Purpoſe for that Uſe and to run of Errands, and pay him with Scraps. When you are ſent on an Errand, be ſure to hedge in ſome Buſineſs of your own, either to ſee your Sweetheart, or drink a Pot

of

of Ale with ſome Brother-Servants, which is ſo much Time clear gained.

There is a great Controverſy about the moſt convenient and genteel Way of holding your Plate at Meals; ſome ſtick it between the Frame and the Back of the Chair, which is an excellent Expedient, where the make of the Chair will allow it: Others, for Fear the Plate ſhould fall, graſp it ſo firmly, that their Thumb reacheth to the Middle of the Hollow; which however, if your Thumb be dry, is no ſecure Method; and therefore in that Caſe, I adviſe your wetting the Bowl of it with your Tongue: As to that abſurd Practice of letting the Back of the Plate lye leaning on the Hollow of your Hand, which ſome Ladies recommend, it is univerſally exploded, being liable to ſo many Accidents. Others again, are ſo refined, that they hold their Plate directly under the Left Arm-pit, which is the beſt Situation for keeping it warm; but this may be dangerous in the Article of taking away a Diſh, where your Plate may happen to fall upon ſome of the Company's Heads. I confeſs myſelf to have objected againſt all theſe Ways, which I have frequently tryed; and therefore I recommend a Fourth, which is to ſtick your Plate up to the Rim incluſive, and in the left Side between your Waiſtcoat and your Shirt: This will keep it at leaſt as warm as under your Arm-pit, or Ockſter, (as the *Scots* call it) this will hide it ſo, as Strangers may take you for a better Ser-

vant,

vant, too good to hold a Plate; this will ſecure it from falling, and thus diſpoſed, it lies ready for you to whip it out in a Moment, ready warmed, to any Gueſt within your Reach, who may want it. And laſtly, there is another Convenience in this Method, that if, any Time during your waiting, you find yourſelves going to cough or ſneeze, you can immediately ſnatch out your Plate, and hold the hollow Part cloſe to your Noſe or Mouth, and, thus prevent ſpirting any Moiſture from either, upon the Diſhes or the Ladies Head-dreſs: You ſee Gentlemen and Ladies obſerve a like Practice on ſuch an Occaſion, with a Hat or a Handkerchief: yet a Plate is leſs fouled and ſooner cleaned than either of theſe; for, when your Cough or Sneeſe is over, it is but returning your Plate to the ſame Poſition, and your Shirt will clean it in the Paſſage.

Take off the largeſt Diſhes, and ſet them on with one Hand, to ſhew the Ladies your Vigour and Strength of Back; but always do it between two Ladies, that if the Diſh happens to ſlip, the Soup or Sauce may fall on their Cloaths and not daub the Floor: By this Practice two of our Brethren, my worthy Friends, got conſiderable Fortunes.

Learn all the new-faſhion Words, and Oaths, and Songs, and Scraps of Plays that your Memory can hold. Thus, you will become the Delight of nine Ladies in ten, and the Envy of ninety nine Beaux in a hundred.

Take Care, that at certain Periods, during Dinner eſpecially, when Perſons of Quality are there, you and your Brethren be all out of the Room together, by which you will give yourſelves ſome Eaſe from the Fatigue of waiting, and at the ſame Time leave the Company to converſe more freely, without being conſtrain-by your Preſence.

When you are ſent on a Meſſage, deliver it in your own Words, altho' it be to a Duke or a Ducheſs, and not in the Words of your Maſter or Lady; for how can they underſtand what belongs to a Meſſage as well as you, who have been bred to the Employment? But never deliver the Anſwer till it is called for, and then adorn it with your own Style.

When Dinner is done, carry down a great Heap of Plates to the Kitchen, and when you come to the Head of the Stairs, trundle them all before you: There is not a more agreeable Sight or Sound, eſpecially if they be Silver, beſides the Trouble they ſave you, and there they will lie ready near the Kitchen Door, for the Scullion to waſh them.

If you are bringing up a Joint of Meat in a Diſh, and it falls out of your Hand, before you get into the Dining Room, with the Meat on the Ground, and the Sauce ſpilled, take up the Meat gently, wipe it with the Lap of your Coat, then put it again into the Diſh, and serve it up; and when your Lady miſſes the Sauce, tell her, it is to be ſent up in a Plate by itſelf.

When

When you carry up a Diſh of Meat, dip your Fingers in the Sauce, or lick it with your Tongue, to try whether it be good, and fit for your Maſter's Table.

You are the beſt Judge of what Acquaintance your Lady ought to have, and therefore, if ſhe ſends you on a Meſſage of Compliment or Buſineſs to a Family you do not like, deliver the Anſwer in ſuch a Manner, as may breed a Quarrel between them, not to be reconciled: Or, if a Footman comes from the ſame Family on the like Errand, turn the Anſwer ſhe orders you to deliver, in ſuch a Manner, as the other Family may take it for an Affront.

When you are in Lodgings, and no Shoe-boy to be got, clean your Maſter's Shoes with the Bottom of the Curtains, a clean Napkin, or your Landlady's Apron.

Ever wear your Hat in the Houſe, but when your Maſter calls; and as ſoon as you come into his Preſence, pull it off to ſhew your Manners.

Never clean your Shoes on the Scraper, but in the Entry, or at the Foot of the Stairs, by which you will have the Credit of being at home, almoſt a Minute ſooner, and the Scraper will laſt the longer.

Never aſk Leave to go abroad, for then it will be always known that you are abſent, and you will be thought an idle rambling Fellow; whereas, if you go out, and nobody obſerves, you have a Chance of coming home without being missed, and you need not tell your Fellow-servants when you are gone, for they will be sure to say, you were in the House but two Minutes ago, which is the Duty of all Servants.

Snuff the Candles with your Fingers, and throw the Snuff on the Floor, then tread it out to prevent stinking: This Method will very much save the Snuffers from wearing out. You ought also to snuff them close to the Tallow, which will make them run, and so increase the Perquisite of the Cook's Kitchen-Stuff; for she is the Person you ought in Prudence to be well with.

While Grace is saying after Meat, do you and your Brethren take the Chairs from behind the Company, so that when they go to it again, they may fall backwards, which will make them all merry; but be you so discreet as to hold your Laughter till you get to the Kitchen, and then divert your Fellow-servants.

When you know your Master is most busy in Company, come in and pretend to settle about the Room, and if he chides, say, you thought he rung the Bell. This will divert him from plodding on Business too much, or spending himself in Talk, or racking his Thoughts, all which are hurtful to his Constitution.

If you are ordered to break the Claw of a Crab or a Lobster, clap it between the Sides of the Dining Room Door between the Hinges: Thus you can do it gradually without mashing the

the Meat, which is often the Fate of the Street-Door-Key, or the Pestle.

When you take a foul Plate from any of the Guests, and observe the foul Knife and Fork lying on the Plate, shew your Dexterity, take up the Plate, and throw off the Knife and Fork on the Table without shaking off the Bones or broken Meat that are left: Then the Guest, who hath more Time than you, will wipe the Fork and Knife already used.

When you carry a Glass of Liquor to any Person who hath called for it, do not bob him on the Shoulder, or cry, Sir, or Madam, here's the Glass; that would be unmannerly, as if you had a Mind to force it down one's Throat; but stand at the Person's Right Shoulder and wait his Time; and if he strikes it down with his Elbow by Forgetfulness, that was his Fault and not yours.

When your Mistress sends you for a Hackney Coach in a wet Day, come back in the Coach to save your Cloaths and the Trouble of walking; it is better the Bottom of her Pettycoats should be draggled with your dirty Shoes, than your Livery be spoiled, and yourself get a Cold.

There is no Indignity so great to one of your Station, as that of lighting your Master in the Streets with a Lanthorn; and therefore, it is very honest Policy to try all Arts how to evade it: Besides, it shews your Master to be either poor or covetous, which are the two worst Qualities you can meet with in any Service. When

I was under these Circumstances, I made use of several wise Expedients, which I here recommend to you: Sometimes I took a Candle so long, that it reached to the very Top of the Lanthorn and burnt it: But, my Master after a good Beating, ordered me to paste the Top with Paper. I then used a middling Candle, but stuck it so loose in the Socket that it leaned towards one Side, and burned a whole Quarter of the Horn. Then I used a Bit of Candle of half an Inch, which sunk in the Socket, and melted the Solder, and forced my Master to walk half the Way in the Dark. Then he made me stick two Inches of Candle in the Place where the Socket was; after which, I pretended to stumble, put out the Candle, and broke all the Tin Part to Pieces: At last, he was forced to make use of a Lanthorn-boy out of perfect good Husbandry.

It is much to be lamented, that Gentlemen of our Employment have but two Hands to carry Plates, Dishes, Bottles, and the like out of the Room at Meals; and the Misfortune is still the greater, because one of those Hands is required to open the Door, while you are encumbred with your Load: Therefore, I advise, that the Door may be always left at jar, so as to open it with your Foot, and then you may carry out Plates and Dishes from your Belly up to your Chin, besides a good Quantity of Things under your Arms, which will save you many a weary Step; but take Care that none of the

Burthen

Burthen falls till you are out of the Room, and, if poſſible, out of Hearing.

If you are ſent to the Poſt-Office with a Letter in a cold rainy Night, ſtep to the Ale-houſe, and take a Pot, until it is ſuppoſed you have done your Errand, but take the next fair Opportunity to put the Letter in carefully, as becomes an honeſt Servant.

If you are ordered to make Coffee for the Ladies after Dinner, and the Pot happens to boil over, while you are running up for a Spoon to ſtir it, or are thinking of ſomething elſe, or ſtruggling with the Chamber-maid for a Kiſs, wipe the Sides of the Pot clean with a Diſhclout, carry up your Coffee boldly, and when your Lady finds it too weak, and examines you whether it has not run over, deny the Fact abſolutely, ſwear you put in more Coffee than ordinary, that you never ſtirred an Inch from it, that you ſtrove to make it better than uſual, becauſe your Miſtreſs had Ladies with her, that the Servants in the Kitchen will juſtify what you ſay: Upon this, you will find that the other Ladies will pronounce your Coffee to be very good, and your Miſtreſs will confeſs that her Mouth is out of Taſte, and ſhe will for the future ſuſpect herſelf, and be more cautious in finding Fault. This I would have you do from a Principle of Conſcience, for Coffee is very unwholſome; and out of Affection to your Lady, you ought to give it her as weak as poſſible: And upon this Argument, when you have a Mind to treat any of the Maids with a Dish of fresh Coffee, you may, and ought to substract a third Part of the Powder, on account of your Lady's Health and getting her Maids Good-will.

If your Master sends you with a small trifling Present to one of his Friends, be as careful of it as you would be of a Diamond Ring: Therefore, if the Present be only half a Dozen Pippins, send up the Servant who received the Message to say, that you were ordered to deliver them with your own Hands. This will shew your Exactness and Care to prevent Accidents or Mistakes; and the Gentleman or Lady cannot do less than give you a Shilling: So when your Master receives the like Present, teach the Messenger that brings it to do the same, and give your Master Hints that may stir up his Generosity; for Brother Servants should assist one another, since it is all for your Master's Honour, which is the chief Point to be consulted by every good Servant, and of which he is the best Judge.

When you step but a few Doors off to tattle with a Wench, or take a running Pot of Ale, or to see a Brother Footman going to be hanged, leave the Street Door open, that you may not be forced to knock, and your Master discover you are gone out; for a Quarter of an Hour's Time can do his Service no Injury.

When you take away the remaining Pieces of Bread after Dinner, put them on foul Plates, and press them down with other Plates over them

them, ſo as nobody can touch them; and ſo, they will be a good Perquiſite to the Black-guard Boy in ordinary.

When you are forced to clean your Maſter's Shoes with your own Hand, uſe the Edge of the ſharpeſt Caſe Knife, and dry them with the Toes an Inch from the Fire, becauſe wet Shoes are dangerous; and beſides, by theſe Arts you will get them the ſooner for yourſelf.

In ſome Families the Maſter often ſends to the Tavern for a Bottle of Wine, and you are the Meſſenger: I adviſe you, therefore, to take the ſmalleſt Bottle you can find; but however, make the Drawer give you a full Quart, then you will get a good Sup for yourſelf, and your Bottle will be filled. As for a Cork to ſtop it, you need be at no Trouble, for the Thumb will do as well, or a Bit of dirty chewed Paper.

In all Diſputes with Chairmen and Coach-men, for demanding too much, when your Maſter ſends you down to chaffer with them, take Pity of the poor Fellows, and tell your Maſter that they will not take a Farthing leſs: It is more for your Intereſt to get a Share of a Pot of Ale, than to ſave a Shilling for your Maſter, to whom it is a Trifle.

When you attend your Lady in a dark Night, if ſhe uſeth her Coach, do not walk by the Coach Side, ſo as to tire and dirt yourſelf, but get up into your proper Place, behind it, and ſo hold the Flambeau ſloping forward over the

Coach

Coach Roof; and when it wants ſnuffing, daſh it againſt the Corners.

When you leave your Lady at Church on *Sundays*, you have two Hours ſafe to ſpend with your Companions at the Ale-Houſe, or over a Beef Stake and a Pot of Beer at home with the Cook and the Maids; and indeed poor Servants have ſo few Opportunities to be happy, that they ought not to loſe any.

Never wear Socks when you wait at Meals, on the Account of your own Health, as well as of them who ſet at Table; becauſe as moſt Ladies like the Smell of young Mens Toes, ſo it is a ſovereign Remedy againſt the Vapours.

Chuſe a Service, if you can, where your Livery Colours are leaſt tawdry and diſtinguiſhing: Green and Yellow, immediately betray your Office, and ſo do all Kinds of Lace, except Silver which will hardly fall to your Share, unleſs with a Duke, or ſome Prodigal juſt come to his Eſtate. The Colours you ought to wiſh for, are Blue, or Filemot, turn'd up with Red; which with a borrowed Sword, a borrowed Air, your Maſter's Linen, and a natural and improved Confidence, will give you what Title you pleaſe, where you are not known.

When you carry Diſhes or other Things out of the Room at Meals, fill both your Hands as full as poſſible; for although you may ſometimes ſpill, and ſometimes let fall, yet you will find at the Year's End, you have made great Diſpatch and ſaved abundance of Time.

If

If your Maſter or Miſtreſs happens to walk the Streets, keep on one Side, and as much on the Level with them as you can, which People obſerving, will either think you do not belong to them, or that you are one of their Companions; but, if either of them happen to turn back and ſpeak to you, ſo that you are under the Neceſſity to take off your Hat, uſe but your Thumb and one Finger, and ſcratch your Head with the reſt.

In Winter time light the Dining-Room Fire but two Minutes before Dinner is ſerved up, that your Maſter may ſee, how ſaving you are of his Coals.

When you are ordered to ſtir up the Fire, clean away the Aſhes from betwixt the Bars with the Fire-Bruſh.

When you are ordered to call a Coach, although it be Midnight, go no further than the Door, for fear of being out of the Way when you are wanted; and there ſtand bawling, Coach, Coach, for half an Hour.

Although you Gentlemen in Livery have the Misfortune to be treated ſcurvily by all Mankind, yet you make a Shift to keep up your Spirits, and ſometimes arrive at conſiderable Fortunes. I was an intimate Friend to one of our Brethren, who was a Footman to a Court Lady: She had an honourable Employment, was Siſter to an Earl, and the Widow of a Man of Quality. She obſerved ſomething ſo polite in my Friend, the Gracefulneſs with which he

tript

tript before her Chair, and put his Hair under his Hat, that ſhe made him many Advances; and one Day taking the Air in her Coach with *Tom* behind it, the Coachman miſtook the Way, and ſtopt at a privileged Chapel, where the Couple were marry'd, and *Tom* came home in the Chariot by his Lady's Side: But he unfortunately taught her to drink Brandy, of which ſhe dy'd, after having pawned all her Plate to purchaſe it, and *Tom* is now a Journeyman Malſter.

Boucher, the famous Gameſter, was another of our Fraternity, and when he was worth 50,000 *l.* he dunned the Duke of *B——m* for an Arrear of Wages in his Service; and I could inſtance many more, particularly another, whoſe Son had one of the chief Employments at Court; and is ſufficient to give you the following Advice, which is to be pert and ſawcy to all Mankind, eſpecially to the Chaplain, the Waiting-woman, and the better Sort of Servants in a Perſon of Quality's Family, and value not now and then a Kicking, or a Caning; for your Inſolence will at laſt turn to good Account; and from wearing a Livery, you may probably ſoon carry a Pair of Colours.

When you wait behind a Chair at Meals, keep conſtantly wriggling the Back of the Chair, that the Perſon behind whom you ſtand, may know you are ready to attend him.

When you carry a Parcel of *China* Plates, if you chance to fall, as it is a frequent Misfortune,

tune, your Excuſe muſt be, that a Dog ran acroſs you in the Hall; that the Chamber-maid accidentally puſhed the Door againſt you; that a Map ſtood acroſs the Entry, and tript you up; that your Sleeve ſtuck againſt the Key, or Button of the Lock.

When your Maſter and Lady are talking together in the Bed-chamber, and you have ſome Suſpicion that you or your Fellow-ſervants are concerned in what they ſay, liſten at the Door for the publick Good of all the Servants, and join all to take proper Meaſures for preventing any Innovations that may hurt the Community.

Be not proud in Proſperity: You have heard that Fortune turns on a Wheel; if you have a good Place, you are at the Top of the Wheel. Remember how often you have been ſtripped, and kick'd out of Doors, your Wages all taken up beforehand, and ſpent in tranſlated red-heel'd Shoes, ſecond-hand Toupees, and repair'd Lace Ruffles, beſides a ſwinging Debt to the Ale-wife and the Brandy-ſhop. The neigbouring Tapſter, who before would beckon you over to a ſavoury Bit of Ox-cheek in the Morning, give it you *gratis*, and only ſcore you up for the Liquor, immediately after you were packt off in Diſgrace, carried a Petition to your Maſter, to be paid out of your Wages, whereof not a Farthing was due, and then purſued you with Bailiffs into every blind Cellar. Remember how ſoon you grew ſhabby, thread-bare, and

and out-at-heels, was forced to borrow an old Livery Coat, to make your Appearance while you were looking for a Place; and ſneak to every Houſe where you have an old Acquaintance to ſteal you a Scrap, to keep Life and Soul together; and upon the whole, were in the loweſt Station of human Life, which, as the old Ballad ſays, is that of a Skipkennel turn'd out of Place: I ſay, remember all this now in your flouriſhing Condition. Pay your Contributions duly to your late Brothers the Cadets, who are left to the wide World: Take one of them as your Dependant, to ſend on your Lady's Meſſages when you have a Mind to go to the Alehouſe; ſlip him out privately now and then a Slice of Bread, and a Bit of cold Meat, your Maſter can afford it; and if he be not yet put upon the Eſtabliſhment for a Lodging, let him lie in the Stable, or the Coach-houſe, or under the Back-ſtairs, and recommend him to all the Gentlemen who frequent your Houſe, as an excellent Servant.

To grow old in the Office of a Footman, is the higheſt of all Indignities: Therefore when you find Years coming on, without Hopes of a Place at Court, a Command in the Army, a Succeſſion to the Stewardſhip, an Employment in the Revenue (which two laſt you cannot obtain without Reading and Writing) or running away with your Maſter's Niece or Daughter; I directly adviſe you to go upon the Road, which is the only Poſt of Honour left you: Therefore you

you will meet many of your old Comrades, and live a ſhort Life and a merry one, and make a Figure at your Exit, wherein I will give you ſome Inſtructions.

The laſt Advice I give you, relates to your Behaviour when you are going to be hanged; which, either for robbing your Maſter, for Houſe-breaking, or going upon the High-way, or in a drunken Quarrel, by killing the firſt Man you meet, may very probably be your Lot, and is owing to one of theſe three Qualities; either a Love of good Fellowſhip, a Generoſity of Mind, or too much Vivacity of Spirits. Your good Behaviour on this Article, will concern your whole Community: Deny the Fact with all Solemnity of Imprecations: A hundred of your Brethren, if they can be admitted, will attend about the Bar, and be ready upon Demand to give you a good Character before the Court: Let nothing prevail on you to confeſs, but the Promiſe of a Pardon for diſcovering your Comrades: But, I ſuppoſe all this to be in vain, for if you eſcape now, your Fate will be the ſame another Day. Get a Speech to be written by the beſt Author of *Newgate*: Some of your kind Wenches will provide you with a *Holland* Shirt, and white Cap crowned with a crimſon or black Ribbon: Take Leave chearfully of all your Friends in *Newgate*: Mount the Cart with Courage: Fall on your Knees: Lift up your Hands: Hold a Book in your Hands although you cannot read a Word:

Deny

Deny the Fact at the Gallows: Kiſs and forgive the Hangman, and ſo farewell: You ſhall be buried in Pomp, at the Charge of the Fraternity: The Surgeon ſhall not touch a Limb of you; and your Fame ſhall continue until a Succeſſor of equal Renown ſucceeds in your Place.

CHAP. IV.

Directions to the COACHMAN.

YOU are ſtrictly bound to nothing, but to ſtep into the Box, and carry your Maſter or Lady.

Let your Horſes be ſo well trained, that when you attend your Lady at a Viſit, they will wait until you ſlip into a neighbouring Ale-houſe, to take a Pot with a Friend.

When you are in no Humour to drive, tell your Maſter that the Horſes have got a Cold, that they want Shoeing, that Rain does them Hurt, and roughens their Coat, and rots the Harneſs. This may likewiſe be applied to the Groom.

If your Maſter dines with a Country Friend, drink as much as you can get; becauſe it is allowed, that a good Coachman never drives ſo well as when he is drunk, and then ſhew your Skill by driving to an Inch by a Precipice; and ſay you never drive ſo well as when drunk.

If you find any Gentleman fond of one of your

your Horſes, and willing to give you a Conſideration beſide the Price; perſuade your Maſter to ſell him, becauſe he is ſo vicious that you cannot undertake to drive with him, and is founder'd into the Bargain.

Get a Blackguard-boy to watch your Coach at the Church Door on *Sundays*, that you and your Brother-Coachmen may be merry together at the Ale-houſe, while your Maſter and Lady are at Church.

Take Care that your Wheels be good; and get a new Set bought as often as you can, whether you are allowed the old as your Perquiſite or not: In one Caſe it will turn to your honeſt Profit, and in the other it will be a juſt Puniſhment on your Maſter's Covetouſneſs; and probably the Coach-maker will conſider you too.

CHAP. V.

Directions to the GROOM.

YOU are the Servant upon whom the Care of your Maſter's Honour in all Journies entirely depends: Your Breaſt is the ſole Repoſitory of it. If he travels the Country, and lodgeth at Inns, every Dram of Brandy, every Pot of Ale extraordinary that you drink, raiſeth his Character; and therefore his Reputation ought to be dear to you; and, I hope, you will not ſtint yourſelf in either. The Smith, the

Sadler's Journeyman, the Cook at the Inn, the Oſtler and the Boot-catcher, ought all by your Means to partake of your Maſter's Generoſity: Thus, his Fame will reach from one County to another; and what is a Gallon of Ale, or a Pint of Brandy in his Worſhip's Pocket? And, although he ſhould be in the Number of thoſe who value their Credit leſs than their Purſe, yet your Care of the former ought to be ſo much the greater. His Horſe wanted two Removes; your Horſe wanted Nails; his Allowance of Oats and Beans was greater than the Journey required; a third Part may be retrenched, and turned into Ale or Brandy; and thus his Honour may be preſerved by your Diſcretion, and leſs Expence to him; or, if he travels with no other Servant, the Matter is eaſily made up in the Bill between you and the Tapſter.

Therefore, as ſoon as you alight at the Inn, deliver your Horſes to the Stable-boy, and let him gallop them to the next Pond; then call for a Pot of Ale, for it is very fit that a Chriſtian ſhould drink before a Beaſt. Leave your Maſter to the Care of the Servants in the Inn, and your Horſes to thoſe in the Stable: Thus both he and they are left in the propereſt Hands; but you are to provide for yourſelf; therefore get your Supper, drink freely, and go to Bed without troubling your Maſter, who is in better Hands than yours. The Oſtler is an honeſt Fellow, and loves Horſes in his Heart; and would not wrong the dumb Crea-

tures

tures for the World. Be tender of your Maſter, and order the Servants not to wake him too early. Get your Breakfaſt before he is up, that he may not wait for you; make the Oſtler tell him the Roads are very good, and the Miles ſhort; but adviſe him to ſtay a little longer till the Weather clears up, for he is afraid there will be Rain, and he will be Time enough after Dinner.

Let your Maſter mount before you, out of Good-manners. As he is leaving the Inn, drop a good Word in favour of the Oſtler, what Care he took of the Cattle; and add, that you never ſaw civiller Servants. Let your Maſter ride on before, and do you ſtay until your Landlord has given you a Dram; then gallop after him thro' the Town or Village with full Speed, for fear he ſhould want you, and to ſhew your Horſemanſhip.

If you are a Piece of a Farrier, as every good Groom ought to be, get Sack, Brandy, or Strong-beer to rub your Horſes Heels every Night, and be not ſparing, for (if any be ſpent) what is left, you know how to diſpoſe of it.

Conſider your Maſter's Health, and rather than let him take long Journies, ſay the Cattle are weak, and fallen in their Fleſh with hard riding; tell him of a very good Inn five Miles nearer than he intended to go; or leave one of his Horſes Fore Shoes looſe in the Morning; or contrive that the Saddle may pinch the Beaſt in his Withers; or keep him without

Corn all Night and Morning, ſo that he may tire on the Road; or wedge a thin Plate of Iron between the Hoof and the Shoe, to make him halt; and all this in perfect Tenderneſs to your Maſter.

When you are going to be hired, and the Gentleman aſks you, whether you are apt to be drunk? Own freely that you love a Cup of good Ale; but that it is your Way, drunk or ſober, never to neglect your Horſes.

When your Maſter hath a Mind to ride out for the Air, or for Pleaſure, if any private Buſineſs of your own makes it inconvenient for you to attend him; give him to underſtand, that the Horſes want bleeding or purging; that his own Pad hath got a Surfeit; or, that the Saddle wants ſtuffing; and his Bridle is gone to be mended: This you may honeſtly do, becauſe it will be no Injury to the Horſes or your Maſter; and at the ſame time ſhews the great Care you have of the poor dumb Creatures.

If there be a particular Inn in the Town whither you are going, and where you are well acquainted with the Oſtler or Tapſter, and the People of the Houſe, find Fault with the other Inns, and recommend your Maſter thither; it may probably be a Pot and a Dram or two more in your Way, and to your Maſter's Honour.

If your Maſter ſends you to buy Hay, deal with thoſe who will be the moſt liberal to you; for

for Service being no Inheritance, you ought not to let ſlip any lawful and cuſtomary Perquiſite. If your Maſter buys it himſelf, he wrongs you, and to teach him his Duty, be ſure to find Fault with the Hay as long as it laſts; and if the Horſes thrive with it, the Fault is yours.

Hay and Oats, in the Management of a ſkilful Groom, will make excellent Ale as well as Brandy; but this I only hint.

When your Maſter dines, or lies at a Gentleman's Houſe in the Country, altho' there be no Groom, or he be gone abroad, or that the Horſes have been quite neglected; be ſure employ ſome of the Servants to hold the Horſe when your Maſter mounts. This I would have you do, when your Maſter only alights, to call in for a few Minutes: For Brother-ſervants muſt always befriend one another, and that alſo concerns your Maſter's Honour; becauſe he cannot do leſs than give a Piece of Money to him who holds his Horſe.

In long Journies, aſk your Maſter Leave to give Ale to the Horſes; carry two Quarts full to the Stable, pour half a Pint into a Bowl, and if they will not drink it, you and the Oſtler muſt do the beſt you can; perhaps they may be in a better Humour at the next Inn, for I would have you never fail to make the Experiment.

When you go to air your Horſes in the Park, or the Fields, give them to a Horſe-boy, or one of the Blackguards, who being lighter than you, may be trusted to run Races with less Damage to the Horses, and teach them to leap over Hedges and Ditches, while you are drinking a friendly Pot with your Brother Grooms: But sometimes you and they may run Races yourselves for the Honour of your Horses, and of your Masters.

Never stint your Horses at home in Hay and Oats, but fill the Rack to the Top, and the Manger to the Brim: For you would take it ill to be stinted yourself; altho', perhaps, they may not have the Stomach to eat; consider, they have no Tongues to ask. If the Hay be thrown down, there is no Loss, for it will make Litter, and save Straw.

When your Master is leaving a Gentleman's House in the Country, where he hath lain a Night; then consider his Honour: Let him know how many Servants there are of both Sexes, who expect Vails; and give them their Cue to attend in two Lines as he leaves the House; but, desire him not to trust the Money with the Butler, for fear he should cheat the rest: This will force your Master to be more generous; and then you may take Occasion to tell your Master, that 'Squire such a one, whom you lived with last, always gave so much a-piece to the common Servants, and so much to the House-keeper, and the rest, naming at least double to what he intended to give; but, be sure to tell the Servants what a good Office

you

you did them: This will gain you Love, and your Maſter Honour.

You may venture to be drunk much oftner than the Coachman, whatever he pretends to alledge in his own Behalf, becauſe you hazard no Body's Neck but your own; for, the Horſe will probably take ſo much Care of himſelf, as to come off with only a Strain or a Shoulder-ſlip.

When you carry your Maſter's Riding-Coat in a Journey, wrap your own in it, and buckle them up cloſe with a Strap, but turn your Maſter's Inſide out, to preſerve the Outſide from Wet and Dirt; thus, when it begins to rain, your Maſter's Coat will be firſt ready to be given him; and, if it get more Hurt than yours, he can afford it better, for your Livery muſt always ſerve its Year's Apprenticeſhip.

When you come to your Inn with the Horſes wet and dirty after hard riding, and are very hot, make the Oſtler immediately plunge them into Water up to their Bellies, and allow them to drink as much as they pleaſe; but, be ſure to gallop them full ſpeed a Mile at leaſt, to dry their Skins and warm the Water in their Bellies. The Oſtler underſtands his Buſineſs, leave all to his Diſcretion, while you get a Pot of Ale and ſome Brandy at the Kitchen Fire to comfort your Heart.

If your Horſe drop a Fore-Shoe, be ſo careful to alight and take it up: Then ride with all the Speed you can (the Shoe in your Hand that every Traveller may obſerve your Care) to the next Smith on the Road, make him put it on immediately, that your Maſter may not wait for you, and that the poor Horſe may be as ſhort a Time as poſſible without a Shoe.

When your Maſter lies at a Gentleman's Houſe, if you find the Hay and Oats are good, complain aloud of their Badneſs; this will get you the Name of a diligent Servant; and be ſure to cram the Horſes with as much Oats as they can eat, while you are there, and you may give them ſo much the leſs for ſome Days at the Inns, and turn the Oats into Ale. When you leave the Gentleman's Houſe, tell your Maſter what a covetous Hunks that Gentleman was, that you got nothing but Butter-milk or Water to drink; this will make your Maſter out of Pity allow you a Pot of Ale the more at the next Inn: But, if you happen to get drunk in a Gentleman's Houſe, your Maſter cannot be angry, becauſe it coſt him nothing; and ſo you ought to tell him as well as you can in your preſent Condition, and let him know it is both for his and the Gentleman's Honour to make a Friend's Servant welcome.

A Maſter ought always to love his Groom, to put him into a handſome Livery, and to allow him a Silver-laced Hat. When you are in this Equipage, all the Honours he receives on the Road are owing to you alone: That he is not turned out of the Way by every Carrier, is

cauſed

caused by the Civility he receives at second hand from the Respect paid to your Livery.

You may now and then lend your Master's Pad to a Brother Servant, or your favourite Maid, for a short Jaunt, or hire him for a Day, because the Horse is spoiled for want of Exercise: And if your Master happens to want his Horse, or hath a Mind to see the Stable, curse that Rogue the Helper who is gone out with the Key.

When you want to spend an Hour or two with your Companions at the Ale-house, and that you stand in need of a reasonable Excuse for your Stay, go out of the Stable Door, or the back Way, with an old Bridle, Girth, or Stirrup Leather in your Pocket, and on your Return come home by the Street Door with the same Bridle, Girth, or Stirrup Leather dangling in your Hand, as if you came from the Saddler's, where you were getting the same mended; (if you are not missed all is well,) but, if you are met by your Master, you will have the Reputation of a careful Servant. This I have known practised with good Success.

CHAP. VI.

Directions to the HOUSE-STEWARD, *and* LAND-STEWARD.

LORD *Peterborough*'s Steward that pulled down his House, sold the Materials, and charged

charged my Lord with Repairs. Take Money for Forbearance from Tenants. Renew Leases and get by them, and sell Woods. Lend my Lord his own Money. (*Gilblas* said much of this, to whom I refer.)

CHAP. VII.

Directions to the PORTER.

IF your Master be a Minister of State, let him be at Home to none but his Pimp, or chief Flatterer, or one of his Pensionary Writers, or his hired Spy, and Informer, or his Printer in ordinary, or his City Sollicitor, or a Land-Jobber, or his Inventor of new Funds, or a Stock-Jobber.

CHAP. VIII.

Directions to the CHAMBER-MAID.

THE Nature of your Employment differs according to the Quality, the Pride, or the Wealth of the Lady you serve; and this Treatise is to be applied to all Sorts of Families; so, that I find myself under great Difficulty to adjust the Business for which you are hired. In a Family where there is a tolerable Estate, you differ from the House-Maid, and in that View I give my Directions. Your particular Province is your Lady's Chamber, where

where you make the Bed, and put Things in Order; and if you live in the Country, you take Care of Rooms where Ladies lie who come into the Houſe, which brings in all the Vails that fall to your Share. Your uſual Lover, as I take it, is the Coachman; but, if you are under Twenty, and tolerably handſome, perhaps a Footman may caſt his Eyes on you.

Get your favourite Footman to help you in making your Lady's Bed; and, if you ſerve a young Couple, the Footman and you, as you are turning up the Bed-cloaths, will make the pretti eſt Obſervations in the World, which whiſpered about, will be very entertaining to the whole Family, and get among the Neighbourhood.

Do not carry down the neceſſary Veſſels for the Fellows to ſee, but empty them out of the Window, for your Lady's Credit. It is highly improper for Men Servants to know that fine Ladies have Occaſion for ſuch Utenſils; and do not ſcour the Chamber-pot, becauſe the Smell is wholeſome.

If you happen to break any *China* with the Top of the Wiſk on the Mantle-tree or the Cabinet, gather up the Fragments, put them together as well as you can, and place them behind the reſt, ſo that when your Lady comes to diſcover them, you may ſafely ſay they were broke long ago, before you came to the Service. This will ſave your Lady many an Hour's Vexation.

It

It ſometimes happens that a Looking-Glaſs is broken by the ſame Means, while you are looking another Way, as you ſweep the Chamber, the long End of the Bruſh ſtrikes againſt the Glaſs, and breaks it to Shivers. This is the extremeſt of all Misfortunes, and all Remedy deſperate in Appearance, becauſe it is impoſſible to be concealed. Such a fatal Accident once happened in a great Family where I had the Honour to be a Footman; and I will relate the Particulars, to ſhew the Ingenuity of the poor Chamber-maid on ſo ſudden and dreadful an Emergency, which perhaps may help to ſharpen your Invention, if your evil Star ſhould ever give you the like Occaſion: The poor Girl had broken a large Japan Glaſs of great Value, with a Stroke of her Bruſh: She had not conſidered long, when by a prodigious Preſence of Mind, ſhe locked the Door, ſtole into the Yard, brought a Stone of three Pound Weight into the Chamber, laid it on the Hearth juſt under the Looking-Glaſs, then broke a Paine in the Saſh Window that looked into the ſame Yard, ſo ſhut the Door, and went about her other Affairs. Two Hours after, the Lady goes into the Chamber, ſees the Glaſs broken, the Stone lying under, and a whole Paine in the Window deſtroyed, from all which Circumſtances, ſhe concluded juſt as the Maid could have wiſhed, that ſome idle Straggler in the Neighbourhood, or perhaps one of the Out-Servants, had through Malice,

Accident,

Accident, or Carelessness, flung in the Stone, and done the Mischief. Thus far all Things went well, and the Girl concluded herself out of Danger: But, it was her ill Fortune, that a few Hours after in came the Parson of the Parish, and the Lady (naturally) told him the Accident, which you may believe had much discomposed her; but the Minister, who happened to understand Mathematicks, after examining the Situation of the Yard, the Window, and the Chimney, soon convinced the Lady, that the Stone could never reach the Looking-Glass without taking three Turns in its Flight from the Hand that threw it, and the Maid being proved to have swept the Room the same Morning, was strictly examined, but constantly denied that she was guilty upon her Salvation, offering to take her Oath upon the Bible, before his Reverence, that she was innocent as the Child unborn; yet the poor Wench was turned off, which I take to have been hard Treatment, considering her Ingenuity: However, this may be a Direction to you in the like Case, to contrive a Story that will better hang together. For Instance, you might say, that while you were at work with the Mop, or Brush, a Flash of Lightning came suddenly in at the Window, which almost blinded you; that you immediately heard the ringing of broken Glass on the Hearth; that, as soon as you recovered your Eyes, you saw the Looking-Glass all broken to Pieces: Or, you may alledge,

alledge, that obſerving the Glaſs a little covered with Duſt, and going very gently to wipe it, you ſuppoſe the Moiſture of the Air had diſſolved the Glue or Cement, which made it fall to the Ground: Or, as ſoon as the Miſchief is done, you may cut the Cords that faſtened the Glaſs to the Wainſcot, and ſo let it fall flat on the Ground; run out in a Fright, tell your Lady, curſe the Upholſterer; and declare how narrowly you eſcaped, that it did not fall upon your Head. I offer theſe Expedients, from a Deſire I have to defend the Innocent; for innocent you certainly muſt be, if you did not break the Glaſs on purpoſe, which I would by no Means excuſe, except upon great Provocations.

Oil the Tongs, Poker, and Fire-ſhovel up to the Top, not only to keep them from ruſting, but likewiſe to prevent meddling People from waſting your Maſter's Coals with ſtirring the Fire.

When you are in haſte, ſweep the Duſt into a Corner of the Room, but leave your Bruſh upon it, that it may not be ſeen, for, that would diſgrace you.

Never waſh your Hands, or put on a clean Apron, till you have made your Lady's Bed, for fear of rumpling your Apron, or fouling your Hands again.

When you bar the Window-ſhuts of your Lady's Bed-chamber at Nights, leave open the Saſhes,

Sashes, to let in the fresh Air, and sweeten the Room against Morning.

In the Time when you leave the Windows open for Air, leave Books, or something else on the Window-seat, that they may get Air too.

When you sweep your Lady's Room, never stay to pick up foul Smocks, Handkerchiefs, Pinners, Pin-cushions, Tea-spoons, Ribbons, Slippers, or whatever lies in your Way; but sweep all into a Corner, and then you may take them up in a Lump, and save Time.

Making Beds in hot Weather is a very laborious Work, and you will be apt to sweat; therefore, when you find the Drops running down from your Forehead, wipe them off with a Corner of the Sheet, that they may not be seen on the Bed.

When your Lady sends you to wash a *China* Cup, and it happen to fall, bring it up, and swear you did but just touch it with your Hand, when it broke into *three Halves*: And here I must inform you, as well as your fellow Servants, that you ought never to be without an Excuse; it doth no Harm to your Master, and it lessens your Fault: As in this Instance; I do not commend you for breaking the Cup; it is certain you did not break it on purpose, and the Thing is possible, that it might break in your Hand.

You are sometimes desirous to see a Funeral, a Quarrel, a Man going to be hanged, a Wedding, a Bawd carted, or the like: As they pass by by in the Street, you lift up the Sash suddenly; there by Misfortune it sticks: This was no Fault of yours; young Women are curious by Nature; you have no Remedy, but to cut the Cord; and lay the Fault upon the Carpenter, unless no Body saw you, and then you are as innocent as any Servant in the House.

Wear your Lady's Smock when she has thrown it off; it will do you Credit, save your own Linen, and be not a Pin the worse.

When you put a clean Pillow-case on your Lady's Pillow, be sure to fasten it well with three corking Pins, that it may not fall off in the Night.

When you spread Bread and Butter for Tea, be sure that all the Holes in the Loaf be left full of Butter, to keep the Bread moist against Dinner; and let the Mark of your Thumb be seen only upon one End of every Slice, to shew your Cleanliness.

When you are ordered to open or lock any Door, Trunk or Cabinet, and miss the proper Key, or cannot distinguish it in the Bunch; try the first Key that you can thrust in, and turn it with all your Strength till you open the Lock, or break the Key; for your Lady will reckon you a Fool to come back and do nothing.

CHAP.

CHAP. IX.

Directions to the WAITING-MAID.

TWO Accidents have happened to lessen the Comforts and Profits of your Employment; First, that execrable Custom got among Ladies, of trucking their old Cloaths for *China*, or turning them to cover easy Chairs, or making them into Patch-work for Skreens, Stools, Cushions, and the like. The Second is, the Invention of small Chests and Trunks, with Lock and Key, wherein they keep the Tea and Sugar, without which it is impossible for a Waiting-maid to live: For, by this means you are forced to buy brown Sugar, and pour Water upon the Leaves, when they have lost all their Spirit and Taste: I cannot contrive any perfect Remedy against either of these two Evils. As to the former, I think there should be a general Confederacy of all the Servants in every Family, for the publick Good, to drive those *China* Hucksters from the Doors; and as to the latter, there is no other Method to relieve yourselves, but by a false Key, which is a Point both difficult and dangerous to compass; but, as to the Circumstance of Honesty in procuring one, I am under no Doubt, when your Mistress gives you so just a Provocation, by refusing you an ancient and legal Perquisite. The Mistress of the Tea-shop may now and then give you half an Ounce,

 but

but that will be only a Drop in the Bucket: Therefore, I fear you muſt be forced, like the reſt of your Siſters, to run in Truſt, and pay for it out of your Wages, as far as they will go, which you can eaſily make up other ways, if your Lady be handſome, or her Daughters have good Fortunes.

If you are in a great Family, and my Lady's Woman, my Lord may probably like you, although you are not half ſo handſome as his own Lady. In this Caſe, take Care to get as much out of him as you can; and never allow him the ſmalleſt Liberty, not the ſqueezing of your Hand, unleſs he puts a Guinea into it; ſo, by degrees, make him pay accordingly for every new Attempt, doubling upon him in proportion to the Conceſſions you allow, and always ſtruggling, and threatning to cry out or tell your Lady, although you receive his Money: Five Guineas for handling your Breaſt is a cheap Pennyworth, although you ſeem to reſiſt with all your Might; but never allow him the laſt Favour under a hundred Guineas, or a Settlement of twenty Pounds a Year for Life.

In ſuch a Family, if you are handſome, you will have the Choice of three Lovers; the Chaplain, the Steward, and my Lord's Gentleman. I would firſt adviſe you to chuſe the Steward; but, if you happen to be young with Child by my Lord, you muſt take up with the Chaplain. I like my Lord's Gentleman the leaſt

leaſt of the three; for he is uſually vain and ſawcy from the Time he throws off his Livery; and, if he miſſes a Pair of Colours, or a Tide-waiter's Place, he hath no Remedy but the Highway.

I muſt caution you particularly againſt my Lord's eldeſt Son: If you are dextrous enough, it is odds that you may draw him in to marry you, and make you a Lady: If he be a common Rake, (and he muſt be one or t'other) avoid him like *Satan*; for he ſtands leſs in Awe of a Mother, than my Lord doth of a Wife; and, after ten thouſand Promiſes, you will get nothing from him, but a big Belly or a Clap, and probably both together.

When your Lady is ill, and after a very bad Night, is getting a little Nap in the Morning, if a Footman comes with a Meſſage to enquire how ſhe doth, do not let the Compliment be loſt, but ſhake her gently until ſhe wakes; then deliver the Meſſage, receive her Anſwer, and leave her to ſleep.

If you are ſo happy as to wait on a young Lady with a great Fortune, you muſt be an ill Manager if you cannot get five or ſix hundred Pounds for diſpoſing of her. Put her often in Mind, that ſhe is rich enough to make any Man happy; that there is no real Happineſs but in Love; that ſhe hath Liberty to chuſe wherever ſhe pleaſeth, and not by the Direction of Parents, who never give Allowances for an innocent Paſſion; that there are a World of handſome, fine, ſweet young Gentlemen in Town, who would be glad to die at her Feet; that the Converſation of two Lovers is a Heaven upon Earth; that Love, like Death, equals all Conditions; that if ſhe ſhould caſt her Eyes upon a young Fellow below her Birth and Eſtate, his marrying her would make him a Gentleman; that you ſaw yeſterday on the *Mall*, the prettieſt Enſign; and that, if you had forty thouſand Pounds, it ſhould be at his Service. Take Care that every Body ſhould know what Lady you live with; how great a Favourite you are; and, that ſhe always takes your Advice. Go often to St. *James*'s Park, the fine Fellows will ſoon diſcover you, and contrive to ſlip a Letter into your Sleeve or your Boſom: Pull it out in a Fury, and throw it on the Ground, unleſs you find at leaſt two Guineas along with it; but in that Caſe, ſeem not to find it, and to think he was only playing the Wag with you: When you come home, drop the Letter careleſsly in your Lady's Chamber; ſhe finds it, is angry; proteſt you knew nothing of it, only you remember, that a Gentleman in the Park ſtruggled to kiſs you, and you believe it was he that put the Letter in your Sleeve or Pettycoat; and, indeed, he was as pretty a Man as ever ſhe ſaw: That ſhe may burn the Letter if ſhe pleaſeth. If your Lady be wiſe, ſhe will burn ſome other Paper before you, and read the Letter when you are gone down. You muſt follow this Practice as often

often as you fafely can; but, let him who pays you beft with every Letter, be the handfomeft Man. If a Footman prefumes to bring a Letter to the Houfe, to be delivered to you, for your Lady, although it come from your beft Cuftomer, throw it at his Head; call him impudent Rogue and Villain, and fhut the Door in his Face; run up to your Lady, and as a Proof of your Fidelity, tell her what you have done.

I could enlarge very much upon this Subject: But I truft to your own Difcretion.

If you ferve a Lady who is a little difpofed to Gallantries, you will find it a Point of great Prudence how to manage: Three Things are neceffary. Firft, how to pleafe your Lady; Secondly, how to prevent Sufpicion in the Hufband, or among the Family; and laftly, but principally, how to make it moft for your own Advantage. To give you full Directions in this important Affair, would require a large Volume. All Affignations at home are dangerous, both to your Lady and yourfelf; and therefore contrive, as much as poffible, to have them in a third Place; efpecially, if your Lady, as it is a hundred odds, entertains more Lovers than one, each of whom is often more jealous than a thoufand Hufbands; and, very unlucky Rencounters may often happen under the beft Management. I need not warn you to employ your good Offices chiefly in favour of thofe, whom you find moft liberal; yet, if your

Lady ſhould happen to caſt an Eye upon a handſome Footman, you ſhould be generous enough to bear with her Humour, which is no Singularity, but a very natural Appetite: It is ſtill the ſafeſt of all home Intrigues, and was formerly the leaſt ſuſpected, until of late Years it hath grown more common: The great Danger is, leſt this Kind of Gentry, dealing too often in bad Ware, may happen not to be ſound; and then, your Lady and you are in a very bad Way, although not altogether deſperate.

But, to ſay the Truth, I confeſs it is a great Preſumption in me, to offer you any Inſtructions in the Conduct of your Lady's Amours, wherein your whole Siſterhood is already ſo expert, and deeply learned; although it be much more difficult to compaſs, than that Aſſiſtance which my Brother Footmen give their Maſters, on the like Occaſion; and therefore, I leave this Affair to be treated by ſome abler Pen.

When you lock up a Silk Mantua, or laced Head in a Trunk or Cheſt, leave a Piece out, that when you open the Trunk again, you may know where to find it.

CHAP X.

Directions to the HOUSE-MAID.

IF your Maſter and Lady go into the Country for a Week or more, never waſh the Bed-

Bed-chamber or Dining-room, until juſt the Hour before you expect them to return: Thus, the Room will be perfectly clean to receive them, and you will not be at the Trouble to waſh them ſo ſoon again.

I am very much offended with thoſe Ladies, who are ſo proud and lazy, that they will not be at the Pains of ſtepping into the Garden to pluck a Roſe, but keep an odious Implement, ſometimes in the Bed-chamber itſelf, or at leaſt in a dark Cloſet adjoining, which they make Uſe of to eaſe their worſt Neceſſities; and, you are the uſual Carriers away of the Pan, which maketh not only the Chamber, but even their Cloaths offenſive, to all who come near. Now, to cure them of this odious Practice, let me adviſe you, on whom this Office lies, to convey away this Utenſil, that you will do it openly, down the great Stairs, and in the Preſence of the Footmen; and, if any Body knocks, to open the Street-door, while you have the Veſſel filled in your Hands: This, if any Thing can, will make your Lady take the Pains of evacuating her Perſon in the proper Place, rather than expoſe her Filthineſs to all the Men Servants in the Houſe.

Leave a Payl of dirty Water with the Mop in it, a Coal-box, a Bottle, a Broom, a Chamber-pot, and ſuch other unſightly Things, either in a blind Entry, or upon the darkeſt Part of the Back-ſtairs, that they may not be ſeen; and, if People break their Shins by trampling on them, it is their own Fault.

Never empty the Chamber-pots until they are quite full: If that happen in the Night, empty them into the Street; if, in the Morning, into the Garden; for it would be an endleſs Work to go a dozen Times from the Garret and upper Rooms, down to the Back-ſides; but, never waſh them in any other Liquor except your own: What cleanly Girl would be dabbling in other Folks Urine? and beſides, the Smell of Stale, as I obſerved before, is admirable againſt the Vapours; which, a hundred to one, may be your Lady's Caſe.

Bruſh down the Cobwebs with a Broom that is wet and dirty, which will make them ſtick the faſter to it, and bring them down more effectually.

When you rid up the Parlour Hearth in a Morning, throw the laſt Night's Aſhes into a Sieve; and what falls through, as you carry it down, will ſerve inſtead of Sand for the Room and the Stairs.

When you have ſcoured the Braſſes and Irons in the Parlour Chimney, lay the foul wet Clout upon the next Chair, that your Lady may ſee you have not neglected your Work: Obſerve the ſame Rule, when you clean the Braſs Locks, only with this Addition, to leave the Marks of your Fingers on the Doors, to ſhew you have not forgot.

Leave

Leave your Lady's Chamber-pot in her Bed-chamber Window, all Day to air.

Bring up none but large Coals to the Dining-room and your Lady's Chamber; they make the beſt Fires, and, if you find them too big, it is eaſy to break them on the Marble Hearth.

When you go to Bed, be ſure take Care of Fire; and, therefore blow the Candle out with your Breath, and then thruſt it under your Bed. *Note*, The Smell of the Snuff is very good againſt Vapours.

Perſuade the Footman who got you with Child, to marry you before you are ſix Months gone; and, if your Lady aſks you, Why you would take a Fellow who was not worth a Groat? let your Anſwer be, That Service is no Inheritance.

When your Lady's Bed is made, put the Chamber-pot under it, but in ſuch a Manner, as to thruſt the Valance along with it, that it may be full in Sight, and ready for your Lady when ſhe hath Occaſion to uſe it.

Lock up a Cat or a Dog in ſome Room or Cloſet, ſo as to make ſuch a Noiſe all over the Houſe, as may affright away the Thieves, if any ſhould attempt to break or ſteal in.

When you waſh any of the Rooms towards the Street over Night, throw the foul Water out of the Street-door; but, be ſure not to look before you, for fear thoſe on whom the Water lights, might think you uncivil, and that you did it on purpoſe. If he who ſuffers, breaks the

the Windows in revenge, and your Lady chides you, and gives positive Orders that you ſhould carry the Payl down, and empty it in the Sink, you have an eaſy Remedy. When you waſh an upper Room, carry down the Payl ſo as to let the Water dribble on the Stairs all the way down to the Kitchen; by which, not only your Load will be lighter, but you will convince your Lady, that it is better to throw the Water out of the Windows, or down the Street-door Steps: Beſides this latter Practice will be very diverting to you and the Family in a froſty Night, to ſee a hundred People falling on their Noſes or Back-ſides before your Door, when the Water is frozen.

Poliſh and brighten the Marble Hearths and Chimney-pieces with a Clout dipt in Greaſe; nothing maketh them ſhine ſo well; and, it is the Buſineſs of the Ladies to take Care of their Pettycoats.

If your Lady be ſo nice that ſhe will have the Room ſcoured with Freeſtone, be ſure to leave the Marks of the Freeſtone, ſix Inches deep round the Bottom of the Wainſcot, that your Lady may ſee your Obedience to her Orders.

CHAP. XI

Directions to the DAIRY-MAID.

FATIGUE of making Butter: Put ſcalding Water in your Churn, although in Summer,

Summer, and churn close to the Kitchen Fire, and with Cream of a Week old. Keep Cream for your Sweet-heart.

CHAP. XII.

Directions to the CHILDRENS-MAID.

IF a Child be sick, give it whatever it wants to eat or drink, although particularly forbid by the Doctor: For what we long for in Sickness, will do us good; and throw the Physick out of the Window; the Child will love you the better; but bid it not tell. Do the same for your Lady, when she longs for any thing in Sickness, and engage it will do her good.

If your Mistress cometh to the Nursery, and offers to whip a Child, snatch it out of her Hands in a Rage, and tell her she is the cruellest Mother you ever saw: She will chide, but love you the better. Tell the Children Stories of Spirits, when they offer to cry, *&c.*

Be sure to wean the Children, *&c.*

CHAP. XIII.

Directions to the NURSE.

IF you happen to let the Child fall, and lame it, be sure never confess it; and, if it dies, all is safe.

Contrive to be with Child as soon as you can,

can, while you are giving Suck, that you may be ready for another Service, when the Child you nurse dies, or is weaned.

CHAP. XIV.

Directions to the LAUNDRESS.

IF you singe the Linen with the Iron, rub the Place with Flour, Chalk, or white Powder; and if nothing will do, wash it so long, till it be either not to be seen, or torn to Rags.

About tearing Linen in washing.

When your Linen is pinned on the Line, or on a Hedge, and it rains, whip it off, although you tear it, *&c.* But the Place for hanging them, is on young Fruit Trees, especially in Blossom; the Linen cannot be torn, and the Trees give them a fine Smell.

CHAP. XV.

Directions to the HOUSE-KEEPER.

YOU must always have a favourite Footman whom you can depend upon; and order him to be very watchful when the Second Course is taken off, that it be brought safely to your Office, that you and the Steward may have a Tit-bit together.

CHAP.

CHAP. XVI.

Directions to the TUTORESS, *or* GOVERNESS.

SAY the Children have ſore Eyes; Miſs *Betty* won't take to her Book, *&c.*

Make the Miſſes read *French* and *Engliſh* Novels, and *French* Romances, and all the Comedies writ in King *Charles* II. and King *William*'s Reigns, to ſoften their Nature, and make them tender-hearted, *&c.*

FINIS.

THE

CONTENTS.

www.ingramcontent.com/pod-product-compliance
Lightning Source LLC
Chambersburg PA
CBHW031623210326
41599CB00021B/3274
9781138358003